SEEDS OF FAITH

SEEDS OF FAITH

DAN BARKER

CFI
An Imprint of Cedar Fort, Inc.
Springville, Utah

The accounts in this book were taken from the journals of various individuals and have now entered the public domain.

A number of the journal entries are courtesy of the Book of Abraham Project (www.boap.org).

Editor's note: Original punctuation and spelling retained in the following accounts.

This is not an official publication of The Church of Jesus Christ of Latter-day Saints. The opinions and views expressed herein belong solely to the authors and do not necessarily represent the opinions or views of Cedar Fort, Inc. Permission for the use of sources, graphics, and photos is also solely the responsibility of the authors.

ISBN 13: 978-1-4621-1441-2

Published by CFI, an imprint of Cedar Fort, Inc.
2373 W. 700 S., Springville, UT 84663
Distributed by Cedar Fort, Inc., www.cedarfort.com

LIBRARY OF CONGRESS CATALOGING-IN-PUBLICATION DATA

Barker, Dan, 1958- author.
Seeds of faith : conversion stories from early Church history / Dan Barker.
pages cm
Summary: Includes conversion stories from early members of The Church of Jesus Christ of Latter-day Saints.
ISBN 978-1-4621-1441-2
1. Church of Jesus Christ of Latter-day Saints--Biography. 2. Mormons--Biography. 3. Church of Jesus Christ of Latter-day Saints--History--19th century. 4. Mormon Church--History--19th century. I. Title.

BX8693.B36 2014
289.3092'2--dc23
[B]

2014004417

Cover design by Shawnda T. Craig
Cover design © 2014 Lyle Mortimer
Edited and typeset by Kevin Haws

Printed in the United States of America

10 9 8 7 6 5 4 3 2 1

Printed on acid-free paper

Table of Contents

Table of Contents

Acknowledgments

This book—or any of my previous books—would never have happened if not for the great people at Cedar Fort. I'm always grateful to Catherine Christensen for her thoughts and suggestions. I'll miss her, but wish her the best in her future endeavors. Again, many thanks go out to those who edit. (I'm the owner of numerous Cs in English, so I'm grateful that there are those with As that can figure out what I'm trying to say and make it look good on paper.) Thanks to those who format and design, and to the sales team who have always gone over the top to getting my books out there. Finally, thanks to my family and their understanding my passion for those pioneers that sacrificed so much so that we can enjoy more.

Preface

In these pages are forty-eight journal accounts, chronicling, for example, what Solomon Chamberlain and Harrison Burgess saw in visions similar to that of Joseph Smith as an adolescent on his father's farm "early in the spring of 1820." Afterward is what could be described as the most investigative search of any of the accounts, provided by John Corrill, along with his attempt to convince Sidney Rigdon of his folly in joining the Church. What was it John discovered about the "imposters" that caused him to want to join the Church? Benjamin Brown, having heard the new teachings and choosing to reject those things he had learned, due mostly in part to the inflated falsehoods the Church was attracting, eventually prayed for a sign. That sign was manifested, coupled with a "severe reprimand" from two Book of Mormon personalities. What was it Benjamin learned from the heavenly visitants? And what about Baptist preacher Zerah Pulsipher? What happened in his barn as he reflected on the Book of Mormon and the teachings of the Mormon elders? In the section "They Knew Something Better Was Coming" is the phenomenal story of three men, none of whom knew each other and were from three different states, led to the Smith home in Palmyra by the same Spirit and would not only shortly join the Church after its organization, but two of the three would be called to the holy Apostleship in 1835.

Along with these many journal entries, and the miraculous events surrounding the conversion of these early Saints, will be the attitude expressed by newspapers and reporters and ministers of the day. I do this to give a glimpse of the prejudice that the early members of the Church faced, the false reports that they had to filter through in their decision to be baptized into the new Church. I also include journal accounts of those who were not members of the Church, but had an active part in bringing forth of the Book of Mormon. Their testimonies are fascinating as they shed more light on the unfolding of the Church.

Many journal accounts state that they had heard about a "Golden Bible." It was this curiosity, that of seeing and reading this book, that led to their conversions. The journal entry of Mary Elizabeth Rollins Lightner sums up the excitement best of seeing and reading for the first time the Book of Mormon. Of the forty-eight entries, she is the only journal recorded as a child.

I will include, at the end of the journal account, additional information of the individual, if there is information available.

Mary E. Rollins Lightner (1818–1913)

Source: "Mary Elizabeth Rollins Lightner," *The Utah Genealogical and Historical Magazine* 17 (July 1926):193–205, 250.

I was born in the town of Lima, Livingston County, state of New York, April 9, 1818. My father, John D. Rollins, came from one of the New England States; I think it was Vermont. My mother, Keziah Keturah van Benthuysen, was born in Albany, state of New York, May 16, 1796. She married my father in 1814 or 1815. Three children were the fruit of this marriage, James Henry, myself and sister Caroline, the youngest. When Caroline was six months old, my father was shipwrecked on Lake Ontario during a terrible storm. Only one person was saved out of all the passengers and crew.

When I was ten years old, we moved to Kirtland, Ohio, and lived in a house belonging to Algernon Sidney Gilbert, mother's sister's husband. We remained there two years, when we heard of the plates of the Book of Mormon, being found by Joseph Smith. Soon the news was confirmed by the appearance of Oliver Cowdery, Peter Whitmer, and Ziba Peterson, with the glorious news of the restoration of the Gospel through the Prophet Joseph Smith. They bore a powerful testimony, by the Holy Spirit, of the truth of the great work they were engaged in; and which they were commissioned by the Father to present to all the world.

Quite a number of the residents of Kirtland accepted baptism. Mother and myself also, in the month of October, 1830. A branch of the Church was organized, and Father Morley was ordained an elder to preside over it. He owned a large farm, about a mile from Kirtland, and some three or four families went there to live, and meetings were held there. A good spirit and one of union prevailed among the brethren for some time. After Oliver Cowdery and his brethren left there for Missouri on their mission to the Lamanites, a wrong spirit crept into our midst, and a few were led away by it. About this time, John Whitmer came and brought a Book of Mormon. There was a meeting that evening, and we learned that Brother Morley had the Book in his possession the only one in that part of the country. I went to his house just before the meeting was to commence, and asked to see the book; Brother Morley put it in my hand, as I looked at it, I felt such a desire to read it, that I could not refrain from asking him to let me take it home and read it, while he attended meeting. He said it would be too late for me to take it back after meeting, and another thing, he had hardly had time to read a chapter in it himself, and but few of the brethren had even seen it, but I pled so earnestly for it, he finally said, "Child, if you will bring this book home before breakfast tomorrow morning, you may take it." He admonished me to be very careful, and see that no harm came to it.

If any person in this world was ever perfectly happy in the possession of any coveted treasure I was when I had permission to read that wonderful book. Uncle and Aunt were Methodists, so when I got into the house, I exclaimed, "Oh, Uncle, I have got the 'Golden Bible'." Well, there was consternation in the house for a few moments, and I was severely reprimanded for being so presumptuous as to ask such a favor, when Brother Morley had not read it himself. However, we all took turns reading it until very late in the night; as soon as it was light enough to see, I was up and learned the first verse in the book. When I reached Brother Morley's they had been up for only a little while. When I handed him the book, he remarked, "I guess you did not read much in it." I showed him how far we had read. He was surprised and said, "I don't believe you can tell me one word of it." I then repeated the first verse, also the outlines of the history of Nephi. He gazed at me in surprise, and said, "child, take this book home and finish it, I can wait."

Before or about the time I finished the last chapter, the Prophet Joseph Smith arrived in Kirtland, and moved into a part of Newel K. Whitney's house (Uncle Algernon's partner in the Mercantile Business), while waiting for his goods to be put in order. Brother Whitney brought the Prophet Joseph to our house and introduced him to the older ones of the family (I was not in at the time.) In looking around he saw the Book of Mormon on the shelf, and asked how that book came to be there. He said, "I sent that book to Brother Morley." Uncle told him how his niece had obtained it. He asked, "Where is your niece?" I was sent for; when he saw me he looked at me so earnestly, I felt almost afraid. After a moment or two he came and put his hands on my head and gave me a great blessing, the first I ever received, and made me a present of the book, and said he would give Brother Morley another. He came in time to rebuke the evil spirits, and set the church in order. We all felt that he was a man of God, for he spoke with power, and as one having authority in very deed.

Additional Information: The name Mary Rollins Lightner may seem familiar to you. Usually her name is coupled with that of her sister, Caroline. When the Jackson County mob was breaking up the printing establishment of W. W. Phelps on July 20, 1833, the revelations which Joseph Smith had received to that point in time were dumped into the street. Mary, Caroline, and John Taylor (not the same individual who would later become president of the Church) risked their lives and were able to save some of the revelations from mob destruction. Later, Mary and Caroline were presented with a Book of Commandments, which they cherished for the remainder of their lives.

Part One

They Knew Something Better Was Coming

The Bible is replete with examples of God's instructions to His children here on the earth. It's impossible to study this book of scripture and not understand that communication between man and heaven was alive and well when the various accounts were first written. It makes sense that a loving Father in Heaven would provide teaching for those seeking Him. However, with the death of the Savior and His apostles, coupled with the loss of priesthood authority, this gift, the association between heaven and earth, was closed for a time. With the closing of heaven's door and the light provided by revelation, spiritual darkness covered the earth. Men, left to their own interpretation of scripture, faltered. It was a severe case of the "blind leading the blind." Nevertheless, as part of the great plan of salvation, the heavens reopened and restored that which was once lost.

Latter-day Saints are familiar with the proceedings leading to that "beautiful, clear day, early in the spring of eighteen hundred and twenty" (Joseph Smith—History 1:14). It's no secret that heavenly sanctioned events had to take place. God is a God of order. What happens on His timeline is not a fluke, as some might suggest. Heavenly Father knew certain events had to take place, even eons before the Restoration: the Reformation (which provided all with access to the Bible), the invention of the printing press, the discovery of America, the Revolutionary War, the social atmosphere which allowed for the affordability and distribution of the Bible to the average American family, the placing of the Smith family in the Palmyra area, and finally the religious revival of the 1820s.

What set the gears in motion in Joseph's mind was the circuit Methodist minister, George Lane after a talk titled, "Which Church Shall I Join?" All that remained was for young Joseph to read James 1:5, as introduced by Reverend Lane. Everything else was set and in place. Touched by this passage of scripture, Joseph pondered, which, with time, led him to the Sacred Grove. The rest, as they say, is history—a history that has been immortalized in hymn, art, print, and millions of testimonies the world over. A history that any Latter-day Saint, past, present, or future will never tire of.

But was Joseph the only one? Was he the only individual who knew something better was coming, that there was more, and that it would require a companion book to the Bible? No, Joseph Smith was not the only one. However, he is the only person in this dispensation to be visited simultaneously by Heavenly Father and His Son, Jesus Christ. Joseph Smith was foreordained in the counsels of heaven for this unique experience. But as stated, there were others visited by heavenly messengers, and these others also knew that there *had* to be additional scripture, four of which (Chamberlain, Patten, Harris, and Marsh) had this knowledge before the Church was reestablished on the earth.

In the next three journal accounts are the amazing experiences of Solomon Chamberlain, Thomas B. Marsh, and Parley P. Pratt. Solomon was visited by a heavenly messenger. His experience was similar to Joseph's. The accounts of Marsh and Pratt do not involve a heavenly visitation; however, their stories becomes very similar to Chamberlain's account when they are touched by the same Spirit to leave the boat they were on at Palmyra. What makes these accounts more incredible is that Chamberlain, Marsh, and Pratt did not know each other. They were from different parts of the country (Chamberlain, New York; Pratt, Ohio; Marsh, Massachusetts). And yet, they knew something better was coming prior to the official organization of the Church.

The section ends with the accounts of William Huntington, David Patten, and Martin Harris. Though these entries are short, their accounts make for an interesting study because, not knowing exactly why, they knew that the true Church was not on the earth and believed that the day would arrive when they would see it in all its glory. What makes their cases compelling is that they did not possess proof other than their own feelings that these things would be; and yet, as Huntington would state in his own words, "I boldly advocated the gospel as our Savior taught it in His days or as the Apostles taught."

Solomon Chamberlain (1788–1862)

Source: Autobiography (1788–1850), Holograph, BYU Harold B. Lee Library.

My father was an honest, hard-working man, a farmer by trade, and earned his bread by the sweat of his brow, and accumulated considerable property, and died when I was about 8 years old, and my mother died about 10 years after. What little property I received from my father's estate did me little or no good, and I began the world like my father, earned my bread by the sweat of my face. I soon learned the cooper's trade and worked the most of my days at that. From the time my father died, till I was 19 years of age I lived a very wicked life. About that time, I had a vision of hell, and which alarmed me very much, and I reformed and had another of three heavens, and their glories, and the third one, far exceeded the others. My visions so alarmed me, I was in sorrow and repentance for many days, on account of my sins, I thought I would give all the world if I could find a man that could tell me what I should do to be saved. I sought much, but could find none. I thought I would go to the Presbyterian Minister and enquire of him, I accordingly went, and asked him what I should do to be saved, he appeared like a man astonished, he said I must wait the Lord's due time, and in His own due time he would bring me in. As all others had failed I thought I would go to God and plead for mercy, and if I went to hell, I would go praying, and I cried unto the Lord night and day, for the forgiveness of my sins. Like Enos of old, till at length the Lord said, "Solomon, thy sins are forgiven thee. Go in peace and sin no more." My heart then leaped for joy unspeakable, I now joined the Methodist Order, and thought they were the rightest of any on the earth.

About the year 1814 or 1815, the Reformed Methodists broke off from the Episcopal Methodists. I was in hope that they were right. [This last sentence was crossed out in the original manuscript.] I found them to be more right than the Episcopal, and joined them. About this time the Lord showed me in a vision, that there were no people on the earth that were right, and that faith was gone from the earth, excepting a few and that all churches were corrupt. I further saw in vision, that he would soon raise up a church, that would be after the Apostolic Order, that there would be in it the same powers, and gifts that were in the days of Christ, and that I should live to see the day, and that there would a book come forth, like unto the Bible and the people would [be] guided by it, as well as the Bible. This was in the year of 1816. I then believed in gifts and miracles as the Latter-day Saints do, for which I was much persecuted and called deluded. This vision I received from an angel or spirit from the eternal world that told me these things.

About the time that Joseph Smith found the gold record, I began to feel that the time was drawing near, that the Lord would in some shape or other, bring forth his church. I made some inquiry through the country where I traveled if there was any strange work of God, such as had not been on the earth since the days of Christ. I could hear of none. I was living about 20 miles east of where the gold record was found, on the Erie Canal. I had occasion to go on a visit into Upper Canada. I took boat for Lockport, when the boat came to Palmyra, I felt as if some genie or good spirit told me to leave the boat. This was a few miles from where the record was found. After leaving the boat, the spirit manifested to me, to travel a south course. I did so for about 3 miles. I had not as yet heard of the Gold Bible (so called) [Book of Mormon] nor any of the [Joseph] Smith family. I was a stranger in that part of the country, a town where I never before had set my foot, and knew no one in the town.

It was now about sundown, and my guide directed me to put up for the night, which I did to a farm house. In the morning, the people of the house asked me if I had heard of the Gold Bible [Book of Mormon]. When they said Gold Bible, there was a power like electricity went from the top of my head to the end of my toes. This was the first time I ever heard of the Gold Bible. I was now within half a mile of the Smith family where Joseph lived. From the time I left the boat until now, I was wholly led by the Spirit or my genie. The women spoke considerable of the Gold Bible that Joseph Smith had found. When she mentioned Gold Bible, I felt a shock of the power of God go from head to foot. I said to myself, "I shall soon find why I have been led in this singular manner."

I soon made my way across lots, to Father Smith's and found Hyrum walking the floor. As I entered the door, I said, "Peace be to this house." He looked at me as one astonished, and said, "I hope it will be peace." I then said, "Is there anyone here that believes in visions or revelations?" He said, "Yes, we are a visionary house." I said, "Then I will give you one of my pamphlets, which was visionary, and of my own experience." They then called the people together, which consisted of five or six men who were out at the door. Father Smith was one and some of the Whitmer's. They then sat down and read my pamphlet. Hyrum read first, but was so affected he could not read it. He then gave it to a man, which I learned was Christian Whitmer, he finished reading it. I then opened my mouth and began to preach to them, in the words that the angel had made known to me in the vision, that all churches and denominations on the earth had become corrupt, and no church of God on the earth, but that he would shortly raise up a church that would never be confounded nor brought down and be like unto the Apostolic Church. They wondered greatly who had been telling me these things, for said they we have the same things wrote [written] down in our house, taken from the Gold record, that you are preaching to us. I said, "The Lord told me these things a number of years ago." I then said, "If you are a visionary house, I wish you would make known some of your discoveries, for I think I can bear them." They then made known to me that they had obtained a gold record, and just finished translating it here. Now, the Lord revealed to me by the gift and power of the Holy Ghost that this was the work I had been looking for.

Here I stayed 2 days and they instructed me, in the manuscripts of the Book of Mormon. After I had been here two days, I went with Hyrum and some others to Palmyra printing office where they began to print the Book of Mormon, and as soon as they had printed 64 pages, I took them with their leave and pursued my journey to Canada, and I preached all that I knew concerning Mormonism, to all both high and low, rich and poor, and thus you see this was the first that ever printed Mormonism was preached to this generation.

I did not see anyone in traveling for 7 or 800 miles, that had ever heard of the Gold Bible (so called). I exhorted all people to prepare for the great work of God that was now about to come forth, and it would never be brought down nor confounded. As soon as the book was printed, I took 8 or 10 of them and traveled for 8 days, and sold one in that time. About this time I thought if I could see the Reformed Methodists I could convince them of the truth of the Book of Mormon. I accordingly went to one of their conferences, where I met about 40 of their preachers and labored with them for two days to convince them of the truth of the Book of Mormon, and they utterly rejected me and the Book of Mormon. One of their greatest preachers so called, by the name of Buckly, (if a mistake not) abused me very bad, and ordered me off from their premises. He was soon taken crazy, and died a miserable death. At this conference was Brigham and his brother Phineas Young. They did not oppose me but used me well. On my way home I stopped at their camp meeting, where I found one of their greatest preachers, whom I contended with concerning the Book of Mormon, by the name of William Lake, who utterly condemned it and rejected it, who spurned at me and the Book and said, if it was of God, do you think He would send such a little upstart as you are around with it? But he soon after died a poor drunken sot. While on my way home I stopped at a Free Will Baptist Church, and preached to a large congregation, and they received the work, but there was no one to baptize them.

The Church was not yet organized, but was soon after, April 6th, 1830. A few days after, I was baptized in the waters of Seneca Lake, by Joseph Smith, (and) emigrated same spring to Kirtland, Ohio, and in the fall of 1831, emigrated to Jackson County, Missouri, and in the beginning of the winter of 1833, was broken up by mobs, and driven out of the county and suffered the loss of all things, with hundreds of my brethren and sisters. Settled again in Clay County and was there broke up and suffered the loss of 3 houses and my plantation. Again settled in Caldwell County and was broke up and also in Daviess County, and was driven out of the counties in the coldest part of the winter and suffered the loss of all things. And great was the suffering of the Saints while in Missouri, that I was a witness to and many times had my life threatened, and sometimes been knocked down, and some of my blood spilt [spilled] by mobs. We were driven from the state of Missouri, and settled in Illinois, at Nauvoo, where we remained in peace for several years, and built a temple. On June 27, 1844, our Prophet and Patriarch was murdered, and about the year 1846 we were broken up and had to flee to the Rocky Mountains.

Additional Information: According to history, the Prophet's younger brother Samuel H. Smith is credited with being the first missionary after the Church was organized. However, going off of

Solomon's account here, it's possible that Solomon, as an unbaptized enthusiast for the cause, may have been the first missionary in this dispensation *prior* to the organization of the Church to leave the country on a "mission."

Parley P. Pratt (1807–1857)

Source: Book of Abraham Project (www.boap.org).

At the commencement of 1830, I felt drawn out in an extraordinary manner to search the prophets, and to pray for an understanding of the same. My prayers were soon answered, even beyond my expectations; the prophecies of the holy prophets were opened to my view; I began to understand the things which were coming on the earth, the restoration of Israel, the coming of the Messiah, and the glory that should follow. I was so astonished at the darkness of myself and mankind on these subjects that I could exclaim with the prophet: surely, "darkness covers the earth, and gross darkness the people."

I was all swallowed up in these things. I felt constrained to devote my time in enlightening my fellow men on these important truths, and in warning them to prepare for the coming of the Lord.

My brother William, who journeyed to the West with me in my seventeenth year, had now been missing to the family for five years, and was supposed to be dead. About the time he disappeared and was lost sight of, he was known to leave the city of New York, where he had been employed, and to pass up the Hudson on a steamer. He was heard of no more; and, as a notice appeared in the papers of the same date that a young gentleman by the name of William Pratt was drowned in the Hudson, on his way up the river, our parents and the family had given him up for lost.

One morning, as I was absent from home on business, about two miles distant, I heard of him; and that he was then residing about ten miles from me. On hearing this I ran nearly the whole distance on foot, and in about two hours had him by the hand. He was much surprised, although he had heard of a man of my name living in the neighborhood; but could not believe it was me. We had each of us taken our chance amid the hardships and toils of a new country for years, and at last found ourselves together about six hundred miles from our starting point.

This was a joyful and unexpected meeting of two brothers. He immediately accompanied me home, and was introduced to my wife and our little farm in the wilderness, where we spent some days together. He admired my wife; but above all my farm. "Brother

Parley," said he, "how have you done all this? When we were last together you had no wife, no farm, no house, no orchard, and now you are here with everything smiling around you." I replied that hard work had accomplished it all. And, continued I, we are now about to leave this quiet home which we have toiled so hard to make, and perhaps, never see it again. "How so?" said he, with much surprise, and somewhat of disappointment. I then unfolded to him the gospel and prophecies as they had been opened to me, and told him that the spirit of these things had wrought so powerfully on my mind of late that I could not rest; that I could no longer be contented to dwell in quiet and retirement on my farm, while I had light to impart to mankind, of which I knew they were in a great measure ignorant. "But," said he, "if I had fifty acres of land, a comfortable house, a fine orchard, a beautiful garden, with meadow land, grain, and above all, such beautiful flowers and so valuable a housekeeper as you have, and all these things the work of our own hands, I am sure I would stay and enjoy the same while I lived; and the world might go on its own jog, and its own way, for all me. Besides, how are you to get your living? This is your all; you have toiled for years to obtain it, and why not now continue to enjoy it?"

"William," said I, "I see plainly you know but little of my circumstances if the changes which have taken place with me since we parted five years ago, nor how vastly wealthy I have become within that time. Why, sir, I have bank bills enough, on the very best institutions in the world, to sustain myself and family while we live."

"Indeed," said he, "well, I should like to see some of them; I hope they are genuine." "Certainly," I replied, "there is no doubt of that. They are true bills and founded on capital that will never fail, though heaven and earth should pass away. Of this I will convince you in a moment."

I then unlocked my treasury and drew from thence a large pocket book, fall of promissory notes like the following: "Whoever shall forsake father or mother, brethren or sisters, houses or lands, wife or children, for my sake and the gospel's, shall receive an hundred fold in this life, and in the world to come lie everlasting." "If ye abide in me, and my words abide in you, you shall ask what you will in my name and I will give it you." "All things are possible to him that believeth."

"Now, William," said I, "are these the words of Jesus Christ, or are they not?" "They certainly are," said he, "I always believed the New Testament."

"Then you admit they are genuine bills?"

"I do."

"Is the signer able to meet his engagements?"

"He certainly is."

"Is he willing?"

"He is."

"Well, then, I am going to fulfil the conditions to the letter on my part. I feel called upon by the Holy Ghost to forsake my house and home for the gospel's sake; and I will do it, placing both feet firm on these promises with nothing else to rely upon." "If I sink, they are false."

"If I am sustained, they are true. I will put them to the test. Experiment shall now establish the truth of Christ's promises, or the truth of infidelity."

"Well," said he, "try it, if you will; but, for my part, although I always believed the Bible, I would not dare believe it literally, and really stand upon its promises, with no other prop."

We parted. He to his business, I to my preparations for a mission which should only end with my life.

In August, 1830, I had closed my business, completed my arrangements, and we bid adieu to our wilderness home and never saw it afterwards.

On settling up, at a great sacrifice of property, we had about ten dollars left in cash. With this small sum, we launched forth into the wide world, determining first to visit our native place, on our mission, and then such other places as I might be led to by the Holy Spirit.

We made our way to Cleveland, 30 miles. We then took passage on a schooner for Buffalo, a distance of 200 miles. We had a fair wind, and the captain, being short of hands, gave me the helm, the sails being all set, and turned in. I steered the vessel the most of the day, with no other person on deck. Of course, our passage cost us little besides my labor. Landing in Buffalo, we engaged our passage for Albany on a canal boat, distance 360 miles. This, including board, cost all our money and some articles of clothing.

Arriving at Rochester, I informed my wife that, notwithstanding our passage being paid through the whole distance, yet I must leave the boat and her to pursue her passage to our friends; while I would stop awhile in this region. Why, I did not know; but so it was plainly manifest by the Spirit to me. I said to her, "We part for a season; go and visit our friends in our native place; I will come soon, but how soon I know not; for I have a work to do in this region of country, and what it is, or how long it will take to perform it, I know not; but I will come when it is performed."

My wife would have objected to this; but she had seen the hand of God so plainly manifest in His dealings with me many times, that she dare not oppose the things manifest to me by His spirit. She, therefore, consented; and I accompanied her as far as Newark, a small town upwards of 100 miles from Buffalo, and then took leave of her, and of the boat.

It was early in the morning, just at the dawn of day, I walked ten miles into the country, and stopped to breakfast with a Mr. Wells. I proposed to preach in the evening. Mr. Wells readily accompanied me through the neighborhood to visit the people, and circulate the appointment.

We visited an old Baptist deacon by the name of Hamlin. After hearing of our appointment for evening, he began to tell of a book, a STRANGE BOOK, a VERY STRANGE BOOK! in his possession, which had been just published. This book, he said, purported to have been originally written on plates either of gold or brass, by a branch of the tribes of Israel; and to have been discovered and translated by a young man near Palmyra, in the State of New York, by the aid of visions, or the ministry of angels. I inquired of him how or where the book was to be obtained. He promised me the perusal of it, at his house the next day, if I would call. I felt a strange interest in the book. I preached that evening to a small audience, who appeared to be interested in the truths which I endeavored to unfold to them in a clear and lucid manner from the Scriptures. Next morning I called at his house, where, for the first time, my eyes beheld the "BOOK OF MORMON" that book of books—that record which reveals the antiquities of the "New World" back to the remotest ages, and which unfolds the destiny of its people and the world for all time to come; that Book which contains the fulness of the gospel of a crucified and risen Redeemer; that Book which reveals a lost remnant of Joseph, and which was the principal means, in the hands of God, of directing the entire course of my future life.

I opened it with eagerness, and read its title page. I then read the testimony of several witnesses in relation to the manner of its being found and translated. After this I commenced its contents by course. I read all day; eating was a burden, I had no desire for food; sleep was a burden when the night came, for I preferred reading to sleep.

As I read, the spirit of the Lord was upon me, and I knew and comprehended that the book was true, as plainly and manifestly as a man comprehends and knows that he exists. My joy was now full, as it were, and I rejoiced sufficiently to more than pay me for all the sorrows, sacrifices and toils of my life. I soon determined to see the young man who had been the instrument of its discovery and translation.

I accordingly visited the village of Palmyra, and inquired for the residence of Mr. Joseph Smith. I found it some two or three miles from the village. As I approached the house at the close of the day I overtook a man who was driving some cows, and inquired of him for Mr. Joseph Smith, the translator of the "Book of Mormon." He informed me that he now resided in Pennsylvania; some one hundred miles distant. I inquired for his father, or for any of the family. He told me that his father had gone a journey; but that his residence was a small house just before me; and, said he, I am his brother. It was Mr. Hyrum Smith. I informed him of the interest I felt in the Book, and of my desire to learn more about it. He welcomed me to his house, and we spent the night together; for neither of us felt disposed to sleep. We conversed most of the night, during which I unfolded to him much of my experience in my search after truth, and my success so far; together with that which I felt was lacking, viz: a commissioned priesthood, or apostleship to minister in the ordinances of God.

He also unfolded to me the particulars of the discovery of the Book; its translation; the rise of the Church of Latter-day Saints, and the commission of his brother Joseph, and others, by revelation and the ministering of angels, by which the apostleship and authority had been again restored to the earth. After duly weighing the whole matter in my mind I saw clearly that these things were true; and that myself and the whole world were without baptism, and without the ministry and ordinances of God; and that the whole world had been in this condition since the days that inspiration and revelation had ceased—in short, that this was a new dispensation or commission, in fulfillment of prophecy, and for the restoration of Israel, and to prepare the way before the second coming of the Lord.

In the morning I was compelled to take leave of this worthy man and his family—as I had to hasten back a distance of thirty miles, on foot, to fulfil an appointment in the evening. As we parted he kindly presented me with a copy of the Book of Mormon. I had not yet completed its perusal, and was glad indeed to possess a copy of my own. I travelled on a few miles, and, stopping to rest, I commenced again to read the book. To my great joy I found that Jesus Christ, in his glorified resurrected body, had appeared to the remnant of Joseph on the continent of America, soon after his resurrection and ascension into heaven; and that he also administered, in person, to the ten lost tribes; and that through his personal ministry in these countries his gospel was revealed and written in countries and among nations entirely unknown to the Jewish apostles.

Thus revealed, written, handed down and preserved, till revealed in this age by the angels of God, it had, of course, escaped the corruptions of the great and abominable church; and been preserved in purity.

This discovery greatly enlarged my heart, and filled my soul with joy and gladness. I esteemed the Book, or the information contained in it, more than all the riches of the world. Yes; I verily believe that I would not at that time have exchanged the knowledge I then possessed, for a legal title to all the beautiful farms, houses, villages and property which passed in review before me, on my journey through one of the most flourishing settlements of western New York.

Surely, thought I, Jesus had other sheep, as he said to his Apostles of old; and here they were, in the wilderness of the world called new. And they heard the voice of the Good Shepherd of Israel; and he brought them to his fold. Truly, thought I, he was not sent (in person) save to the lost sheep of the house of Israel, as he told the woman of Canaan; and here were a portion of them. Truly, thought I, the angels sung with the spirit and with the understanding when they declared: "We bring you glad tidings of great joy, which shall be to ALL PEOPLE."

In his mortal tabernacle he confined his ministry and that of his Apostles to the land of Judea; but afterwards, released from the bonds of mortal life, or rather death, and clothed with an immortal body, and with organs strong and lasting as the immortal mind, he possessed all power in heaven and on earth; he was then enabled to extend his ministry to heaven, earth or hell. He could take the wings of the morning, and, with the speed of light, make his way to the Heaven of Heavens; and converse and counsel among the sons of God; or receive counsel from his Father in Heaven; or, leaving again the starry worlds, he could descend to the dark and gloomy abodes of the spirits in prison and preach to them the gospel—bursting off their shackles and unlocking their prison doors; while these once dark abodes were now brilliant with light, and, instead of prison groans, were heard joyful acclamations of deliverance to the captive, and the opening of the prison to them that are bound; or coming again to visit the earth, he could soar away beyond the waves and tempests, which had before set bounds to the geographical knowledge of man, and stood up as an impregnable barrier to the intercourse of nations; and there, in other tribes and tongues, make known the riches of his grace, and his triumph over death. And when ages had passed, and nations slumbered in the dust—when cruelty and bloodshed had blotted almost every trace of priesthood and apostleship from the earth; when saints had been worn out and overcome times, laws and ordinances changed; the Bible itself robbed of its plainness; and all things darkened and corrupted; a pure and faithful record of his ministry to other nations is forthcoming from among the archives of the dead, to reveal the "mystery of iniquity;" to speak, as with a voice of thunder, in rebuking the evil and revealing the fullness of the gospel. Such was the Book of Mormon—much its effect upon the startling nations.

Having rested awhile and perused this sacred book by the roadside, I again walked on.

In the evening I arrived in time to fill my appointment. I met a crowded house, and laid before them many interesting truths, which were listened to with deep interest.

The next evening I had another appointment, and the people came out in great numbers, and were filled with the spirit of interest and inquiry.

They urged me very much to continue my discourses among them; but I felt to minister no more till I had attended to some important duties for myself. I had now found men on earth commissioned to preach, baptize, ordain to the ministry, etc., and I determined to obey the fullness of the gospel without delay. I should have done so at the first interview with Elder Hyrum Smith; but these two appointments were already out, and thirty miles' travel required all the time I had.

I now returned immediately to Hyrum Smith's residence, and demanded baptism at his hands. I tarried with him one night, and the next day we walked some twenty-five miles to the residence of Mr. Whitmer, in Seneca County. Here we arrived in the evening, and found a most welcome reception.

This was the family, several of whose names were attached to the Book of Mormon as witnesses—Mr. Joseph Smith having translated much of the book in Whitmer's chamber.

I found the little branch of the Church in this place full of joy, faith, humility and charity. We rested that night, and on the next day, being about the 1st of September, 1830, I was baptized by the hand of an Apostle of the Church of Jesus Christ, by the name of Oliver Cowdery. This took place in Seneca Lake, a beautiful and transparent sheet of water in Western New York.

A meeting was held the same evening, and after singing a hymn and prayer, Elder Cowdery and others proceeded to lay their hands upon my head in the name of Jesus, for the gift of the Holy Ghost. After which I was ordained to the office of an Elder in the Church, which included authority to preach, baptize, and minister the sacrament, administer the Holy Spirit, by the laying on of hands in the name of Jesus Christ and to take the lead of meetings of worship.

Additional Information: Parley was called to the Apostleship in February of 1835, faithfully serving for over two decades until his murder in Arkansas in May 1857.

Thomas Baldwin Marsh (1799–1866)

Source: "History of Thomas Baldwin Marsh [by himself]," The Latter-day Saints' Millennial Star 26 (1864):359–60, 375–76, 390–92, 406. (Written by himself in Great Salt Lake City, November, 1857.)

I was born in the town of Acton, Middlesex County, Massachusetts, November 1, 1799. My father, James Marsh was born in Douglas, Massachusetts, March 27, 1751. My mother, Mary, daughter of Titus Law, was born in Acton, Massachusetts, March 18, 1759.

I spent my early life in farming at Westmoreland, New Hampshire, until I was fourteen years of age, when I ran away and went to Chester, Vermont, where I worked on a farm three months; then went to Albany, New York and engaged in a public house as a waiter, where I remained eighteen months, when I went to New York and engaged in the city hotel and remained two years; when I returned to my old situation in Albany, and after serving a year returned to New York City Hotel for two years; then removed to Long Island, New York, where I engaged as groom to Edward Griswald, in whose service I remained one and a half-years; during which I became acquainted with Elizabeth Godkin, and married her on the 1st November, 1820.

Immediately after marrying I commenced in the grocery business, in New York, in which business I remained one and a half years, but did not succeed. I then engaged in a type foundry in Boston, where I continued seven years.

While engaged in this business I joined the Methodist Church and tried for two years to be a genuine Methodist, but did not succeed any better in getting Methodist religion than I did in the grocery business. I compared Methodism with the Bible, but could not make it correspond. I withdrew from all sects, and being about to leave Boston my old class leader wished me to take a good certificate, but I informed him I did not want it. I had a measure of the spirit of prophecy and told him that I expected a new church would arise, which would have the truth in its purity. He said to me, you no doubt mean to be a leader in that new sect. I told him I had no such intentions. He said, he prayed that the Lord would make me a firebrand in the midst of that new religious body, as reformation was necessary. My wife unknown to me, however, got a certificate for herself and me on one paper. I informed her that I never would attend, but I would find a suitable class for her if she wanted to join.

I remained in Boston several years engaged in the type foundry. During this period I became acquainted with several friends whose opinions concerning religion were like my own. We kept aloof from sectarians, and were called by them Quietists, because we resembled so much a sect in France known by that name professing to be led by the Spirit.

I believed the Spirit of God dictated me to make a journey west. I started in company with one Benjamin Hall, who was also led by the Spirit. I went to Lima, Livingston County, New York, where I staid [stayed] some three months, and then left for home. I called on my return at Lyonstown, on a family, whose names I do not recollect. On leaving there next morning the lady enquired if I had heard of the Golden Book found by a youth named Joseph Smith. I informed her I never heard anything about it, and became very anxious to know concerning the matter. On enquiring, she told me I could learn more about it from Martin Harris, in Palmyra.

I returned back westward and found Martin Harris at the printing office, in Palmyra, where the first sixteen pages of the Book of Mormon had just been struck off, the proof sheet of which I obtained from the printer and took with me. As soon as Martin Harris found out my intentions he took me to the house of Joseph Smith, Sen., where Joseph Smith, Jun., resided, who could give me any information I might wish. Here I found Oliver Cowdery, who gave me all the information concerning the book I desired. After staying there two days I started for Charleston, Massachusetts, highly pleased with the information I had obtained concerning the new found book.

After arriving home and finding my family all well, I showed my wife the sixteen pages of the Book of Mormon which I had obtained, with which she was well pleased, believing it to be the work of God. From this time for about one year I corresponded with Oliver Cowdery and Joseph Smith, Jun., and prepared myself to move west.

Learning by letter that the Church of Jesus Christ had been organized on the 6th day of April, 1830, I moved to Palmyra, Ontario County, in September following, and landed at the house of Joseph Smith, Sen., with my whole family. During the month I was baptized by David Whitmer, in Cayuga Lake, and in a few days I was ordained an elder by Oliver Cowdery with six elders, at Father

Whitmer's house. Joseph received a revelation appointing me a physician to the Church.

Additional information: Thomas B. Marsh would also be called to the Apostleship in 1835, serving as President of the Quorum of the Twelve; however, he would eventually apostatize from the Church during the troubled Missouri years of 1839. Years later, in 1857, Marsh trekked west to Salt Lake City and reunited with the Church.

See *Church History in the Fulness of Times* (Salt Lake City: The Church of Jesus Christ of Latter-day Saints, 1989), 199.

William Huntington (1784–1846)

Source: Typescript, BYU Harold B. Lee Library. This version edited for standard grammar.

About 1832, I was moved upon by the spirit of God to look into the situation of the churches. I found the ordinances changed [and] the covenants broken. The fear of God was taught by [the] precepts of men. They had a form of godliness, but denied the power thereof. From such things, I felt my duty to turn away. I withdrew from the church [Presbyterians][and] stood alone. I searched the scriptures daily. [I] found the faith once delivered to the saints was not among men. The power of the priesthood was lost. In searching the scriptures and history, I found where it [the priesthood] was gone or, in other words, John the Revelator said it had gone into the wilderness. I found in searching the scriptures, that the Church should return, bringing with her the gifts and graces as it formerly had in the Apostle's day. I boldly advocated the gospel as our Savior taught it in his days or as the Apostles taught.

I told the people I believed I should see a church in my day based on the gospel plan as was in the Apostle's days. In this frame of mind I stood for some two or three years, anxiously contending for the faith once delivered to the saints. In 1833, I found the Book of Mormon. I read the book, believed in the book [and felt] that it was what it was represented to be. My mind thus being prepared to receive the gospel accordingly, in the month of April 1835, myself and my wife both united with the Church of Jesus Christ of Latter-day Saints.

Additional Information: Not only did William know that the true church didn't exist on earth at the time he was searching for truth, but it was also impressed on his mind at the time that alcohol was not for the body, at which time he never drank alcohol again.

Seehttp://historyofmormonism.com/index.php?s=William+Huntington (04/11/2014).

David Wyman Patten (1800–1838)

Source: Journal (c.1800–1838) in Extracts from the Journals of David W. Patten, Wilford Woodruff, Charles C. Rich and Heber C. Kimball "History of David W. Patten," Millennial Star 26 (1864).

In the early part of my life, I was often called upon to repent of my sins, and the Spirit of the Lord did often reprove me. In the twenty-first year of my life the Lord visited me by his Holy Spirit, and called upon me again to repent. I rejected the call at first, but, upon mature reflection, considered it was reasonable the Lord should require obedience, and I turned to the Lord and found his favor. I lived in the enjoyment of his Spirit for three years, during which time, by dreams and visions, many things were made known unto me, which were to come; and from the teachings I received of the Holy Spirit, I was looking for the Church of Christ to arise in its purity, according to the promise of Christ, and that I should live to see it.

From this happy state I fell away and lived, in a measure, in darkness until the year 1830, when my mind became again aroused by the Spirit of God to a sense of my situation, and I began to pray mightily to God that he would pardon my sins and grant me his Holy Spirit. About this time the sound of the Book of Mormon came to my ears, and I was greatly agitated in mind about it, and desired to see it. I saw the book that same summer, but had no opportunity of reading it further than the preface and testimony of the witnesses. A fear came upon me, and I dare not say anything against it. From that time I began to cry to God for saving faith.

Nothing took place worthy of note until May, 1832, when on receiving a letter from my brother in Indiana, giving me information of the rise of the Church of Christ, the reception of the Holy Ghost and the gifts thereof by the Saints. My brother informed me that he had received the Holy Ghost by the laying on of the hands of the Elders of the Church. This caused my heart to leap for joy, and I resolved to go immediately and see for myself. I soon became satisfied that the work was true, and was baptized on the 15th of June, 1832, in Greene Co., Indiana, by my brother, John Patten.

Additional Information: David Patten was called to the original Quorum of the Twelve Apostles in February 1835. He served in it until his death at the Battle of Crooked River in Missouri in 1838. It's because of his death, and the falling away of Thomas B. Marsh, that Brigham Young would become the President of the Church after the death of Joseph Smith.

Martin Harris (1783–1875)

Source: *Journal of Edward Stevenson*, vol. 32, cit. Joseph Grant Stevenson, "The Life of Edward Stevenson" (Brigham Young University, 1955), 163–164.

[Salt Lake City, September 4, 1870, Sunday morning: Testimony of Martin Harris, written by my hand (Edward Stevenson) from the mouth of Martin Harris]:

In the year 1818, fifty-two years ago I was inspired of the Lord and taught of the spirit that I should not join any church, although I was anxiously sought for by many of the sectarians. I was taught I could not walk together unless agreed. What can you not be agreed in? In the trinity, because I cannot find it in any Bible. Find it for me and I am ready to receive it. Three persons in one God—one personage I can not concede to, for this is anti-Christ, for where is the Father as Son. I have more proof to prove nine persons in the trinity than you have three. How do you do so? John tells us of the seven spirits sent into all the world. If you have a right to make a personage of one spirit, I have of the seven—and the Father and Son are two more, making nine. Other sects also tried me. They say three persons in one God, without body, parts or passions. I told them such a God I would not be afraid of. I could not please or offend him. [I] would not be afraid to fight a duel with such a God. The Methodists teach two [one word illegible] them exceed from one. I told them to [retract] to my saying, "God would hold me accountable for the use I made of it. All of the sects called me "Bro" [Brother] because the Lord had enlightened me.

The spirit told me to join none of the churches, for none had authority from the Lord, for there will not be a true church on the earth until the words of Isaiah shall be fulfilled. When interrogated closely, I told them, "If any church [be] the church of Christ, the Christians then claim me. But join and lectuien [?] as much as any other. The time has not come for you to take that name. At Antioch they were called Christians in derision. No thanks for your name, so I remained, for there was no authority, for the spirit told me that I might just as well plunge myself into the water as to have any one of the sects baptize me.

So I remained until the Church was organized by Joseph Smith, the Prophet. Then I was baptized by the hands of Oliver

Cowdery, by Joseph Smith's command, being the first after Joseph and Oliver Cowdery. And then the spirit bore testimony that this was all right, and I rejoiced in the established Church. Previous to my being baptized, I became a witness of the plates of the Book of Mormon in 1829. In March the people rose up and united against the work, gathering testimony against the plates, and said they had testimony enough, and if I did not put Joseph in jail and his father for deception, they would me. So I went from Waterloo twenty-five miles southeast of Palmyra to Rogerses, Suscotua [sic] County, New York, and to Harmony, Pennsylvania, 125 [miles] and found Joseph. Rogers, unknown to me, had agreed to give my wife one hundred dollars if it was not a deception, and had whet his knife to eat the [word illegible] of the plates as the Lord had forbid Joseph exhibiting them openly.

Additional Information: Harris's life is well documented. He left the Church but was later rebaptized. Martin Harris once stated, "I never did leave the Church; the Church left me."

See William H. Homer Jr., "'Publish It Upon the Mountains': The Story of Martin Harris," *Improvement Era,* July 1955, 505.

Part Two

Heavenly Manifestations

This following section includes journal entries of angelic visitations (Harrison Burgess), a visit from two of the three Nephites (Benjamin Brown), the individual's spirit leaving his body and an interview on the "other side" (Nathan Porter), the whispering of the Spirit (Levi Hancock), a column of light (Zerah Pulsipher), and a deceased grandfather letting a grandson know he was making the right choice (Jacob Hamblin). Ironically, in spite of the heavenly manifestations, it did not mean that they all enwrapped themselves in Gospel principles and desired baptism. In fact, there were times when some rebelled and chose to take matters into their own hands, essentially ignoring Heavenly Father's will.

This may sound ludicrous. How can anyone disregard heavenly communication? And yet, even today, people do this. The classic example is Jonah. Here was a man that received a direct command to call a city to repentance, but he discounted the encounter and the call. Jonah realized quick that you can run, but cannot hide from the Lord.

In these journal entries are miraculous examples of heaven's love, provided by divine indicators in the form of personages or the Holy Ghost. Some of these individuals saw heaven's hand in the experience and embraced the Gospel. But in the case of John Lowe Butler, he rebelled like Jonah. However, also like Jonah, he submitted to Heavenly Father's will and eventually joined the Church.

Zerah Pulsipher (1789–1872)

Source: Autobiography (c. 1803–1862). Typescript, BYU Harold B. Lee Library.

I soon wound up my business in that country and went to Pennsylvania, in Susquehanna County. A new country where there were much good timber. I built a mill, cleared a farm and married a wife by the name of Mary Brown. A very agreeable companion by whom I have a large family of kind children. I stayed in that country about eight years and labored very hard rafting on the Susquehanna River, and many times my life was much exposed but I stayed in that country about eight years and removed to Onondaga County in the state of New York. I then lost my only son by the fall of a tree which caused much grief to me in that place.

I had many agreeable friends and good society there. I bought a farm and built a mill. I also built a meeting house for the Baptist Church which I was then associated with. In the summer of 1831 I heard a minister say than an ancient record or Golden Bible in Manchester near Palmyra which remark struck me like a shock of electricity at the same time thought it might be something that would give light to my mind upon principles that I had been thinking of for years and many times I had remarked that if the pure church with its gifts and graces was not on the earth, if so I had not found it. But I should be happy enough to find it in my day.

I embraced it accordingly in the fall of 1831 there was a Book of Mormon brought in to town I succeeded in getting it I directly read it through twice gave it a thorough investigation and believed it was true and the winter following Jerod [Jared] Carter came that was from a mission to Vermont or Lake George. As soon as he came into town I, with two Methodist Preachers went to see him after a reasonable introduction I questioned him upon the principles of the ancient gospel with all its gifts belonging to it. I asked him if he believed it, he answered in the affirmative. I asked him if he had ever laid hands on the sick and they had recovered. Yes, he said, he had in many instances.

He preached the following evening to a crowded congregation, held up the Book of Mormon and declared it to be a revelation from God. I could not gain-say anything he had said, he sat down and gave liberty for remarks, the congregation seemed to be in amaze, not knowing what to think of what they had heard. I arose and said to the congregation that we had been hearing strange things and if true they were of the utmost importance to us. If not true it was one of the greatest impositions and as the preacher had said that he had got his knowledge from heaven and was nothing but a man and I the same, that I had just as good a right to obtain that blessing as he, therefore I was determined to have that knowledge for myself which I considered it my privilege, from that time I made it a matter of fervent prayer.

I think about the seventh day as I was thrashing in my barn with doors shut, all at once there seemed to be a ray of light from heaven which caused me to stop work for a short time, but soon began it again. Then in a few minutes another light came over my head which caused me to look up. I thought I saw the angels with the Book of Mormon in their hands in the attitude of showing it to me and saying "this is the great revelation of the last days in which all things spoken of by the prophets must be fulfilled." The vision was so open and plain that I began to rejoice exceedingly so that I walked the length of my barn crying "Glory Hal-la-lu-ya to the God and the Lamb forever."

For some time it seemed a little difficult to keep my mind in a proper state of reasonable order, I was so filled with the joys of heaven. But when my mind became calm I called the church together, (Note: he was their minister) and informed them of what I had seen. I told them of my determination to join the Church of Latter Day Saints, which I did and a large body of my church went with me. I was ordained to the office of an elder and went to preaching with considerable success at home and abroad. I had the privilege of baptizing Wilford Woodruff on the 31st of December, 1833, at Richland, New York.

Additional Information: In Doctrine and Covenants 124:138, Zerah is mentioned by name and called as one of the seven Presidents of the Quorum of the Seventy. He was excommunicated for a time, but later was reinstated into the Church.

John Pulsipher (1827–1891)

Source: Book of Abraham Project (www.boap.org).

I include the following entry of John Pulsipher, son of Zerah, for further information on Zerah's coming in contact with the Book of Mormon.

I, John Pulsipher, was born in the town of Spafford, Onondago County, state of New York, North America, on the 17th of July, 1827, this being the year that Joseph Smith got the plates which contain the Book of Mormon. When I was four years old, said book was published and one copy came into our town. Father got it and read it. He, with the neighbors, Elijah Cheney, S. Roundy and others, would sit and read and talk day and night 'till they read it thru and thru. They believed it was brought forth by the power of God, to prepare the way for the second coming of the Son of Man. It was just what they were looking for. The church of Jesus Christ was organized on the 6th of April, 1830, in the state of New York. After the angels of the Lord restored the priesthood to men on the earth, elders were ordained and sent to preach the Gospel to the world. The first elder that came into our town—viz., Jared Carter—baptized father and mother and the children that were old enough, and a number of the neighbors organized a branch of the Church, ordained father an elder and left him to preside over it. This was in January, 1832.

Additional Information: John moved west with the Church to the Salt Lake Valley, enjoying full fellowship until his death.

See http://history.lds.org/overlandtravels/pioneerDetail?lang=eng&pioneerId=2432 (04/11/2014).

Benjamin Brown (1794–1878)

Source: Autobiography (1794–1853) in Testimonies for the Truth. Liverpool: S. W. Richards (1853).

Five years more passed, and I was still unconnected with any religious party. At this time, what were called "Protracted Meetings," or religious services, continuing for days, and sometimes weeks, were very popular in America. In common with the rest of the "Universalists," I felt unfavorable to these meetings, but such magnificent reports of their results—the wholesale "conversion of souls," led me to attend one. I humbled myself, and determined to divest my mind of all prejudice, and put myself at least in a position to receive all the good that could be obtained. Before going, I covenanted with the Lord, that if he would reveal his mind and will unto me, whatever sacrifice or duty he might require at my hands, I would do it. Little did I think of the way my truthfulness would be tried, or possibly I might have shunned such a contract.

As soon as I began to attend, I felt the Spirit of the Lord operating upon me, so that I seemed filled to overflowing with its teachings, a continual stream of glorious truths passed through my mind, my happiness was great, and my mind was so absorbed in spiritual things, that all the time the meetings lasted, which was about fifteen days, I scarcely eat [sic] or drank anything. At other times, that which I subsisted on during these fifteen days, could not possibly have sustained life, but the Spirit of the Lord so operated on my system, that I felt full at the time, and had no desire to eat or partake of anything.

The subject of "Freemasonry" was just then agitating the public mind, so that many of the churches were divided about it, more especially the one to which most of the members attending this meeting belonged, being divided into "Masons" and "Anti-Masons." This meeting was called the "Masonic party." The other minister of the same church held Anti-Masonic principles, and refused to meet with the Masonic party, and kept most of his party away. This caused a great deal of quarrelling and contention, and much anger and bad feeling, of which I knew but little until afterwards. I had heard of the two parties, but had not interested myself in the matter, and consequently did not care much about it.

While sitting in the meeting, listening to the preaching, being much interested in what was being said, the Spirit of the Lord came upon me, and revealed that I was to visit the minister of the Anti-Masonic party, Judge Cushing, and tell him of his foolishness and wickedness in increasing the spirit of division between those who ought to be united as brethren in one common interest. It rained hard at the time, and feeling rather taken up with the preaching, I thought I would delay until the close of the meeting. This mission to me was a very hard task. How was I, a man from the thrashing-floor, to reprove a minister, and, moreover, a judge? But a few minutes had scarcely elapsed, before the Word of the Lord came to me again, with greater power than before, that I was to go at once! I had covenanted with the Lord, and I felt determined to fulfill, if it killed me; so I sprang to my feet, took my hat, and departed from the meeting.

I found the judge at a public inn, engaged in making some purchase. I requested to speak with him for a few minutes in private. He said he would attend to me presently. I sat down, but I had hardly done so before the Spirit of the Lord was again upon me, like fire in my bones, commanding me to deliver my message directly. I again requested to speak with the judge, stating that my business was urgent. He complied this time, and retired with me outside the house. The Spirit of the Lord gave me utterance, and filled my mouth with words, and I laid before him, in language which was given me, the impropriety of his conduct. The same Spirit bearing witness, the judge acknowledged his folly, said he would amend, and told me that he had had many sleepless nights on the same subject. He also said that, directly as I sat down, something told him for what I had come, although I was a stranger to him. In fact, he knew nearly as well before I had spoken, as after. This confirmed my faith that the Lord had sent me, but it was a great trial to my feelings at the time.

However, I had another trial to undergo, which occurred some days after, during the same meeting. While the minister was preaching, it was revealed to me to rise up and declare to the congregation, that they, before coming together to pray for the conversion of others, ought first to be reconciled one to the other, so that their gifts of prayer might be accepted by the Lord. The Spirit also said, that some in the congregation were guilty of oppressing the poor, taking unlawful usury, oppressing the hireling in his wages, and many other sins of the kind. I waited until the preacher had finished his discourse, during which the idea of having to rise and speak before this congregation of about fifteen hundred people, most of whom being members of Christian societies, I considered better persons than myself, filled me with fear, and the perspiration rolled off me profusely. Could such a thing have availed, I would sooner have given five hundred dollars than have buckled up to this task, but there was no escape, I had covenanted, and the moment the minister ceased speaking I delivered my message. It was received very well by the congregation, many fancying I was converted to their faith, and, being blessed with such gifts, a bit of a prize.

On coming out, two men, one a justice of the peace, and the other a colonel, came up to me. The justice asked why, if I had anything against him, I did not, as the scripture directs, go to him privately, and not expose him before all the congregation. The other said, "If you have got a man by the throat, you need not think that because it is pleasant to you, it is so to him." I told them that as the cap seemed to fit they might wear it. But I was much surprised, for I was not aware they were present.

About a day previous to the close of this meeting, I received a more important communication than either of the previous ones. A knowledge was given me that the ancient gifts of the gospel —speaking in tongues, the power to heal the sick, the spirit of prophecy, etc., were just about to be restored to the believers in Christ. The revelation was a perfect knowledge of the fact, so sure and certain, that I felt as though the truth had been stereotyped upon me. I knew it from the crown of my head to the sole of my foot—in the whole of my system, being filled with the Holy Ghost! I can compare it to nothing better than the change made on a clean sheet of paper by a printing press, leaving an indelible impression behind.

As the Spirit did not tell me to whom these things were to be restored, I at first fancied, in my ignorance, that the people with whom I had been meeting were about to be blessed with these things, so I joyfully visited the minister of the meeting, and laid before him the intelligence I had received. But, to my great astonishment, I met with an utter repulse. He told me, "It was all of the devil, for such things had ceased forever!" Had any one knocked me down with a beetle, I could not have felt more sensibly the opposition between the spirits by which we were actuated. I soon found, by the bold and determined way in which he fought against the principle of present revelation, etc., that it was not to him or his people that these gifts would be given. So I sought for them elsewhere. A few days after, curiosity led me to visit the Latter-day Saints, amongst whom I witnessed a fulfillment of the prediction, for I beheld a manifestation of the gifts of prophecy and tongues, and received the latter myself.

Notwithstanding that the above confirmation which I received of the truth of the Church of the Latter-day Saints, was very great, I did not feel sufficiently convinced to be induced to join them at once. I had experienced the Spirit of the Lord in a similar way elsewhere, so that when the elders of the Church, at this meeting, urged upon me to yield obedience to the gospel they preached, which possessed such evidences as the manifestation of the ancient gifts, I treated the elders very lightly, and replied, that as for the gift of tongues, I could speak in tongues as well as any of them. So I could, for directly one of them manifested this gift, the gift of tongues rested upon me, and gave me the same power. Thus did the devil seek to blind me, and turn that testimony which the Lord had given me for the truth, almost into an evidence against it!

However, I procured a Book of Mormon, and took it home to read, determined to investigate until I was fully satisfied. But I had scarcely begun to read, before I felt greatly to dislike the book. Ere I had perused ten pages, I rejected it altogether. Acting in this bigoted manner, I had resigned myself to the evil influence that was gaining power over me, so that, directly after, I felt a similar dislike seize me towards the Bible. Its statements of miracles, etc., appeared to me to be compounds of the grossest absurdity possible. I could see no light or good in it at all! and actually resolved never to read it again! But oh, the darkness that seized me as soon as I had made this resolution! The light that was in me became darkness, and how great it was, no language can describe. All knowledge of religious truth seemed to forsake me, and if I attempted to quote scripture, my recollection failed, after the first word or so! So remarkable was this, that it excited reflection, and caused me to marvel, and finally I determined to repent of my resolve respecting the Bible, and I commenced to read again.

The book was hardly in my hand, when, as in a moment, my light and recollection returned as usual. This made me rejoice, and immediately the idea flashed across my mind, "What have you done with the Book of Mormon? Behave as fairly to that." I soon reprocured it. But, even this time, I felt prejudiced against the book. I resolved, however, to read it through, and I persevered in its perusal, till I came to that part where Jesus, on visiting the continent of America, after his resurrection, grants the request of three of the twelve whom he had chosen, to permit them to live until his second coming on the earth (like unto John spoken of in the Bible). Here my mind half yielded to the belief which arose within me, that perhaps it might be true, whereupon I took the book and laid it before the Lord, and pleaded with him in prayer for a testimony whether it was true or false, and, as I found it stated that the three Nephites had power to show themselves to any persons they might wish, Jews or Gentiles, I asked the Lord to allow me to see them for a witness and testimony of the truth of the Book of Mormon, and I covenanted with him, if he complied with my request, that I would preach it even at the expense of my life, should it be necessary.

The Lord heard my prayer, and, about five days after, two of the three visited me in my bedroom. I did not see them come, but I found them there. One spoke to me for some time, and reproved me sharply on account of my behavior at the time when I first attended the meeting of the Saints, and treated so lightly the gift of tongues. He told me never, as long as I lived, to do so again, for I had grieved the Spirit of the Lord, by whose power that gift had been given. This personage spoke in the Nephite language, but I understood, by the Spirit which accompanied him, every word as plainly as if he had spoken in English. I recognized the language to be the same as that in which I had heard Father Fisher speak at the meeting. Such a rebuke, with such power, I never had in my life before or since, and never wish to have again. I was dumb before my rebuker, for I knew that what he said was right, and I felt deserving of it.

How these men went, I do not know, but directly they were gone, the Spirit of the Lord said to me, "Now, you know for yourself! You have seen and heard! If you now fall away, there is no forgiveness for you." Did I not know then, that the Book of Mormon was true, and that Joseph Smith was a Prophet of the Lord? Surely I did, and I do now, as surely as I know that I live. The world wonders at the zeal and faith of "Mormon" missionaries in diffusing their principles over the world; but the surprise of the world would soon cease did they know by what evidences the truth of the faith of the Latter-day Saints had been evidenced unto them, for by such proofs as the above, and by the revelations of the Holy Ghost, in tongues, prophesyings, visions, etc., has the work of the last days been attested unto thousands upon thousands, and in ways so peculiar, and attended with such circumstances, that no power of sophistry or reason can possibly show these proofs to be the effects of a fanatical mind or a diseased imagination.

And even could these proofs be overturned, the Latter-day Saints have the still stronger proofs found in the evidences of glorious principles, never before discovered, harmonizing with each other, and every known truth, and clearing up and connecting scripture statements from beginning to end, unlocking the great science of life, shedding light on our existence, and discovering, in the arrangement and combination of these truths, an infinite intelligence that none but a mind that knew the end from the beginning could display! Bear me witness, every spirit that has drunk at the fountain of these truths, the glory, majesty, sublimity, and completeness of which, have again and again made your hearts leap with joy, and cause you to feel that surely such principles are of God, for they have their Father's name enstamped upon their foreheads!

I was not baptized directly, as I hoped to have the pleasure of seeing my wife comply with the same ordinance, when we could enter the Church together. In the meantime I prosecuted my inquiries.

Shortly after inquiring of the Lord concerning the truth of the judgments preached by the Latter-day Saints as being at hand, and impending over this generation, I was shown, in answer, by a vision, the various scenes described in the revelations of the ancient prophets. The inhabitants of the earth appeared before me in their various occupations—plowing, sowing, fishing, and engaging in mechanical business. I saw them, under the infliction of the plagues, etc., lift their eyes towards heaven, curse God, and die. I also saw many other things as predicted by ancient prophets. Thus do I know the truth of the Bible, as well as of the Book of Mormon, and I am a witness for both!

A whole year and a half I deferred my baptism, still waiting for my wife, who, although at first favorable to "Mormonism," had become a determined enemy to the Church. When I went to hear the "Mormons" preach at Westfield, a village where the Twelve Apostles were holding their first conference, curiosity had drawn great numbers to hear them, so that they had crowded meetings all the time.

The second day of this conference, I, with four others, was baptized by Elder McLellin, and confirmed the same night. While undressing on the bank of the creek, preparing for the ordinance, Satan made a last effort to prevent my entering the Church. A man coming along by the waterside came up to me and said, "I wish to speak to you for a few minutes before you go into the water." Thinking of course that he was a friend, or a member of the Church, who intended to give me some instruction as to my behavior when in the water, I listened to him, and, having got me to retire some rods off, he said, "Have you heard what has come out?" "No," I replied, "what about?" "Why," he continued, "concerning the Mormons, it has been discovered that it is all an imposture, a regular hoax to deceive the people. The affair has just come to light. If you wait only a little, you'll hear all about it." At first this completely stunned me, for I was listening very attentively, considering him one of the Church, and for a moment I began to question, but quickly recollecting the manifestations I had received, I told him he was a child of the devil, and I pushed past him to the water, and was baptized at once. This was on the 15th of May, 1835.

My wife, who had managed to be present when I was going to the water, and even threatened that she would not live with me, was, for a long while after, perhaps a year and a half, bitterly opposed to the work, but I knew from the Lord that she would come into the Church, and I told her so. As the way she was at last brought in was very curious, I will mention it. She dreamed one night that a large company of visitors had come to her house, for whom she had to prepare supper. On going into her buttery to procure the necessary food to cook, she could only find a small potato, about the size of a robin's egg, lying on a wooden trencher. However, with this small stock, she commenced, and by some wonderful means converted this little affair into a splendid preparation of pies, puddings, etc. When they were ready, she stood still, wondering how it had all been done, for, as may be supposed, it puzzled her sorely to conceive how, from a little potato, and that on a wooden trencher, she had produced such an elegant entertainment. Just at this moment, while she was thus marveling, I was awakened from my sleep, with a command sounding in my ears that I was to say to my wife, "don't you remember hearing that you should not despise the day of small things?" I was to speak at once, without waiting. So I awoke her, and without any preface did as I was bid.

The wonderful concurrence of these words with her dream, and the self-evident interpretation of it, referring as it did to her past conduct, (for one of the principal reasons of the opposition she felt to my joining the Church was, that she considered it disgraced her to have her husband belong to a Church that was so poor, and everywhere spoken against,) so impressed itself upon her mind, with other confirmations, that she was baptized, and has remained firm to the Church ever since.

Additional Information: Benjamin Brown was the bishop of the 4th ward in Nauvoo, the bishop of the 15–16th ward in Winter Quarters, and the bishop of the 4th ward in Salt Lake City for 16 years.

See http://www.familylinks.us/BB-m.html. (04/11/2014).

Harrison Burgess (1814–1883)

Source: Autobiography (1814–1848) in Kenneth Glyn Hales, ed. and comp. *Windows: A Mormon Family*. Tucson, Arizona: Skyline Printing, 1985.

I was born September 3, 1814 in the town of Putnam, Washington County, state of New York. I lived with my parents until 14 years and a part of the time afterward and being the eldest of my father's family, I was kept constantly at work and had but little opportunity of acquiring an education.

My father made no profession of religion but led a moral and virtuous life. My childhood was not marked with any crime although I paid but little or no attention to religion until the 17th year of my age. In July, 1832, when I first heard the fullness of the gospel proclaimed by Elder Simeon Carter, [and at this time] I was convinced that the scriptures were true and the Book of Mormon was a divine revelation from heaven. I was baptized [by Elder Simeon Carter and confirmed a member in the Church of Christ of Latter-day Saints by Elder Orson Pratt] and spent the following winter in going to school, working for my board and in meeting with the Saints.

In the spring of 1833, I started in company with Brother John S. Carter to the state of Vermont where we labored about two months and [We came to the Benson Branch where I was ordained a priest under the hands of Brother Carter with whom I continued to travel] then returned to New York State.

On the third Sabbath in May while speaking to a congregation I declared that I knew the Book of Mormon was true, the work of God. The next day while I was laboring something seemed to whisper to me "Do you know the Book of Mormon is true?" My mind became perplexed and darkened, and I was so tormented in spirit that I left my work and retired into the woods in misery and distress and therein cannot be described. [The ? all the while seemed to say I know the Book of Mormon is true?" I remained in this situation about two hours before it came into my mind the faith that the Brother of Jared had in obtaining a knowledge of God.] Finally, I resolved to know whether I had proclaimed the truth or not, and commenced praying to the God of Heaven, for a testimony of these things, when all at once the vision of my mind was opened, and a glorious personage clothed in white stood before me and exhibited to my view the plates, from which the Book of Mormon was taken. [I guess I took a short mission in the state of New York, ? proclaimed the truth in great boldness.]

Additional Information: Harrison served in Zion's Camp, was ordained to the First Quorum of the Seventy in 1835 by Sidney Rigdon, and served as a bishop for a short time in Pine Valley (Southern Utah) shortly before his death in 1883.

See http://www.gapages.com/burgeh1.htm. (04/11/2014).

Nathan T. Porter (1820–1897)

Source: Published by Porter Family Organization, Feb. 25, 2000.

In the month of July (1830) of this same year, there came two ministers traveling through the country on their way to the western boundary of the State of Missouri, calling themselves Elders of the Church of Jesus Christ of Latter Day Saints. They called upon my father (Sanford), having learned that he was a singular man in his religious belief. Contending (to argue earnestly) for the old Apostolic Doctrine, and the faith once delivered to the saints, that he believed in visions, and the ministering of angels. He standing aloof from every sect and creed, declaring that they were all out of the way, and therefore stood disconnected with any. Now this being the case, and it being a day in which the gifts and blessings of the gospel in the manifestations of the Holy Spirit by visions, the ministering of angels, speaking in tongues, interpretation of tongues, etc., were deemed by all Christian world, so called. It becomes expedient that I should give a statement as to how my father (Sanford) became impressed into this belief. I will therefore refer back to his early history on this subject. And I will say at the age of about 25 years he was almost, if not quite, a profound atheist. Yea almost to that of an atheist, which is to deny the existence of a God. He came so near as to doubt there being one. Reason and the law of nature was his standard. Therefore any manifestations that was not natural or reasonable wording to the common cause of things, was by him entirely discarded. His reasoning was from cause to effect, and that there was no effect without a natural cause which produced it. And that this proceedeth from what is called by the atheist, the God of Nature without any divinity whatever. Therefore all those who believe in a Divine Being, he set down as phantasy, and all supernatural manifestations, a phantom of the brain, imaginary. And now as I said my father had advanced so far into skepticism as to doubt there being even a God of nature. But that all things came by chance, and that there was no existence after death. Now the thought that after death, he would be as though he had never been, being annihilated with all his faculties of both body and mind. Thus becoming extinct without any further existence whatever was more than he could endure. Therefore he began to be harrowed up in his mind with this awful thought. Looking upon death as a leap in the dark without one ray of light to glimmer in the last moments of sinking humanity. Thus he became troubled by day and by night. Yet he endeavored to prevent the knowledge of his true situation becoming known to anyone, lest he should be imposed upon by the impositions and flatteries of a hireling Priesthood. For he looked upon all the religious pretensions as a bundle of Priest craft, got up by the Priests for gain. One contending against the other. Each looking for his gain from his quarter. And he (Sanford) looked upon the Bible as a bundle of falsehood, with all manner of inconsistencies. Therefore to prevent his concern of mind from being known, he walked the barn by day and the house by night.

Now on the third night after the rest of the family had retired to bed, consisting of my mother (Nancy Warriner) and eldest brother and sister who were in a profound sleep, as he (Sanford) was walking the room, being bowed down with anguish of soul, he cried out, "Oh, is there a God? If there is, may I know the way that is right." As he uttered this there came an audible voice saying, "There is a God, and thou shalt be shown three times this night the way that is right, that thou needest never doubt." Not withstanding it being a mild voice, yet it pierced to the very center so that his whole frame shook to the extremity of every limb. As soon as he had recovered from the shock the first thought was that some person, having learned of his situation had come, and putting his mouth at the top of the door had spoken those words with the intent of making him believe it to be spoken by some supernatural being. But withstanding, he had openly declared that no such being existed, only in the imaginations of the ignorant. No sooner had he received this impression than he was filled with indignation. And springing to the fire he seized the poker, threw open the door, and to his surprise a light snow had fallen, but it had cleared off and the stars shown bright. Now says he to himself, "I have a good chance to track you, my lark." He went out and looked carefully all around the house. But to his surprise not a footprint of any living thing could be seen. The next conclusion was that this person had succeeded in getting into the house during the day, and had secreted himself upstairs, and had spoken through a crack near the door. The sound having come from the walls of the house as he stood fronting it. He came into the house, barred the door and lighting the candle took a chance and started up stairs. As he was ascending he thought to himself I will only leave the breath of life in him. Having not the least doubt but what he was there as he could be nowhere else. Keeping a close watch that he should not dodge by him. He soon found himself at the top of the stairs and raising the light he took a searching glance into every part of the room. But saw no person and nothing that would scare any person, except an old barrel standing in one corner of the room. Now that he was in or behind that barrel was to him certain. Therefore keeping a close watch he proceeded to the barrel, looked behind it, then emptied out its contents consisting of old carpet rags, and not so much as a mouse was discovered. He now gave up the search and returned below entirely confounded in his doctrine and subdued in his spirit. He had now met with a manifestation, but could assign no natural cause by which it was produced. He knew that he had heard a voice, and understood distinctly the sound, but could find no trace of any being who could of uttered it. Therefore he settled down with the conviction that there was a God, and that the voice had proceeded forth from Heavenly Beings sent by Him.

Therefore under this impression he seated himself before the fire marveling at what had transpired and the mildness of the voice. And yet how it caused his whole frame to shake. And that the pain and anguish of soul was gone, leaving his mind calm and serene, with the exception of a dread to hear the voice again, feeling that he could not endure the shock again. For he supposed he would hear the voice again telling him the way that is right, in fulfillment of the promise. He sat for some time, but no voice came. He finally thought he would lay down upon the bed and cover up, and thus he could lay and hear what the voice should say. As he (Sanford) lay down he thought the pillow felt unusually soft to his face, but in a twinkling, as it were, he was caught away with lightning speed from things of earth. Thus with a conductor by his side, he found himself standing in a world of light. Whether in the body or out of the body he could not tell, but to use his own language he said, "I felt of myself and thought it was no dream. But that it was really myself." They stood upon what he called a railing encircling a body of light extending up so high that he could not see the top thereof. This light was all in motion as it were, life dwelling in the light. He could see as it were thousands of miles. So clear was the light, yet there were no sun, moon or stars to be seen. He saw people as numerous almost as the sand of the sea, seated around this light in what he called "box pews or sells", having the appearance of those in a honeycomb, one forming a portion of another. These were only large enough to admit of two persons, male and female. There were a great many cells or mansions that were empty. Yet there were none that were occupied without a male and female.

Thus they were paired all. All these were bowing to the light with humble reverence, full of praise and thanksgiving to God and the Lamb. Those who were the nearest to the light were the most happy, even beyond description. This was expressed in their countenance, which he said surpassed anything he ever beheld in beauty and loveliness. But further back from the light they were less happy, as the light shone less upon them. Thus he looked back until he saw those who were out in darkness. And oh, the awful anguish of soul that was pictured in every continuance. They were in the attitude of waving their hands and gnawing their tongues for pain. He could not enter the scene, and turning to his conductor he enquired as to who they were? His answer was that "They were those spoken of in the scriptures, who were liars, whoremongers and adulterers." He asked if their torment ever would have an end? The answer was, "It had a beginning and it may have and end." He asked what the light was that he saw, as to which all those were bowing to, who were so happy? He said, "It was God."

The angel conductor went on telling him things, even all that he wished to know about God, and that which was written of Him in the scriptures, referring him to many passages giving him chapter and verse. He told him that there was no true Church of God then on the earth. That the churches were all out of the way, and he forbade him to join any of them. My father asked if there would a true church arrive? The answer was, "There will". He asked if he would live to see it? He says, "You will". After he was told all he desired to know the angel says, "Come we must go back". He looked from whence they came, and behold a dark abyss. He said, "Oh, let me stay". His answer was, "You cannot stay". Says my father, "Why can I not stay". Says he, "You are not good enough". My father asked, "If he would ever be any better?" He says, "You will occupy this mansion," pointing to the one by which they stood. He referred him to the scripture where the Savior said, "'In my house are many mansions', and now as Christ said to Peter, 'when thou art converted strengthen thy brethren'. So say I unto you, when thou art converted tell this to the world". Say my father, "They will not believe me if I do". He says, "What is that to thee. Do as you are bid. There are some who will believe. Come let us go". In an instant they were on the wing, as it were. He awoke feeling a very singular sensation throughout his whole system, like unto a person's arm or leg having been asleep, as it is called, causing a prickly sensation. Thus it appears that his spirit must have left his body and that which he thought was his natural body, standing in that world of light, was in reality the body of his spirit. (But to return) As he awoke, he endeavored to awaken my mother that he might relate to her what he had seen. But a profound sleep had come upon her so that when he endeavored to awake her she would partially wake up, but immediately fall asleep again. He therefore lay meditating upon what he had seen and heard, but only for a short time, as he was soon taken as before by the same conductor who showed and told him the same things, word for word. And thus it was once more repeated in fulfillment of the promise that he should be shown three times that night the way that was right so that he need never doubt. And so it was he doubted no more as to God and Godliness, but stood alone declaring what he had seen and heard from him who could not lie. And thus he met opposition. Confounding all who opposed the word of God and the testimony which he had received.

I will now return to my account of those ministers who called upon my father, as before stated. He received them cordially as he was accustomed to with all who wished to converse upon the Holy Scriptures. After they had rested and refreshed themselves a little he entered into conversation with them. They testified that an angel from heaven had appeared to one Joseph Smith, residing in Ontario County, New York, who revealed unto him the Gospel, as taught by Christ and his apostles, with all the gifts and blessings enjoyed by the ancient saints. Also an ancient record, written upon gold plates by an ancient people once inhabiting this continent, and hid up by one of their last prophets to come forth by the hand of God in the last days unto the remnant of their seed. Which, they said was the Indian Tribes of this continent, according to the record. This record was found by Mr. Smith, under the direction of the angel, in a small hill near his residence, called by those ancient people Cumorah. With this record was found an instrument called the Urum and Thummum, being two transparent stones placed in two rims of a bow. By means of this, through the gift and power of God, Mr. Smith was enabled to translate the engravings on these plates, into the English language, which is now published to all the world, containing the fullness of the gospel of Christ set forth as revealed by himself unto this people, after his resurrection and ascension into heaven. After they had given an outline of this marvelous discovery, they presented this book to my father for perusal entitled the Book of Mormon. After he had read the book carefully through and had made all the inquiries he wished, as to their doctrine, they asked my father what he thought of it. He replied that it was nothing more nor less than the old Apostolic Doctrine. They then asked if he was not willing to join them. He replied that he was not, for as he had told them he had been forbidden to join any church that was on the earth. And therefore he should join none except it should be made manifest, by him who could not lie, that it was his duty.

They (missionaries) replied that he (Sanford) was forbidden to join any that was then on the earth, but the Latter Day Saints had arisen since that time. And as he (Sanford) had informed them, that he was told that a true church would arise. "That is so," says my father. "But I have no evidence further than your testimony that you are that church. Therefore I shall never join you until I know of a surety that you are of that true church which should arise." They tarried several days during which they held several meetings in the neighborhood, which my father attended attentively. At the close of the last meeting one of them, whose name was Lyman Wight, the other John Carrol, came to my father and asked, "If he was not yet convinced that it was his duty to join them". He said, "He was not, as he had received no assurance that it was his duty, and had no manifestation as yet that they were right". Mr. Wight looked steadily on the ground for a few moments, then looking up says to my father, "If you are convinced that we are right, will you come tomorrow morning and let us know". Now they were to start the next morning on their way. His (Sanford's) answer was, "If it is made known to me that you are right, I will let you know if I have to follow you to Pekin or to Missouri, or I will follow you to the end of the world." "That" says he, "Is all I ask". And bidding him (Sanford) good night, they separated. My father returning home pondering upon the singular expression "if you are convinced will you come and let us know tomorrow morning?" As though he would be shown within that time. He repaired to bed at quite a late hour still meditating on what had passed during the day and evening. He finally fell asleep and remained until the dawn of day when he awoke without any manifestation whatever as to the strange ministers or their doctrine. But as he still lay pondering in his mind, thinking that perhaps they were like all others, deceiving and being deceived. He was instantly taken in vision, as formally by the same conductor, who informed him that these men were servants of the living God, and that their testimony was true. That God had set up His church and kingdom on the earth. That the gospel was now revealed in its purity, and that it was his duty to embrace it. As he awoke from this trance or vision he immediately set out to inform those ministers that he was ready to join them with full purpose of heart. They (missionaries) were stopping at the place of the before mentioned.

As he drew near the house, he saw Elder Wight walking down the road toward him. As they met he looked up to my father with a smile and said, "Well Mr. Porter, are you ready to join us now?" He replied that he was and had come to inform them of the fact as he promised him he would. He turned and accompanying on to the house where my father related the circumstance of his convictions. After which they made arrangements to hold a meeting at father's house the following day, where they would attend to the ordinance of baptism. Therefore they returned with my father. The word was soon noised abroad of the meeting and that my father was going to unite with those strange people calling themselves Latter Day Saints. Thus quite a multitude assembled at the time appointed. After the close of the meeting they repaired to a suitable place for baptism. After they had sung and prayed by the water edge, Elder Wight took my father by the hand and led him down into the water and says unto him, "Are you willing to forsake all your sins, and take upon you the name of Jesus Christ, and enter into covenant before God that you will live by every word that cometh forth from his mouth?" When my father had answered in the affirmative, he says calling him by name, ". . . having authority given me of Jesus Christ, I baptize you in the name of the Father and the Son and of the Holy Ghost. Amen." He then immersed him in the water and came up out of the water. And thus he baptized my father, mother, brother and one sister. (Family records show that Sanford Porter, his wife Nancy Warriner, and three children, Chauncy Warriner Porter, Malinda Porter and Sarah Porter were baptized on 10 August 1831.) They held a confirmation meeting in the evening and confirmed them members in the Church of Jesus Christ of Latter Day Saints, by the laying on of hands, with the promise of the Holy Ghost, which fell upon them. And they rejoiced with exceeding great joy. They also ordained my father to the office of an Elder. And after giving him the necessary instruction with regard to the duties of this calling, they departed on their way having an appointment ahead about six miles distance at the house of one Jonathan Sumner, whom they also baptized and ordained to the office of a elder.

Additional Information: Nathan Porter would serve six missions for the Church, five to the eastern states and one to Gibraltar (Spain). Interestingly, on four of his missions, he served with the same companion, Elder Edward Stevenson. This is the same Edward Stevenson who convinced Martin Harris to move west and reunite with the Saints in Zion. This being the case, it's probable that Nathan was with Elder Stevenson on this visit to Martin Harris.

Levi Hancock (1803–1882)

Source: Autobiography (1803–1836). Typescript, Harold B. Lee Library.

I worked and paid my board and room and then I would go and see my old friends. The widow Miller sent for me and wanted I should come and do some work for her. I went and completed the work she had for me to do, then went to the Babcocks. I bought some goods and put in his store and he said I might trade as many goods as I could buy. But I gave away my goods to the poor and never made one cent. I found I couldn't live that way and I went to work again. I thought I would go to the widow Millers. I stayed there and in the winter I took some sleigh rides with the young people. I found that would not do in that place it cost too much to hire the horses and sleighs so I put my heart into my work again and in the spring I concluded I would look me up a companion. I thought best to build first on my land in Rome. I went to work and tried to get material to build with and thought I would work out for the same. I was fully bent on settling down but to love one girl more than the others I could not do. The young ladies there were all my friends, I never did insult one in all my life and never did keep company with anyone. Never did I ask for the company of any girl further than to ask them to go to the dance. Often I would have compliments from them how they thought as much of me as they did their brothers. In this way I lived through the summer of 1830.

In the fall I concluded I would go and see Samuel Alger in Chagrin so I hired a horse of my good friend Mrs. Miller and started out. I arrived at his house that evening by taking the near road. I set down and presently Alvah came in and asked me if I had heard the news? "What news", asked I.

"Why," said he, "four men have come and have brought a bock [Book of Mormon] with them that they call history and a record of the people that once inhabited this land."

"Oh, said I to myself, that sounds interesting and I would like to hear more. I began to inquire about it.

Alvah said, "Why, do you not recollect of reading what the Savior said, how he had other sheep which were not of this fold at Jerusalem?" "Oh, yes I do," said I.

"Well," said he, "they were here and he [Savior] came and taught them the same doctrine that he taught them at Jerusalem." "And," said he, "they baptize for the remission of sins and are building up the church as the apostles used to do in the days of Christ. Tomorrow they are to hold a meeting at Mr. Jackson's in Mayfield." "Yes," said he, "they lay hands on those they baptize and bestow on them the Holy Ghost." At these last words I gathered faith and there seemed to fall on me something pleasant and delightful. It seemed like a wash of something warm took me in the face and ran over my body which gave me a feeling I cannot describe. The first word I said was, "It is the truth, I can feel it." "I will go and hear for myself tomorrow." This was on a Saturday so the next day I took my mother behind me on the horse and went to Mr. Jackson's. We got there a few minutes before the meeting. After I had been there a short time, I saw the people begin to assemble. I got in the chamber where there had been a few boards pulled up (which had been laid down loose before) to give the spectators a fair chance of hearing. In the chamber I took a seat beside a lawyer by the name of Card. He sat with his pencil and paper and commenced to scribble as the speaker arose and began to talk. I sat with both ears open for the first word he spoke. I believed all he said as much as though I knew he was Jesus Christ. After he had talked a short time, he opened the Book of Mormon and read what Christ said to his disciples who had gathered around the Temple in the land of Nephi. "Of the three days of darkness that had been upon the land. . . ." When he had got through reading and talking about the new revelation. He then went to exhorting the people to read the scriptures and see if they did not tell of the doctrine. They teach us that there must be something sent from God in order to prepare the people for the glorious reign of Christ.

Then the words of Isaiah 11th chapter on a part of the chapter as far as the eleventh verse. After this man had spoken, whose name was Parley P. Pratt, I had found out. He gave liberty for anyone to reply. Sidney Rigdon then spoke and said he had been trying to preach the Gospel for a long time and now he had done. He thought he should never preach again and confessed he was completely used up and advised the people not to contend against what they had heard. After this man had spoken there arose another young man whose countenance bespoke a spirit of peace and love. He [probably Oliver Cowdery] said he had been an eyewitness to the things declared and the book reported to be a revelation was truth, however strange it may appear to the people.

Parley P. Pratt then said, "If anyone wants to be baptized, let them come forward. My father went and was baptized and also my sister Clarrisa and some few others.

I went home to fathers and then the Devil began to rage. There was one man by the name of Phelps that appeared to be mad and he exerted himself every way he could to discourage us from believing. He told of the many impositions that had been palmed upon the people and where that would not do but that we still believed and meant to prove the work and not condemn it nor the men who brought it until they had proved themselves unworthy of our confidence by some mean trick.

Next morning I went back to Mayfield and asked where the men were that had been baptizing there, with a firm determination to be baptized. I found that they had gone to Kirtland.

I then asked one of Mr. Jackson's sons if he would go to Kirtland with me. He said he would go if I would stay all night. I stayed the night with him and the next morning we started for Kirtland, Ohio. Upon arriving there we found that Parley P. Pratt was engaged in baptizing. I dismounted my horse and went and asked Parley P. Pratt if he would baptize me. He said, he would if I believed. I told him I believed that Jesus is the son of God, and felt within my heart that the things he had told us were the truth. He then baptized me.

Additional Information: At the issuing of the Extermination Order, many of the elderly, women, and children managed to make the trek across Missouri to Quincy, Illinois due in large part to Levi Hancock and his brothers. They had sixteen guns between them that they refused to turn in to the mob at Adam-ondi-Ahman, the day the government requested the firearms. The Hancock brothers successfully protected these Saints from further mob violence. Levi was also a General Authority (Quorum of the Seventy), one of a number of bodyguards to the Prophet Joseph Smith, and a spiritual leader of the Mormon Battalion.

John Lowe Butler (1808–1861)

Source: Autobiography (1808–c.1858). Typescript, BYU Harold B. Lee Library.

In 1832, I prayed and searched the word of God diligently and could find no relief to my mind. I still went to meeting, but my mind was greatly troubled, so that I did not care to work but little for I thought if I should gain the whole world and lose my own soul it would be no advantage to me whatever. So one day I rode out to see a brother Baptist and made known to him all my troubles. He began as usual and answered me and said that the Lord would continue to chastise until I would preach their faith. This had great weight upon my mind, so I started for home and while on my way a rebellious spirit took hold of me and I made up my mind that I would stop going to meeting for it was all contention and nothing to be depended upon and if I read the word of God I could not comprehend it, and when I prayed I could get no answer and finally I concluded that I would be as independent as God himself. If he would not answer me when I pray, I would quit praying to Him, and as he would not give me an understanding of the scriptures I would quit searching them and lay all aside.

When I got home I told my wife what I intended to do and when I had told her it hurt her feelings very much indeed. I then went to put up my horse; my barn was up by my orchard. When I got there I found that a wind storm had passed over when I was away and had destroyed several of my fruit trees by blowing them down, and had blown off a great deal of fruit from the other trees. When I saw what had happened I began to feel very angry to think that the Lord should send such a storm to do me so much damage, and still feeling the same independent spirit, I stood up, looking toward the heavens saying I would not preach such stuff as my Baptist brethren told me I would have to preach and if he thought he would make me to try it and I would quit praying to him for he would not answer me and I would be as independent as he.

While in this exercise of mind there were several streaks of lightning passed before me in the heavens. I said I know you can strike me dead with lightning but pop away if you wish for I will neither preach, pray, go to meeting, nor read the scriptures any more. I felt as though I was seven or eight feet high. I then got some corn tops for my horse and started to feed him and when in the act of stepping in and putting the fodder into the rack, there was a voice spoke to me saying, "I will set on you a refiner's fire." I turned about to see who it was that spoke to me, but I saw no person. I then looked around the barn but saw no person. I certainly thought that someone spoke to me for the voice was so audible, but yet, I still heard no one, neither saw I anyone. This set me to thinking of what I had been doing. I had been defying God and so forth. As I went down to the house I concluded to read one more time old Malachi; it speaks of refiner's fire, etc. and when I got into the house I told my wife what had happened when putting up my horse. I then sat down to read for the last time old Malachi. I read it through twice and closed the book with a determination never to open it again, but made up my mind to go once more and pray and it for the last time.

I started to a place in the field where I often went to pray. I got about fifty steps from the house. My whole mental powers seemed to be drawn out to God to know the truth, and the true order of his kingdom, and if I could only know what, I would do anything, even to the laying down of my life if necessary. While in the exercise of mind, there was a voice that spoke to me saying, "Stand still and see the salvation of God and that will be truth." That instant a light shone round me. I was filled with the Spirit of the Lord and saw clearly that God would save all the workmanship of his hands and truth would stand or be set up in our midst and it will not need propping up as the sects of the day had continued to do.

From this time I began to look for something to come forth different to what we then had in any church. I often told my brethren that the truth would stand alone and might be told by an illiterate man. It could not be put down. Things passed on tolerable well those times. I went to meeting and they would call upon me to speak, and sometimes I would be so filled with the spirit that I did not know what I did say, but those that heard me said that it was a warning to repent, etc.

In 1831, on the 17th of November, my wife bore unto me a son. I was keeping school at that time, for I was unable to do much hard work, being very sickly from my boyhood, suffering very much from the rheumatics. I still attended the meetings, but gained nothing by it, for the Spirit of the Lord was not there and where the Spirit of the

Lord is not, there is little to be learned. In 1833 on the 20th of April, another son was born unto us. He only lived about four months. We named him William Alexander; the other boy was named Kenyon Taylor. In 1834 on June 13, a daughter was born unto us; we called her Charity Artemesia. On the following March, the first day, 1835, when at a Baptist meeting, a word came that two Mormon elders would preach on that evening at my Uncle John Lowe's. I said I would go and hear them. My Baptist brethren opposed me, but I told them I was going to hear them for myself. They then appointed two brethren to go with me, and when we got to meeting seated together one on each side of me, the elder rose up to speak.

I expected they would speak from their Golden Bible, but they did not and to my astonishment, they commenced preaching the first principals as set down in the New Testament. This astonished me. I knew every word they said to be truth for I had the testimony of it. I asked them a few questions and they kindly answered them. I then told them that my house was a home for them as long as they wished while they were preaching. My Baptist brethren sat on either side of me and said to one another how John is taken up with them. See his mouth is wide open to swallow it all. This doctrine will just suit him for it is what he has been seeking after; he will leave us now and join these Mormons; he never was satisfied with the Methodist, so he left them and joined us, and he did not believe in our doctrine. Now he will join these Mormons and believe everything that they preach.

I invited the elders to come to my house and hold meetings there if they wished. I then started for home thinking and weighing over in my mind the doctrine and principals that had been held forth that evening by the elders of the Church of Jesus Christ of Latter-day Saints. My mind was lit up more than it had ever been before and I could begin to see clearly the things pertaining to the kingdom of God. I arrived home and my mother was then staying with us. I told them of the principles of the gospel. My mother said, "Well, John, what do you think of these Mormons?" I told her that I thought that they preached the true and everlasting gospel or they were the greatest imposters that I had ever seen or heard. "Yes," said the old lady, "that is just like you; you were not content with the Methodists, then you joined the Baptists, and they do not suit you. Now you will join these Mormons." I suppose I told her the Lord said try all things and hold fast to that which is good. The next morning I started to work in my clearing, but I had not gotten more than one hundred yards from the house when the same rebelliousness came over me. I then turned right around and went back to the house, took up my Bible and began to search the scriptures and pray to the Lord to hear and answer my prayer and to bless me with an understanding heart, so that I could see and know for myself. I knew it was the nearest right of anything I had heard yet, and I believed that it was this that the Lord had said to me to stand still and wait for the truth.

I continued to call upon the Lord and to read the scriptures. I was determined to find out more about these Mormons so I went to hear the elder's preach again on the next Thursday. They preached about the order of the kingdom and I had never heard anything so plain in all my life before; a child could understand it all. It was just the thing that I had been hankering after and now I felt to rejoice and was perfectly satisfied they were sent of God as the saints of old. I went home, thanking my Heavenly Father for the blessings that he had bestowed upon me from time to time and I felt to go forth and obey his commandments. I asked my wife what she thought of the Mormon elders. She said she thought they were men of God, and that it was the only true church of God and the only way to be saved.

On Friday, the next day, I was lying on my bed reading and resting my mind. I traveled back over my past history and was thinking from the first time that I had serious reflections up until the time that the voice spoke to me and told me to stand still and see the salvation of God and that would be truth. And the voice of the same spirit said, "This is truth that you have been hearing, now choose or refuse." Now I was at a standstill to know what I should do. I saw the sacrifice I had to make in losing my good name and also what little property I had that it would go to if I joined these Mormons, but then it was the truth that we had heard and the elders were sent of God to preach the true and everlasting gospel. What could I do? I had promised the Lord that I would serve and obey him and even lay down my life for the gospel's sake if necessary. And what was my property against my life, why nothing at all, and if I lost my good name it would be to gain a better one. So while I lay on my bed, I covenanted with my Eternal Father to obey the first choice. I then felt better and to rejoice that I was so blessed of God. I then felt the spirit of God to rest down upon me with this testimony that it was right. So on the next Monday, the 9th day of March, 1835, about 2 o'clock in the afternoon, I was led into the waters of baptism by Elder James Emmett and baptized for the remission of my sins. There were some six or eight baptized the same day, my wife being one of the number. There were more baptized after that. The elders appointed a confirmation meeting to be held at my home on the 12th, Thursday evening. There were nine confirmed and the Holy Ghost was poured out upon us; five spoke in new tongues, myself being one of the number. The elders continued to preach and baptize until 22 were baptized and they then organized a branch of the Church of Jesus Christ of Latter-day Saints, ordained Benjamin Lewis an elder and myself a teacher.

Additional Information: John served two missions to the Sioux Indians. He later served as a bishop in Spanish Fork, Utah from 1856 to his death.

See http://josephsmithpapers.org/person/john-lowe-butler (04/11/2014).

Jacob Hamblin (1818–1886)

Source: *Three Mormon Classics, Jacob Hamblin,* James A. Little comp. (Salt Lake City: Bookcraft, 1988), 203–211, 214.

In February, 1842, a neighbor called at my house and told me that he had heard a "Mormon" Elder preach. He asserted that he preached more Bible doctrine than any other man he had ever listened to, and that he knew what he preached was true. He claimed that the gospel had been restored to the earth, and that it was the privilege of all who heard it to know and understand it for themselves.

What this neighbor told me so influenced my mind, that I could scarcely attend to my ordinary business.

The Elder had left an appointment to preach again at the same place, and I went to hear him. When I entered the house he had already commenced his discourse. I shall never forget the feeling that came over me when I saw his face and heard his voice. He preached that which I had long been seeking for; I felt that it was indeed the gospel.

The principles he taught appeared so plain and natural, that I thought it would be easy to convince any one of their truth. In closing his remarks, the Elder bore testimony to the truth of the gospel.

The query came to my mind: How shall I know whether or not these things are so, and be satisfied? As if the Spirit prompted him to answer my inquiry, he again arose to his feet and said: "If there is anyone in the congregation who wishes to know how he can satisfy himself of the truth of these things, I can assure him that if he will be baptized, and have hands laid upon him for the gift of the Holy Ghost, he shall have an assurance of their truth."

This so fired up my mind, that I at once determined to be baptized, and that too, if necessary, at the sacrifice of the friendship of my kindred and of every earthly tie.

I immediately went home and informed my wife of my intentions.

She told me that if I was baptized into the "Mormon" Church, I need not expect her to live with me anymore.

The evening after the Elder had preached I went in search of him, and found him quite late at night. I told him my purpose, and requested him to give me a "Mormon Bible." He handed me the Old and New Testaments.

I said, "I thought you had a new Bible. He then explained about the coming forth of the Book of Mormon, and handed me a copy of it.

The impressions I received at the time cannot be forgotten. The spirit rested upon me and bore testimony of its truth, and I felt like opening my mouth and declaring it to be a revelation from God.

On the 3rd of March, 1842, as soon as it was light in the morning, I started for a pool of water where had arranged to meet with the Elder, to attend to the ordinance of Baptism. On the way, the thought of the sacrifice I was making of wife, of father, mother, brothers, sister and numerous other connections, caused my resolution to waver.

As my pace slackened, some person appeared to come from above, who, I thought, was my grandfather. He seemed to say to me, "Go on, my son; your heart cannot conceive, neither has it entered into your mind to imagine the blessings that are in store for you, if you go on and continue in this work."

I lagged no more, but hurried to the pool, where I was baptized by Elder Lyman Stoddard.

It was said in my confirmation, that the spirits in prison greatly rejoiced over what I had done. I told Elder Stoddard my experience on my way to the water.

He then explained to me the work there was for me to do for my fathers, if I was faithful, all of which I believed and greatly rejoiced in.

On my way home, I called at the house of one of my neighbors. The family asked me if I had not been baptized by the "Mormon" Elder. I replied that I had. They stated that they believed what he preached to be the truth, and hoped they might have the opportunity of being baptized.

The following day Elder Stoddard came to my house, and told me that he had intended to leave the country, but could not go without coming to see me. For what purpose he had come, he knew not.

I related to him what my neighbors had said. He held more meetings in the place, and organized a branch before leaving.

When my father learned that I had joined the "Mormons," he said he thought he had brought up his children so that none of them would ever be deceived by priestcraft; at the same time he turned from my gate, and refused to enter my house.

Other relatives said that my father knew better than to be deceived as I had been. I answered them by predicting that, much as he knew, I would baptize him into the Church before I was two years older.

All my relatives, except one brother, turned against me, and seemed to take pleasure in speaking all manner of evil against me. I felt that I was hated by all my former acquaintances. This was a great mystery to me.

I prayed to the Lord and was comforted. I knew that I had found the valuable treasure spoken of by our Savior, and I was willing to sacrifice all things for it.

My wife's father took great pains to abuse and insult me with his tongue. Without having any conception how my prediction would be fulfilled, I said to him one day, "You will not have the privilege of abusing me much more." A few days after he was taken sick, and died.

Soon after the death of her father, my wife asked me, good-naturedly, why I did not pray in the house or with her. I replied that I felt better to pray by myself than I did before unbelievers. She said that she was a believer; that her father had appeared to her in a dream, and told her not to oppose me anymore as she had done; and that he was in trouble on account of the way he had used me. Soon after this she was baptized, which was a great comfort to me.

In the autumn of 1842, Elder Stoddard returned to the country where I lived, to labor in the ministry, and ordained me an Elder.

About the same time my wife was taken very sick. By her request, I administered to her, and she was immediately healed. I visited my father and told him that signs followed the believer, as in the days of the apostles; that I was a believer, and had been ordained an Elder in the Church of Jesus Christ of Latter-day Saints, and that the signs followed my ministrations.

He ordered me out of his house for believing such nonsense. I went out, reflecting as to whether or not I had done wrong in predicting that I would baptize him in less than two years.

Sometime after this he was taken sick, and I went to see him. My mother told me he had the spotted fever, and that there was no hope of his recovery. She believed he was dying, and so it appeared to me; but I thought that Good could and would save him if I prayed for him.

I retired to a private place, and prayed to the God of Abraham to have mercy on my father and heal him, that he might have an opportunity of obeying the gospel, and said:

It was a moonlight night, and when I returned to the house my mother stood at the door. She spoke to me very kindly, and said:

"Jacob, the fever has left your father; he has spoken and wants to see you."

As I approached him he said, "The fever has left me, and your mother says that you came to me and went away again. What has made such a sudden change? Do you know?"

I answered that I had prayed for him, that I was a believer in the gospel of the Son of God, and in the signs following those that believe.

"Well," said he, "if it is the gospel, I would like to know it; but if it is priestcraft, I want nothing to do with it."

Soon after the sickness of my father, I sold my home, gathered up my effects and started for Nauvoo, Hancock Co., Illinois.

In passing my father's house I found him quite well, and he desired me to remain over night. He showed much interest in the principles of the gospel, and, when I left his house in the morning, the Spirit manifested to me that my father and his household would yet accept the truth. . . .

The following winter I assisted in guarding the Saints in and around the city of Nauvoo. My brother Obed lived about thirty miles out in the country. He was taken sick, and sent for me to come and see him.

On arriving at his house, I found that he had been sick nearly three months, and that doubts were entertained of his recovery. I anointed him with holy oil in the name of the Lord Jesus, laid on hands, and prayed for him, and told him that he should recover, which he did immediately.

This occurrence had much influence on my parents. They both attended the following April conference. At its close, my father asked me if I did not wish to baptize him and my mother. As they were both desirous that I should do so, I baptized them in the Mississippi river, on April 11th, 1845.

My father told me that it was not any man's preaching that had convinced him of the truth of the gospel, but the Lord had shown it to him in night visions. Said he, "It is your privilege to baptize your parents, for you have prayed for them in secret and in public; you never gave them up; you will be a Joseph to your father's house."

Part Three

Their Dreams Pointed to the Church

Human beings dream. The mind never stops. It continues to think even while we lie on our beds in a subconscious state. Most of what we dream doesn't make much sense, and for the most part is forgotten shortly after we awaken. However, there are times when a dream seems so real that it was as if the dreamer were actually cognizant at the time. These dreams are rarely forgotten. To the spiritually enlightened, such dreams likely mean something.

Luman Shurtliff is the first journal account in this part, and for a good reason. All the early converts in this part received dreams; however, with Luman, he received three, all of which are highly symbolic. Sharing his dreams with his wife, he was able to interpret what it was that Heavenly Father was trying to tell him. In fact, his dreams are somewhat reminiscent of the dream that Joseph interpreted after being sold into Egypt.

The other four accounts are also remarkable. The dreams of Jonathan Crosby, Joseph Holbrook, Sarah Rich, and James Rollins pointed them to the Church. Some dreamed of the missionaries coming, as was the case with Crosby and Rich. (Crosby, in addition, also dreamed of a new book of scripture.) The dream of James Rollins is significant in the sense that he saw Joseph and Hyrum Smith before he met them in life.

Luman Shurtliff (1807–1884)

Source: Autobiography (1807–1847). "Biographical Sketch of the Life of Luman Andros Shurtliff." Typescript, BYU Harold B. Lee Library.

Noah Packard and a Mr. Umphry came to Franklin and into our neighborhood preaching. They were Mormon elders. I went to the schoolhouse to hear them speak. Mr. Umphry had been a Methodist preacher and his discourse was so mixed with Methodist, I could learn but little. Mr. Packard little more than bore his testimony to what had been said. They were new beginners in Mormonism and went on west. I was affected in a curious manner when in company with these men; I loved them, but knew not why.

When they returned from the west it was Sunday and we were in meeting. I was speaking. When they came in and were seated, soon the sacrament was passed and they were skipped the bread, it not being offered them. This hurt my feelings although they were strangers and Mormons. I did not feel satisfied and arose and told the people my feelings pointedly. When I sat down, one of them arose and said they had no hard feelings as they should not have accepted it had it been offered them.

I talked with them after and they told me I need not oppose the gospel for I would yet blow the gospel trump. On making inquiry for the truth of the Book of Mormon, they said to me, "Ask God and he will show you."

When these men left, I wept like a child without knowing why or the cause of it. After they were gone, their teachings and sayings lay with weight upon my mind and I had a great desire to see the Book of Mormon or the Golden Bible, but where it could be found, I knew not; neither did I know which way to turn.

Mormonism troubled me and my wife continually. While talking of these things, I remembered that Mr. Packard and Mr. Umphry said if we would ask God in faith, he would show us the truth and so we agreed to pray to God to show us the truth. Accordingly, at our evening prayer, we unitedly asked the Lord to show us if the Mormon book was true, and show us the truth of the work called Mormonism.

Soon after we laid down, I dreamed. I thought I was standing in the northeast corner of my room. It was as light as day but not daylight. I could see plain and clear. I stood facing the east. I stooped forward and had a large-sized hog by the nose and was examining it. It was a white hog but dirty. One ear was close to the head. There was off one inch from the head and the tail was also gone. The hair was long and very rough looking. It had a well-built frame but was very poor. When I was through looking at this hog I looked a little to the northeast and there stood another white hog, perfect in every part. Its beauty exceeded in every part any hog I ever saw. This hog stood, its head up and looking toward Kirtland.

In the morning when we awoke, I told Eunice I had dreamed a rather singular dream and this dream seemed to show that the Book of Mormon was quite inferior to the Bible. I told her of my dream. "Why," said Eunice, "I should think it was the Bible that was inferior." As quick as though the scene changed and the two hogs represented the two books. The Bible, poor, lean, disfigured, and robbed by translators of many of its precious parts. The Book of Mormon, white and pure from the hand of the Almighty and perfect in all its parts like all the work of God.

In a short time I began to think it was a dream, and could I rest my salvation on a dream? I should be ashamed to have people know I had left my religion and embraced another because I had dreamed about a couple of hogs. And so the devil reasoned with me until I became so confused, I concluded to wait and see what further evidence I could get before I joined the Mormons.

Some time in February, 1832, one of the neighbors informed me that Joe Smith and Sidney Rigdon were to preach at Ravenna, the county seat of Portage County, the next day and if I would go he would take me with him in his sleigh as I was lame and could not walk. I gladly accepted the offer and we rode there together.

Sidney Rigdon preached, talking about the prophecy which read: "And they shall run and not be weary, walk and not faint; they shall mount up as on eagle's wings." Mr. Smith bore testimony to what Mr. Rigdon had said. I did not get much information by this meeting. I thought I had heard Sidney Rigdon preach, when a Baptist, much better, but I had seen the Prophet, not such a looking man as I expected to see. He looked green and not very intelligent. I felt disappointed and returned home rather cast down.

In June 1832, while I was still searching after the principles of eternal life, I thought I would humble myself, and with my wife, again ask God to show us our situation and enlighten our minds in relation to Mormonism.

We did as well as we could. In a dream that night I thought I was standing on a platform with a bunch of bushes before me which were laden with the most delicious beautiful-looking fruit I ever saw and much of it was in my reach. I picked none of it. A little lower down and on my side stood my brother Wales. He was in reach of some of the fruit but not of the best quality. Under the bushes standing on the ground, was my brother Selah, the Campbellite elder. He was trying to reach some of the fruit, but could get only some of the smallest and most inferior quality.

When I awoke the interpretation was thus: I had been seeking earnestly the principles of eternal life which this fruit represented. I was in reach of it and in a fair way to obtain it. Wales was less believing and less anxious and was making, or trying to make but little proficiency. Selah, who was unbelieving was gaining nothing or but little in the principles of eternal life.

This was also a dream and soon wore off or lost its weight on my mind. I was left in darkness and doubt as before. I was damned and truly afflicted in mind night and day and saw no light path to walk into.

I again tried to turn my attention to the Campbell doctrine.

In the fall of 1832, I asked God to give me knowledge of my condition and that night I dreamed the earth was covered with snow, about six inches of snow. I was riding horseback around a small circle, with Selah and Mr. Haden, our preacher, on horseback also. Mr. Haden's horse had but two legs, one behind and one before and it made very awkward work of traveling. Selah's horse had but three legs, two behind and one before and made very little or no headway in traveling. I then examined my horse. It was a good horse in all his parts, but he was standing still.

In the morning I understood that the horse of William Haden and Selah represented the Campbell religion and my horse represented the Mormon religion and showed the perfect state of the religion I was investigating.

But, alas, again I was troubled; sorrow and affliction were my lot. I had spoken in public for five or six years and the people seemed pleased with my instruction. Now I had received some of the Mormon principles and when I spoke I could not help presenting something of the Mormon faith. This would excite Selah or some others and they would oppose me. This I saw was likely to divide our church for about one-third was leaning to Mormonism.

About this time a cousin of Wale's wife brought a Book of Mormon to his house for us to read. They read it but it did not make much impression on their minds. Wales let me have the book and I read it carefully and with great anxiety to know of its truth. When through reading, my mother asked me what I thought of the Mormon book. I told her that I was satisfied that the Book of Mormon was not made by man and I did not believe any man living by his knowledge of the Bible could do it and have it harmonize and agree with prophets, revelations and teachings of Christ and the apostles as that book did.

This appeared to surprise her.

I believed this book was gotten up by God or the devil; that no man could of himself do that, for I knew it was a great work. I now felt worse than before and did not believe in any church as far as I was acquainted and I resolved to leave that place the first opportunity.

In July 1833, I swapped my little farm for 120 acres of wild land in Sullivan, Lorain County, Ohio, 60 miles west of Franklin. Wales also traded his land for 130 acres of land joining mine in Sullivan. In the month of August we started to build each of us a house.

I should have enjoyed myself well if my mind had been at ease about religion. Alas! I carried a hell in my heart. One of my neighbors, a Mr. James Durfey, was an elder in the Mormon profession. He visited me; I tried to hide my feelings and reasoned against him, but all in vain.

July 23, 1835, our first son was born. We called him Lewis Warren.

A few hours before the birth of this child, I went down to Wales' with my two little girls. As I returned, the shadows of night were fast falling around me, and millions of insects were bidding a lonely farewell to the passing day and hailing with joyful songs the approaching night. Meditating upon the pleasant scenery around me, the thoughts of my soul arose to the God of the universe. A pleasant feeling was upon me and my mind turned toward my wife. The sweet whisperings of the Spirit to me was, "The child about to be born is a son, chosen and faithful, and shall be a great man in Israel." I have kept this saying mostly to myself.

In the summer of 1836 I saw I was fast approaching a state of infidelity and had but little confidence in anything and believed nothing. I was sick of living so but what could I do? I knew not what to do. I knew not where to go. I had been in torment for four long years and grew more miserable every year. I saw nothing but darkness before me and surrounded with evil influences. If I prayed it availed nothing. If I went to meeting I was in fear I should be called on to preach and would sit and shake like a man who was very cold.

I read the Bible much and was well acquainted with the contents so far as the letter was concerned, but as to the spirit, I knew nothing. I meditated by day and by night came to no conclusions that I could trust. I feared I would soon be a ruined man.

On talking with my wife on this subject, we made up our minds to humble ourselves and again lay our case before the Lord and plead mightily with the Lord to convince us of the truth or the falsity of the Mormon doctrine.

Accordingly, we took a sack of dry wool and in the evening laid it out in the yard and called on the Lord with all the faith and energy we could obtain that if Mormonism was true and of God that the wool might be wet in the morning and this should be a sign unto us.

Early in the morning I went out and found the wool as dry as when put there. It then came into my mind that we had tempted the Lord our God in this thing. If the work was of God, he had shown us three times and we had rejected his testimony. This circumstance had a tendency to make us feel worse than before.

Two Mormon elders had prophesied that I should yet preach the Mormon doctrine. At times the spirit in me manifested that when about 30 years old I should begin to preach the gospel of Jesus Christ as prophesied on my head, yet four years had passed away since that prophecy was given, and to me there was not as much prospect of it now as when delivered.

About 20 years ago, when I was a little boy at school, my cousin Vincent, much older than myself, caught me playfully and threw me headfirst into a snowdrift. I crawled out, when he got me again and threw me in the second time, I scrambled out and again he threw me into the snow. As I came out I said, "Three times you have baptized me and yet I don't believe." He replied, "Why Luman, what did you say?" This observation of his impressed the affair on my mind so that I did not forget the circumstance but seldom thought of it until now.

I had been twice baptized, once by the Baptists, and once by the Campbellites and now if I joined the Mormons and this proved false, I should yet be an unbeliever.

As to the church I left in Franklin, the members that were fond of hearing me speak soon dropped off and moved away, and Selah sold his property and moved out of town. Thus the church broke up. My brother, Wales, moved his family from Sullivan back to Franklin and set up a grocery on the canal. I remained about the same, only my trouble increased and unless my hands were employed and my mind occupied, I was miserable.

I promised the Lord if he would show me the way and give me knowledge of the true gospel, I would preach it as long as I lived. In the sincerity of my heart, I made this covenant time and again.

One morning in August, 1836, I told my wife I thought I would make a trip to Kirtland, the seat of Mormonism and see if I could find out the truth or falsity of this doctrine from there.

I started on my journey on foot, and when I called on my folks in Franklin and told my relatives that I was going to Kirtland, my folks were silent, except father, and he said he was glad I was going, for Mormonism had troubled me for a long time and he hoped I would be satisfied. This somewhat encouraged me. After I had spent a few days in Franklin, I went to Kirtland.

I was a stranger there except for a Mr. Packard who had been at my house in Franklin, but I knew nothing of where he lived. As I passed the Kirtland Temple, I inquired of some boys for Noah Packard. They said they were his boys and would go with me to their home.

Mr. Packard was gone on a mission. Mrs. Packard was a cousin of mine by marriage, but I had never seen her. She received me very kindly, but as soon as I sat down in the house, I began to feel miserable. A fear or dread came upon me. We had some conversation, and at bedtime she called on me to pray. I had made it my practice not to excuse myself when called upon to perform any act of Christianity. We knelt down and I tried to pray but that prayer I could not finish and could think of nothing. My pride was humbled; this made me feel horrible in the extreme.

Sleep did not trouble me much that night. This was Friday evening.

The next morning I was up early and looked over the city of the Mormons. In the afternoon a funeral sermon was delivered in the temple by Jared Carter, a smart speaker, but I learned nothing in particular. The fact was the horizon of my mind was so obscured by clouds of darkness and doubt of long standing that I could see nothing as I ought.

The evil spirit came upon me and had that power over me that at times I would shake like a man with the ague. At another time I would be standing on some emenance [?] weeping like a whipped child, and knew no reason why; then lost in meditation, wandering about the city like a man of little sense.

While in this situation, my tormentor whispered in my mind and said my little boy Lewis was dead and if I did not go home immediately he would be buried and I would not see him more. I then called to mind that the babe was not quite well the morning I left as usual. This strengthened or confirmed the whispering of that spirit and in spite of all my effort to the contrary, it much troubled my mind.

My leg had been crippled for four years now, and began to trouble me more than common. I stated previously that I did much hunting and killed many deer. In the fall of 1832, one morning when the first snows fell, I walked out to kill a deer and had not walked far when I saw a splendid buck. I shot him and when skinning one of his legs, my knife which was sharp pointed, slipped and the point stuck in the joint of my left knee. Then I thought nothing of it, and when through dressing the deer, I went home in considerable pain.

When I got home my wife said, "You have killed a deer, but I was afraid something had happened to you." I replied, "I killed a deer and crippled myself." Why I said this I did not know; I did not think it would injure me. After this I suffered a great deal and sometimes I would be confined to my bed for weeks together. Every effort to cure it was made but it did no good. Surgeons had decided the knife had tapped the joint and the oil oozed out. At best, I could walk with difficulty.

Well, I was in Kirtland with this leg and it was getting worse fast, and it appeared if I stayed a day or so, I might be obliged to stay some time, and if my boy was dead, I might see him no more.

Thus, Saturday night found me a poor miserable man. Sunday I went to meeting. There I found a man by the name of Hyrum Daton [Hiram Dayton] with whom I had a slight acquaintance some years before. I told him I had come to Kirtland to learn the truth of

Mormonism, and I had learned nothing new. I should return tomorrow and trouble my head no more about Mormonism. Yet, I would like to see and have a chat with some of the leading men before I left. Mr. Daton [Dayton] kindly offered to go with me to Brother David Whitmer and give me an introduction to him. As all of the higher officers were absent, I thought this would be my best way of learning what I wanted to know, and as Mr. Whitmer was one of the witnesses of the Book of Mormon, I thought I could learn something.

We walked to Mr. Whitmer's. I got the necessary introduction and took dinner and spent the afternoon in hearing him relate things about the angel showing him the plates from which the Book of Mormon was translated. I also asked him all the questions I had a wish to ask. I had read and heard it all and learned nothing new.

When tired of sitting, we walked out to where we could overlook the flats, where I told him briefly in as few words as possible, my belief and unbelief. I said I did believe the gospel they preached as far as I read it in the Bible, but I could not say that I believed that Joseph Smith, Jr. was a true prophet of God for I did not. Neither did I believe the Book of Mormon to be a revelation from God for I did not. Then facing him I said, "Now you know what I believe and what I do not believe, and if you think I am a fit subject for baptism, I am ready to go to the water; if not, I intend to start home tomorrow and never trouble my head any more about Mormonism."

Mr. Whitmer was silent a few seconds and then replied, "I will go to the water and baptize you or get one of my quorum to do it." On the way to the river, he called on Sylvester Smith and at sunset Sunday, August 21, 1836, I was baptized a member of the Church. David Whitmer confirmed me.

I felt very comfortable and at ease. I slept well that night and in the morning I went to the office and bought a Book of Mormon and started home. I had not traveled far when my leg became worse and the pain severe. I had to walk slow. Upon reflection I saw it must be three or four days before I could get home, and if my boy was sick, he might die.

I knew my neighbors would ask me questions a soon as I got home, and what could I tell them? I could tell them I had been baptized and confirmed a member of the Church and what evidence have I obtained more than I had years ago? Not any. Have I received the Holy Ghost since I was baptized? No. No more than when I was baptized before. Did I believe the Book of Mormon? No. No more than I did four years ago. Do I believe that Joseph Smith, Jr. is a prophet of God? No, I do not. At this I was shocked at my situation and began to call on the Lord in earnest.

While I was praying, something came on my head resembling cold water and passed gradually down through my whole system, removing all pain, and made me a sound man from the top of my head to the soles of my feet.

As soon as this was passed, I heard a sweet melodious voice about me say, "Joseph Smith, Jr. is a prophet of the Most High God, raised up for the restoration of Israel in these last days, and the Book of Mormon which you hold under your arm is true and brought forth for the restoration of the scattered remnants of Jacob."

As this passed off, I cast my eyes to the south. A little way from me I saw my wife standing with my little boy sitting on her left arm with the right arm on her left shoulder and with her right hand pointing to me as if she was saying, "See father, there is father." They both were well and all right. This passed, I was in the road, a sound man, praising God.

After a few miles I began to think what I would say to my neighbors when I got home. I would tell them I knew the Mormon doctrine was true and I had seen and knew much and could do something great. I did not look to God for his aid and help but was boasting in my knowledge and strength. A disagreeable feeling began to come over me and when I comprehended the boasting spirit I had received, I humbled myself before God and after some time, obtained forgiveness and by this learned a useful lesson.

On arriving home, I found all well and I thanked God continually for his forbearance and great mercy and long suffering in sparing my life to the present time, even after I had rejected the testimony that I had asked of him and at last, after four years, condescended to make known to me the trust of that great work, healed my body that I might labor in this great work. Thanks be to God for his goodness to me!

My neighbors were as still as a summer's morning. I had been a cripple there with them three years and they knew and saw it. I was now among them, sound and a healthy man. I was weighed down with sorrow and fettered with affliction. I now rejoiced in the Lord and my soul was full of joy, and my neighbors seemed to mourn.

The middle of September [1836], myself and family went to Franklin on a visit. While there, Brother Noah Packard came and my wife, Eunice was baptized on the 20th of September, 1836, and confirmed a member of the Church.

Jonathan Crosby (1807–1892)

Source: Autobiography of Jonathan Crosby, typescript, Utah State Historical Society. Holograph is also located in the Utah State Historical Society.

Again, when I was eleven years old the Destroyer was after me, for I was taken with "Putrid Disentery" which brought me near the point of death. My mother also became sick of the same disease and died the 30th of July, 1818. My mother, at her death, left two little girls; one, four years old, the other, three months. After nine years from the death of mother, my father married again. During that time, he hired a house-keeper but we, the children, did not receive the instruction at home that our mother used to give us. About this time (1818) Sunday schools were set in order, and protracted meetings held, sometimes a whole week, and every exertion made, and means used to convert sinners. All denominations held them but would not unite their meetings. Each held their meetings by themselves (Baptists, Methodists, and Congregationalists) but their members would go from one to the other. We used to attend Sunday School, and repeat scriptures, hymns, and the Catechism and when I became old enough they put me to teaching a class. School held one hour only.

When sixteen years old I became a member of the choir, and played the bass viol therein until the fullness of the gospel took me away. I was frequently urged and exhorted to get religion (be converted, join the Church) but I could not see it. Their reaching had no affect on me. With all their hell-fire and brimstone, they could not frighten me. Something seemed wrong. I said to thee: If the Bible is true, why don't you preach, teach it all alike? Why all this division in the world? Where is the faith and gifts of the gospel that were enjoyed by the ancient Saints? They could not answer me satisfactorily so I would not be converted.

When I was seventeen years old I got hurt and had a sore on my side. The Destroyer thought he had me then, and the neighbors thought I was going to die but our Father in Heaven thought differently. By His blessing my life was spared, not by the faith of anybody except that they had faith in the doctor who attended me. But the Lord blessed the means used, and I was restored, although I was not able to do anything for six months or more and I have felt the effects of it all my life.

Nothing uncommon transpires from that time until I was twenty-six years old. In the months of January and February there was a singing school in town?, and my oldest sister Emily and myself attended it. She was then eighteen years old. She took a violent cold, which settled on her lungs, also inflammation of the bowels, all which confined her in bed with a hard cough resulting in the spitting up of her lungs. The doctor that attended her did not understand her case, being a young man, and not having had much experience, she pined away and died on the 6th of June following, which was a heavy blow to me. To see her, a fair, beautiful young woman as she was, fade away and suffer as she did and die, was almost more than I could bare. I felt as though I would be willing to take her place if she could live and get well. It affected me so much that I thought I should not live long.

And people thought I was becoming converted, and getting religion. To be sure, I was trying to find out which of the religious sects was right for I wanted to obey the truth. I read the Bible and comments on it by Doddrige and others, and our minister labored with me, but I could not be satisfied. However, he urged me to join the church, and I concluded to do so accordingly, in the month of September, 1833. I was propounded for admission into the Church. This was the custom with them, the applicant giving notice of his intention to join two or three weeks before admission. In the meantime, they had to undergo an examination and if found worthy, would be admitted.

After I concluded to join the church, and was propounded, I felt more miserable than ever. I could not sleep of nights, and there was a great burden upon me which seemed to me more than I could bear, and I prayed the Lord to release me from it and show me the right way. Sometime before this, I think, I dreamed that some new preachers came with a book containing new doctrine, and which threw new light on the Bible, and their preaching was different from that of all others and that I rejoiced in it. But when I awoke the dream somewhat left me, and I thought no more about it. The next sabbath after I was propounded, I went to meeting again and it being quite early, I went into a store kept by two young men and they told me that two young men, preachers, had come to town, had put up at the tavern, and would preach in the hall that evening; that they had a new book, a record, which had been found, and was an addition to the Bible. Well, I said, I am glad of it, I hope they have got the truth. I can't see the propriety of so much division in the world about religion. I shall go and hear them.

After the close of the afternoon meeting, I walked home two miles, this distance we lived from town, did my chores and hurried back. This was near the last of September. The meeting commenced at early candle light, and the hall was filled. They opened by prayer, but I believe there was no singing for the young preachers were not singers. They were mere boys; one 18, the other 19 years old. One of them arose, took the Bible and read a little I think from the 11th chapter of Isaiah, then commenced his discourse. He treated upon the dealings of God with the children of men from Adam, down to the present day, and of the downfall of Israel, and of their restoration, and of the renewal of the covenant in these last days. And such a flood of scripture was quoted, chapter and verse without reading it or looking in the book, that everybody marveled. I rejoiced exceedingly, and they all saw that I was interested, and so I was. The spirit of God was upon me, and I went home prophesying.

The next morning they came to my father's house. I was in the field digging potatoes. My sister came out and called me, and I left my work and went to the house. I was glad to meet them, and invited them to take a walk with me about a mile to a man who was a Methodist. He was well-educated, and strong in argument on theological questions. I thought if there was a man in the world that could whip them out, he could do it.

This Mr. Harris was tending his mill. I introduced them and Mr. Harris took the Mormon book, looked it over a moment, asked some questions about it which they answered; also in regard to the ordinances of the gospel, particularly baptism, which they also answered. He then stopped his mill and invited us into the house. After we were seated, he conversed awhile with them, but entered into no argument with them, at which I marveled. And I said to him sometime afterward, "I brought those men to you for you to whip them out in argument." He said, "They have the truth, and I can't do it, neither can anyone." "Well," I said, "I did not believe you could, but I wanted them tested." I knew it, their preaching was true, and I rejoiced exceedingly.

We had another meeting that evening and everybody, nearly, took notes, and seemed much interested. I thought surely the people will receive this, but the ministers set up against them, and called them false teachers. They labored with me, and urged me to keep away from them and let them go; that if they stayed, some persons would be deceived and led astray by them. Well, said I, if they teach the truth I am in duty bound to receive it, and which is the duty of everyone. But, I said to the minister, if you will go and hear them and show to the people that they are false teachers, and prove them to be imposters (and you ought to be able to do it) then I will leave them. So I prevailed on him to go and hear the again. And after the elders had finished their discourses, they gave liberty to anybody to speak that wished to. Then the minister, Mr. Cligget, arose and said: "These men are false teachers," and left the house, and the people followed him. I saw him a few days after that, and said to him, Why didn't you show us how and wherein those men were false teachers? Do you think we are going to take your word for it without proof? Fact is, they teach the truth and you know it.

Those elders stayed about there for two months, and I supposed a good many people would obey the gospel. But how disappointed I was when I found that only one young man besides myself, and four females, received their teachings. The cross was very heavy on me and I was about to let the elders go away without obeying the gospel, but the Spirit said to me, Perhaps you will not have another opportunity. Likewise I had two sores on me; one was a burn, and the Spirit said, those sores will never get well if you do not obey the gospel. The sores had been on me a long time, and I could not heal them with anything I could put on them and they grew larger all the time, although quite small at first.

These reflections were so heavy upon my mind that I was weighed down with sorrow. I went to the next meeting without taking any clothing for baptism, which was on Monday, the 2nd day of December, 1833. A few persons were to be baptized in the forenoon and then the elders were going to leave the place, and I was going to take them on their way for ten miles in a sleigh as there was plenty of snow on the ground. Well, I went to the baptizing but did not expect to be baptized but when the elders saw my sad feelings they urged me to obey the ordinance of baptism, and even some persons who did not intend to be baptized themselves advised me to be, and one person offered to lend me clothing so I accepted the offer and was baptized and confirmed. After that, the burden left my mind and I felt free and light as air and my sores were soon healed. The other man who was baptized at the same time, whose name was David Nelson, the elders ordained a priest. He had been a baptist by profession and a member of that Church. We held our little meetings (only six? of us) every sabbath, but the neighbors would also come in to hear us. The Lord blessed us, and we had good times.

Additional Information: Many families, after they reached the Salt Lake Valley, were called to serve colonizing missions in the region from Mexico to Canada. Jonathan and his family were called to colonize Hawaii from 1850 to 1852.

See http://josephsmithpapers.org/person/jonathan-crosby (04/11/2014).

James Henry Rollins (1816–1899)

Source: A Life Sketch (1816-1839) of James Henry Rollins. Typescript, BYU Harold B. Lee Library.

The Rollins lived in Vermont and New Hampshire. There were three brothers who emigrated to America and settled in the Eastern States a while, then two of the brothers went south. Their names were James, John Porter and Henry Rollins. My father, John Porter, was interested in cattle and sheep, and he was going on a trip to Canada with a large boat load of cattle, when a storm came up and wrecked the boat, and he went with the load to the bottom of Lake Erie, about the year 1820 or 1821.

My mother was left a widow with three small children, myself and two sisters younger than me, Mary Elizabeth and Caroline [This is the same Mary Elizabeth whose story was shared in the preface of this book]. My mother's sister, Elizabeth Van Benthuysen then the wife of Sidney A. Gilbert, took me to raise as their own. They moved from New York to Mentor, Ohio, in 1825, and a year after that moved to Kirtland, Ohio, at which place my Uncle Sidney went into the mercantile business with Orson [Newel K.] Whitney, and I did chores for them, and as soon as I was old enough was employed in their store as clerk.

I continued working thus until Oliver Cowdery and Parley P. Pratt, and some other brethren came to Kirtland and brought the Book of Mormon in the fall of 1830. These brethren were on their road to find the Center Stake of Zion. They preached the Gospel to my uncle and aunt and the Whitneys and several others, and they were converted and joined the Church of Jesus Christ of Latter-day Saints. I did not join them, as I did not thoroughly understand it, but read the Book of Mormon through, and I had to read at night by firelight, as candles were very scarce at that time, and I lay on the floor on my back with my head to the fire and read at nights, the only time I had to read.

Brothers Cowdery and Pratt put some elders in charge and they were afraid to denounce the actions of individuals who were at that time operated upon by different kinds of spirits such as receiving revelations on parchment, and professing to receive them from heaven; others lying like they were dead, in meetings, on coming to rushing to the river and going through the form of baptism in the flowing ice until they had to be taken out, as was the case with Burr Riggs. After seeing all these, I pleaded with the Lord to show me if this spirit which was operating on certain individuals was His spirit. After much praying I was shown in a dream or vision Joseph and Hyrum. I saw them standing side by side through a wall which seemingly was transparent and was the color of amber. The light which enveloped them and me was not as the light of the sun, but such as penetrated me from head to foot. They beckoned me to follow them to the door, which opened to the north. They appeared as though they were waiting for me, and they received me in a very pleasing manner as I entered. After a very short time they bade me to follow them, which I did. They crossed a very long hall running east and west, the end of which I could not see; then entering a door which opened to the south, we three entered; they showing and pointing out the beauties of the place. I cannot describe the beautiful things I beheld. Nothing on earth can compare with the things I seen in my dream. They then passed to another door to the south; they opened it and entered, if I entered myself all remembrance was taken from me of that place. I never could think of anything I seen if I entered. After this I was shown by a guide, which was at my side. He showed me many things which has transpired since, and are being literally fulfilled to the very letter. My guide also showed me a liquid billow of fire, on either side of me; as it rolled along it consumed everything upon the earth, the extent or the length thereof either was I could not discern. I asked my guide as I stood over this fire which had no flame, what it was; he said, it was what is to come and the destruction which was to roll over the earth to cleanse it, and make it pure. He then took me back and showed me many things which I would have to pass through. He told me to hold fast the Iron Rod, which, at that time, I did not know the meaning of, or neither did he explain it to me.

The adversary, previous to this had tried hard and was determined to crush me. I plead with the Lord to help me, and said, "Oh Lord, take it away. I want none of it, don't let if follow me." It immediately vanished and my spirit was taken from my body at least for 10 hours before it returned.

And all these things shown me has surely been an anchor and solace to me in the many trials and tribulations which I have passed through. I am now 80 years of age, and am having this written from what I can remember, thinking perhaps some of my children and descendants would like to read them what I have passed away.

My first acquaintance with the Prophet Joseph Smith.

As early as February, 1831, I first met Joseph Smith in my Uncle Sidney Gilbert's house. This was the first day he arrived in Kirtland, and while he was in the house conversing with my uncle and aunt, I being at the front gate, saw a wagon turn over as it was coming down the slippery hill, and heard a woman and 2 or 3 children screaming. This was Joseph's family. I ran in and told Joseph and Uncle about it, and Joseph ran to assist them without his hat. My first impression was, that if any of the occupants were hurt seriously that Joseph could heal them, but none of them were hurt. Joseph and my uncle returned to the house. He asked my uncle if I was his son. He said, "No, I was his wife's nephew," "Well," he said, "the Lord has shown him great things." I truly had seen Joseph and Hyrum in my vision in December 1830.

After the turning over of the wagon Joseph and his wife, Emma, came to my uncle's house for the purpose of finding a house to suit her. Soon after this, more or all of the Smith family arrived in Kirtland. From this time on I became personally acquainted with the Smith family. Joseph Sen., his wife, Lucy Smith, Hyrum, Samuel, William, Don Carlos, and Lucy Smith, the youngest daughter, also Jenkins Salsberry and wife. All these I saw almost daily while I remained in Kirtland. I first saw Father Joseph Smith's wife, Lucy, and Don Carlos, on Sunday, the next day after they arrived at a meeting held at Isaac Morley's house. They were so very much fatigued from their journey, and during the meeting Don Carlos fell asleep in his chair, and after several had spoken he awoke and arose and bore as strong a testimony as I ever heard, of the truth of the work. Samuel H. Smith was a man of few words and was very industrious and hard working. William Smith afterwards came to the store and asked for me to go with him on his shooting expedition up and down the river. They often consented to let me go with him. Don Carlos and myself were great chums and were quite attached to each other. In a short time I took leave of the Smiths to prepare to start westward. Joseph went to Kirtland in the spring of 1831, and the first conference of the LDS Church was held in that place. During the summer of 1831 many Elders were sent westward to Missouri, according to a revelation given June 1831, Joseph Smith,

Sidney Rigdon and Sidney Gilbert with his wife accompanying him, she being the first Mormon woman that went to Independence. I accompanied them, at the first of October we prepared to start, as we had to go from Kirtland across the western reserve to the Ohio River, which we did in wagons; taking the families of W. W. Phelps, Isaac Morley and several other families; also my mother's family, two sisters and myself. We were delayed when we got to Arrow Rock, one hundred miles below Independence, on account of the great flow of ice. The steamer turned back, and we remained there with W. W. Phelps for at least 5 weeks, when the wagons came from Independence, where we arrived about the 1st of January, 1832. Joseph Smith the Prophet came to Independence about the last of April, or the first of May. He came to my uncle's house and saluted my uncle and aunt, and then he came to me, and said, "Henry, I want to baptize you if possible before I leave." I was then working in my uncle's store and asked him if I could go with him to the Whitmore settlement, that he wanted to baptize me. My uncle said he could not spare me that day for the majority of the people came in on Saturday to do their trading, and he had no other help that he could depend on but me. When Joseph returned from the Whitmore settlement, he authorized Oliver Cowdery to baptize me instead of Him, which he did not get to do. I was finally baptized by John Carroll on the 1st of June 1832, about 1½ miles west of the Temple block.

Additional Information: "After being baptized, James Henry Rollins became a faithful member of the Church, and a valiant friend to Joseph Smith. When the Saints moved to Nauvoo, Joseph sent for him to come help him in Joseph's Red Brick Store. He did whatever the prophet asked of him, and on May 3, 1842, recalls carrying water to the upper room of the red brick store where the brethren were preparing the room for special ordinances. The next day on May 4, 1842, nine people received their endowments there."

See http://jameshenryrollinspioneer.blogspot.com/ (04/11/2014).

Joseph Holbrook (1806–1885)

Source: Autobiography (1806–1846). Typescript, BYU Harold B. Lee Library.

The next season I continued to labor on my farm. In the course of the summer many vague reports were in circulation about a certain sect of people who were called Mormonites. In the course of the season my Aunt Phebe Angel and her family moved from Rhode Island to Genesee County about the 1st day of September, 1832. I heard there was to be a Mormon meeting in China, four miles distant. I said I would go and hear this strange sect but upon arriving and waiting some time at the place of the meeting, the Elder John P. Greene sent word by his son Evan W. Greene and Lorenzo D. Young that he would not be able to attend. Mr. Green had sent by the bearers two of the papers the Evening and Morning Star printed in Jackson County, Missouri, containing the articles of the church and also the prophecy of Enoch which they requested a Mr. Carline, a universal preacher, to read to the congregation. They made a few remarks after they were read which gave me some little light as to Mormonism. I met the young man in the floor of the school house and asked them where I could get a Book of Mormon. They said they did not know. I then told them I would go 50 miles the next day to get one if they could direct me where. They said they could not tell me. I told them where I lived and if they could direct any elder there in the future, they would be welcome as I wished to learn more about this new revelation to man.

About this moment my cousin, Mary Ann Angel heard my anxiety to get a Book of Mormon, and whispered to me and said she had one she would lend me in about two weeks as she had it promised for that time. I said I would go home with her and see it. She said I could do so. I saw the Book of Mormon and read the testimony of the witnesses and looked at some of the gospel. I felt much rejoiced—to think that an angel had come from God and brought such good news. I thanked my cousin for the favor of seeing the book, hoping she would not disappoint me in having the privilege of reading it in two weeks. The weeks passed away and I thought much of Mormonism, I believed all I heard and saw. I felt much to rejoice for the words came often to my mind. "Blessed are ye for ye believe and have not seen." The two weeks brought my cousin Mary Ann Angel with the Book of Mormon to my house with her father James Angel and the Mormon Elder John P. Greene. I spent two or three hours with them while my wife was getting dinner. This was on Friday and I commenced reading that evening, but being brought up not to spend any time on a weekday to read, I thought I must work and as my cart was in the field where I left it the day before where I was digging potatoes, I went to digging potatoes, but soon found I could not content my mind at work.

I returned to the house, took the Book of Mormon, and read for a few hours but as this was so unusual a thing for me to stop work in the daytime, my wife became alarmed and thought I had better be at work than spending the time reading such deception, which called my attention again to my potato digging. I had not dug long before I wished with all my heart I knew all there was in that book. I went out into a large place nearby where the thistles were very large and thick. I knelt down to pray. I no sooner closed my eyes than it seemed as though the whole thistle plantation was in motion. I opened my eyes. I could see nothing the matter. I closed my eyes the second time when it seemed as if there was a whistle wind among the thistles, yet I felt no wind. I continued my prayer for the forgiveness of my sins and for the Lord to lead me right and show me the truth of Mormonism. When I rose, I said I would go to the house and read the Book of Mormon, work or no work. This was the after-part of Saturday. I read that day and night late. On Sunday, I read again. My wife took the child in the morning and went about 3/4 mile to my brother's, saying she would not be in the house and hear such nonsense. I read and prayed a number of times that day, being all alone and marvelled much that the thistle should be so troubled at my prayers and my wife should be so disturbed she could not stay at home for she was always fond of sitting down and reading evenings and Sundays. I read the Book of Mormon through in two days and three nights and carried it home on a Monday morning to my cousin, Mary Ann Angel. She asked me what I thought of it. I told her I believed it was true and that God was at the bottom of the work. She said she felt glad for she believed also but had not said much about it. I told her I would like to see some of the Mormon elders. She said she would send them along to my house, if she had an opportunity. I thanked her and told her I was ready to fulfill my promise to her some few years before that I would have religion when the right kind came along and I believed this was the right kind.

About this time, one of my neighbors brought me a subscription paper to sign to pay a minister missionary from Massachusetts to the heathen in Weathersfield. He said he would preach one year for $300.00 so I signed for $1.00 which he said was liberal seeing I did not belong to any church. I told him that I did not know that I should ever hear him preach but someone else would and that would keep them out of greater mischief.

These things passed along for some time when Elder John P. Greene called and stayed all night with me much satisfaction concerning the coming forth of the Book of Mormon of the Prophet Joseph Smith, Jr. I became more and more established as to the truth every day of my life as things came to my mind. My connections became much alarmed about my being a Mormon and my grandfather Abraham Morton on my mother's side and my Uncle Benjamin Morton called at my house one day and inquired as to my faith in Mormonism. I told them I believed it was true so far as I could see and I was glad of it.

They then raised their objections which were, I was bringing disgrace upon myself and family and upon my connections which were, they said, there was not another young man in the country for the time had minded the public feelings that I had and they said that if I wanted to be religious they thought I could be as well suited in the Methodist, Presbyterian, Baptist or some other as to be led away after vain delusion.

I told them that so far as disgracing myself was concerned I cared but little ABOUT it, but for their sakes, I might feel somewhat different. I told them I would say nothing about Mormonism for two or three weeks and try my feelings but if it was true I should know it and embrace it. They went away quite satisfied for they knew my promise was good to be carried out and lived to.

But to me it was a long three weeks for when I was in company and heard derision made of Mormonism my conscience would smite me and say, "You know that it is true," but I kept my word until the three weeks were up and they thought I would never say any more about it. But at the expiration of the three weeks I was invited to the raising of a frame barn when one of the neighbors said I understand you have given up Mormonism. I told them I had been under promise of friends for a few weeks and that I was free to speak my mind again and that Mormonism was true. My grandfather Morton and uncle were in hearing [distance], and their hopes were blasted. I further said that from that time forth, I would speak of the truths of Mormonism. I felt much relieved from that time forth.

Mr. Blanchard, the missionary I had signed the dollar for his preaching, was very concerned about me and my family. He told my wife in my absence falsehoods about the coming forth of the Book of Mormon, of the Prophet Joseph Smith, Jr., etc., which kept her in much fear also as she thought I was about to deceive her as well as myself, but still I believed Mormonism.

As there had been no meeting in this vicinity, I had to catch what I could from the Bible as the Book of Mormon had been a key to the Bible to me and it was now a new book, having the seals broken, light and life and salvation on its pages.

In December [1832] one night, I dreamed I was in a certain city where people were engaged in their various business matters when all of a sudden a voice was heard from the heavens saying, "Up, get ye out of this city for behold I will destroy this people, and flee ye into the west." The people all heard the voice and knew it was from heaven. They halted, looked amazed for a moment and then pursued their course as before. Shortly the voice was heard the second time. The people were seemingly less alarmed than before and again the third time. [The voice] spoke the third time the same words with the same warning, but the people paid no attention to it, so I stopped and marvelled and said I am not going to stay here so I started out of the city to the west. I found about a dozen more had taken the same warning as myself and we all met at the outside of the city. We went down a long hill when we came into a large valley running north and south and also a large river running in the midst of the valley running north. It was both wide and deep and there appeared no way to cross the river. Some said let's go up the river and others said let's go down the river, but I said we were commanded to go to the west. I am going right straight into the river. I no sooner got into the river than I found myself on the other bank on the west side and it was said unto me, you are now baptized. I thought that those who were with me on the other side were with me now, but I did not see how they came.

Now there were three large roads presented before me. One led partly up the river bearing around a hill, one partly down the river bearing around the same hill, while the other went straight forward up the hill, but the hill looked hard to ascend while those wound around to the right and left appeared easy and would finally come to the same spot at the top of the hill. The travel in each road was about equal. Those that were with me said, let's take the right or left hand road, it will take us much easier to the top of the hill, but I said we are to go straight to the west. I am going to take the middle road up the hill. As the several roads were sandy or loamy, I could see the footsteps of men and women and children who had traveled up those roads before me. And as I began to travel up the straight forward road up the hill, it did seem as though the hill became more level, but after traveling on for awhile there was a very bad place in the hill. There were roads that turned off at the foot of this bad hill to right and left and appeared to wind around the hill and come to the top. The same arguments were used by those that were with me as before that it would be much easier for [us] to take these winding roads that lead around the hill for what is the use of being so particular which road we travel if we only get to the top of the hill.

I told them I would not turn away from the straight forward road although it did appear that nearly one-half of the people did turn away from the straight forward road. And I did not see them at the top of the hill. Thus I continued my journey finding often a bad hill in the straight forward road while the byroads at the foot of each hill took away much of the travelers and as I came near the end of my journey the obstacles in the road were much more hideous to look at while the byroads look much more pleasant. At last I came to the top of the last hill on a level plain. The road had become a small path. I turned around to see what had become of those who had left the straight forward road when it was said to me, "Few there are that will ever come to the top of the hill, few there are that will be saved." I marvelled greatly and thanked the Lord that He preserved me to come to the top of the hill on a level with my brethren while thousands that had set out on the same journey had turned away at the bottom of the hill in those byroads and are lost, while the roads became as on a level with my brethren while thousands that had set out were lost, while the roads became plain before me that I saw every road that turned away was wrong. They would fork and those forks would fork again until they ended in total dimness where there is no road. And those travelers often wandering for thousands of years before they could again reach the bottom of the hill and have the privilege of coming up as before. And these that turned away near the top of the hill or near the end of the journey, it took much the longest. I looked to see if my wife was coming, saying, I think she will be along soon as she at this time didn't fully believe Mormonism, and I saw the city I had left given over to destruction of every kind by the judgments of God and the wickedness of the people and lo and behold I awoke. It was a dream.

About the last of December 1832, when going to a mill, I met two elders, Aaron C. Lyons and Leonard Rich, from Warsaw, about 12 miles distant. They informed [me] there would be a meeting on the 6th of January 1833, at Elder Lyons' house and invited me to come down and bring my wife and those who would like to come.

On Saturday, January 5, 1833, I took my ox team and cart with my wife Nancy, my Aunt Phebe Angel and cousin Mary Ann Angel and went to Warsaw to Elder Aaron C. Lyons to be there on Sunday. Brother Lyons gave us a cheerful welcome on our arrival that night. In the morning I told Brother Lyons and Rich I would like to be baptized if they thought I was worthy as I had brought my clothes for that purpose. So after breakfast I was baptized with my Aunt Phebe Angel by Leonard Rich, Mary Ann having been baptized about one week before. We were confirmed by Aaron C. Lyons about 11:00 o'clock A.M. They had a meeting, the first I had ever been to. Different elders occupied the time during the day and evening. Windsor C. Lyons then spoke in tongues which was the first I had ever heard. My wife became convinced that Mormonism was true. On Monday, the 7th day of January [1833] she was baptized also by Leonard Rich and confirmed by Aaron C. Lyons. I was also ordained a teacher in the Church of Christ under the hands of Aaron C. Lyons, a high priest, and was directed to teach the principles to all who might wish to hear, and received my license which I shall enclose in this journal.

I returned home on the same day much rejoiced to think that my wife was with me in the faith of the gospel, but found that I got myself into business for I met with opposition on all hands and from every quarter, but this kept me the more faithful. I visited my brother Chandler and his wife and told them there would be a meeting the next week at my house and invited them to attend with sister, and also a meeting at my Aunt Phebe Angel's in China. I continued to go from house [to house] and carry the Book of Mormon to them and try to get them to read it. The result was that my brother, Chandler, and his wife, Eunice, my sister, Phebe, and Dwight Hardin, who was boarding at my house, father Owens and mother and many others in the vicinity were added to the church in the course of a few months. Brother Lyons and Rich and some other elders met with us often until the church in this place numbered about 85 members. Many had the gift of tongues and interpretation with prophesying by the gift of the Holy Ghost, and the church did meet together often to preach, exhort and speak to another of the things of the kingdom which gave them much love for one another, strengthening their faith, etc.

Additional Information: Joseph wrote the music to the Church hymn, "Jesus, Lover of My Soul." (Hymn 102 in the current Church hymnal.)

See http://www.lds.org/music/library/hymns/jesus-lover-of-my-soul?lang=eng (04/11/2014).

Sarah DeArmon Pea Rich (1814–1893)

Source: Autobiography (1814–1893). Typescript, BYU Harold B. Lee Library.

In the summer of 1835 two Mormon elders came to preach at my father's house by request of my father, as he had met them in the town of Belleville, nine miles from my father's house. I, together with my father and mother were at that time members of the Reformed Methodist Church. The two elders came and held a meeting and preached on the first principles of the gospel, and related to the people about their being a prophet in their church, and told us about the Book of Mormon, and about an angel appearing to the prophet and others; all of which was new doctrine to the people, so as it was in the afternoon they held their meeting, my father invited them to stop all night, which invitation they accepted as they were then on their way to Kirtland, Ohio, some five hundred miles from where we then lived.

So after supper was over a number of neighbors gathered in to hear the strange talk, but I felt anxious to see the Book of Mormon they had told us about and I asked one of the elders if I could the see the book and read some in it that evening. So he gladly handed me the book, and I asked the company to excuse me for the evening and most of the night I spent in reading that book. I truly was greatly astonished at its contents that it left an impression upon my mind not to be forgotten:—For in fact the book appeared to be open before my eyes for weeks but the next morning those men bid us goodbye and started on their journey for Ohio. So our family had many things to say about this strange people; but still the things they told us left a deep impression on our minds, not easy to be forgotten.

But yet we did not think of ever meeting with those strange men again; and after they had been gone six weeks, I had a dream concerning them. I dreamed on a Friday night that they would come to our house the next evening just as the sun would be setting, and they would first come in sight at the end of a long lane in front of our house. I also dreamed that I met them on the porch and of the remark that was made both by them and of the remark made by myself, which I will relate later on.

So in the morning father and mother were going to Belleville, a town nine miles away, and while we were at breakfast I asked my father if he would not try to come home early that evening. He answered., "Why are you so particular, is your young man coming?" I said, "No, father, but those two Mormon elders will be here tonight." "Why," said my father, "have you heard from them?" I said, "No, but I dreamed last night that they would be here, and I feel sure it will be so." Father said I must be crazy for those men were hundreds of miles away. I said, "Father, hurry home this evening for I am sure they will come." He only laughed at me, and he and mother went off to town. Then said my sister, "Let us prepare for those men for they will surely be here." She too, laughed at me, but as it was Saturday we went to work baking and preparing for Sunday, as that was our custom to do on Saturday; and as the day passed on I began to look once in awhile down the lane for those men.

Sure enough, just as the sun was setting they made their appearance just where I dreamed I first saw them. I met them on the porch, and bid them the time of day by saying, "I have been looking for you to come." "Why," said they, "had you heard we were coming?" "No," said I, "but I dreamed last night that you were coming and I felt sure you would be here." "Well," said one of the elders, "and we had a vision that we were to return here and baptize you and build up a Church in this region." I said, "Well, that is something for the future," but bid them to take chairs and be comfortable for my father and mother drove into the yard and as I was standing on the porch my father said to me, "Well, Sarah, where are your Mormon elders?" I told him they were in the house, at the same time they stepped out onto the porch to meet my father, who seemed struck with astonishment remembering what I told him in the morning about my dream.

But after supper was over the evening was well spent in conversing about the principles of the gospel which they were preaching to the people, and we became more and more interested in what they told us. So in the morning, it being Sunday, Father took a horse and went and notified the neighborhood that there would be preaching at our house that evening by the Mormon elders. And when time arrived for the meeting the house was filled, and all listened with the greatest of order to a beautiful discourse upon the coming forth of the Book of Mormon, and of the appearing to Joseph Smith of the angel, and many were astonished to hear such strange doctrine, for it truly was something new to the people.

And after the meeting was dismissed, a great number stopped and spent the evening, asking questions until a late hour. But before dismissing the meeting it was agreed that they should preach again on Tuesday evening following at the same place.

So the word went far and near, and they came from all the settlements in reach, and the house and porch was full of hearers. The elders preached on the first principles of the gospel, and were listened to with the greatest of attention. So when meeting was dismissed the elders had many invitations to preach in different places.

By this time I was truly convinced that their doctrine was from God, and on the next morning I went forth and was baptized; it was on the 15th of December, and they had to cut the ice and baptize me. I had made it a business of prayer to my Father in Heaven to show me is this the work of God, and He did so. I was truly convinced that it was the true gospel, and never have for one moment doubted it since; and it has now been fifty-four years since I embraced Mormonism; and I feel thankful to my Heavenly Father that I over heard and embraced the truth of His latter-day work.

Additional Information: After the Saints were pushed from Missouri to Quincy, Illinois, Sarah became sick. The following is the blessing she received from the hands of Joseph Smith Sr.:

I got along finely for a few days, but took a back set which came near proving fatal, for I grew worse all the time, until my life was despaired for six weeks no one thought I would recover except my husband, Mr. Rich he would not give up but said all the time that I would not die. Finally he sent back to Quincy, five miles, for Father Smith, the Prophet Joseph Smith's father, he was then the Patriarch of our Church, for I thought I was going to die in a very short time.

So Father Smith came, and when he came to the bedside and looked at me he said he thought I would die. Mr. Rich quickly answered Father Smith: "She won't die." The old gentleman hung his head for a few moments and then looked and then said, "Let us administer to her, and I will give her a Patriarchal blessing." He did so and Spirit of the Lord was so poured out upon him that he blessed me with a long life, and said I should speedily recover, and gave me such a blessing that all in the room were weeping for joy, for they had all been looking for me to die. When he got through the blessing he stood a moment looking at me and then said, "I did not have faith when I commenced blessing Sister Rich that she would get well, but the Lord poured out His Spirit upon me to give her the blessing, and promised her a long life, and many blessings and said he, "every word will be fulfilled."

Part Four

Joseph Smith and Perspective

It was said to Joseph Smith, even before the Church was organized, that his name would be known for good and bad in the world. He encountered this immediately when he shared with a minister his account of the First Vision. Joseph later wrote, "It caused me serious reflection then, and often has since, how very strange it was that an obscure boy, of a little over fourteen years of age, and one, too, who was doomed to the necessity of obtaining a scanty maintenance by his daily labor, should be thought a character of sufficient importance to attract the attention of the great ones of the most popular sects of the day, and in a manner to create in them a spirit of the most bitter persecution and reviling. But strange or not, so it was, and it was often the cause of great sorrow to myself" (Joseph Smith—History 1:23).

It was not all bad though. Those that understood and knew Joseph appreciated him. There were those that weren't even members of the Church that respected and esteemed him, and that was because of perspective. Just recently in my ward we had a high council visitor come and speak. His talk was centered on judging others and how wrongful judgment is passed when we lack perspective. He told of a time when he was involved as a participant at a BYU basketball camp along with his son and the autistic son of his brother. Part of the basketball camp's activities was a father-son flag football game that pitted the fathers against their sons. During the game, his autistic nephew decided it would be better if he tied on his flags. Sure enough, he got the ball and tore for the end zone. A number of the dads pulled at his flags, but since they had been tied on, obviously they didn't come off. The young man scored the touchdown. Some of the fathers were understandably upset and headed in the direction of the young man. The uncle could see what was about to happen and intercepted the fathers. He told them that this young man was autistic, that he didn't understand. He said he could see these fathers melt when they understood the big picture. The uncle then spoke to his nephew and explained to him that the flags could not be tied. The flags were untied and, through the encouragement of the very fathers that were about to berate this boy for having "cheated," went on to have a MVP performance.

I'll bring this back to Joseph Smith by sharing another example. I had the privilege of serving in the Massachusetts Boston Mission over three decades ago. While serving in the New Market, New Hampshire area, my companion and I decided to street board in a local mall. Partway through the day, a man came up to me and I walked him through the First Vision display. With time he began to chuckle. I asked him what he found so amusing. His exact words to me were, "God, angels, and a 14-year-old boy. Yeah, right!" I could see that he would not be teachable, so I left him with my testimony.

Many months later, I was attending church in my new area in Keene, New Hampshire. My companion and I had to give talks that day in sacrament meeting. We were both sitting on the stand waiting for the meeting to begin when I noticed a man walk into the chapel. I had no idea who he was, thinking that he was a visitor. After the meeting, members were congratulating my companion and myself on our talks. I noticed this "visitor" standing at the perimeter of the members, patiently waiting his turn to speak with us.

When all had departed the chapel and only my companion and this man were left, he shook our hands, first thanking us for our talks. He then stated to me, "I can tell by the look in your eyes that you have no idea who I am." He was right. As far as I knew, I had never seen him before. He continued, "But I remember you well." He then asked, "Do you remember street boarding in the Newington Mall in Portsmouth and speaking to a man that laughed at you?" It all came flooding back. "Yes, I remember," I responded. He said, "I'm that man." He apologized for having laughed at me, and then stated, "When you bore your testimony, something hit me inside. I couldn't stop thinking about what you said. With time, I looked up the elders in my area and eventually joined the Church."

Without perspective, his initial reaction was to laugh; however, after being taught by the missionaries and being touched by the

Spirit he had a change of heart. His perspective had changed with added knowledge. He then desired to join the Church.

In the upcoming section are seven journal accounts. Five accounts are by individuals who eventually joined the Church. The account of Nancy Tracy is thought-provoking. At first she lacked perspective and was antagonistic to the Church and its Prophet. As the light of the Gospel entered her soul and as she gained perspective, there was a corresponding change in her attitude. The final two accounts are from individuals who were not members of the Church and who would never join. These are interesting because the two men that wrote them traveled together, met the Prophet at the same time and under the same circumstances, but ended up having very different feelings because of perspective. One account is negative while the account of Josiah Quincy (who would later become mayor of Boston) is not always, and for the most part is in fact positive.

Wandle Mace (1809–1890)

Source: Autobiography (1809–1846). Journal of Wandle Mace. Typescript, BYU Harold B. Lee Library. (As told to his wife, Rebecca E. Howell Mace)

In September, 1837, I exhibited at the Mechanic's Fair held in Niblo's Garden, and was awarded a diploma by the Mechanic's Institute of New York for a post mortising and rail sharpening machine, good for saving labor. George Bruce President.

I sold patent rights to a large amount and with this means I was enabled to settle all the obligations of my brother, John and myself which were incurred from failure in business, when we found ourselves several thousand dollars worse than nothing. Now we were again free from all such obligations. I also bought a piece of land in Illinois, about four miles away from Quincy, from a Mr. Begaudus, a resident of that place, for which I paid $3,200. I was very particular about the deed. I would not receive one made out in New York, but it must come direct from Quincy. I received the deed from Quincy all right, but alas! alas! It proved to be forged.

I now disposed of this business to my brother, John, and turned my attention to making portable mills. I bought the patent right with all the "title, interest, etc.," in what was called a conical grinder, with improvements in threshing machine and horse power, for which I paid $1,500 in company with Mr. William Shay. We done a good business. I was engaged in this business when Elder Parley P. Pratt cane [came] along preaching the gospel.

About this time Mrs. Dexter, a friend of my parents, came from Troy upon a visit with her friends in the city. On one of her visits to my house she made me acquainted with the situation of her youngest daughter, which was extremely miserable. This daughter was married to a profligate fellow who had communicated to her a loathsome disease. He had administered to her calomel and powerful acids, which had produced a terrible state of salivation, and she was fearful that he designed to destroy her life. Mrs. Dexter craved protection for her daughter with her infant. I gave them an upper room in my house where they would be safe from him for the present. Although I was greatly prospered in business I did not neglect the opportunity of meeting with my associates to search the scriptures, and sometimes

I visited the meetings held by the Methodists as prayer meetings. On one occasion of this kind they took for their subject a saying of Paul, "Contend earnestly for the faith once delivered to the Saints." Several persons present spoke upon the subject, very earnest and full of zeal. They clapped their hands, etc. and seemed to think they had exhausted the subject. They then invited me to speak.

I spoke upon the same subject—viz, "contend earnestly for the faith once delivered to the Saints." I endeavored to show how far short we came of having that faith. When that 'faith' was delivered to the Saints, they were told to "Heal the sick, cast out devils, open the eyes of the blind, and to raise the dead," and "as freely as you have received, freely give." I asked, "Have we that faith?" Surely not. Can we heal the sick, cast out devils, open the eyes of the blind or raise the dead? Have we any of the gifts of the spirit? If we had, we could do all these things as did the apostles. These gifts are the result of the faith that was delivered to the Saints. I spoke at some length in this strain and sat down.

As soon as I had taken my seat several were on their feet in a moment to confront me and denounce those Bible truths I had presented to them. They declared they were not needed in this age and it was ridiculous for any person to entertain such views. Confusion reigned and the meeting closed.

I had noticed a stranger in the meeting, a portly looking man, sitting by Mr. Elijah Fordham, with whom I was acquainted, as we frequently met each other at the meetings held at the house of Mr. La Tourett. At the close of the meeting Mr. Fordham came forward and very warmly pressed my hand and congratulated me upon the remarks I had made. He then introduced me to the stranger, who seemed very much interested in the meetings, as Mr. Pratt from Ohio.

Mr. Pratt expressed his pleasure at my remarks in the meeting and said he would like a further conversation with me. I told him I was always ready for conversation upon such topics. He inquired if tomorrow afternoon at four o'clock would be convenient. I said "Yes," and gave him my address and he visited me next day at the time appointed. My wife prepared tea, after which we entered into conversation upon the doctrines taught in the New Testament. He spoke of repentance and of the necessity of baptism for the remission of sins by one holding authority, and the laying on of hands for the gift of the Holy Ghost. This kind of talk suited me exactly, but where could that authority be found? In the course of our conversation he learned from me this that I was waiting and watching for the gifts of the gospel as they once existed. I would no more connect myself with any denomination unless that denomination had with them apostles and prophets, Jesus Christ being the chief cornerstone.

Said he "Brother Mace,"—he called me Brother Mace from the first—"Do you know that you are a singular man." I replied, "No, I believe in the scriptures and in the doctrines recorded in the New Testament, but why do you say singular?" He said, "I said singular to find a man in this great city of learning and ignorance, of riches and poverty, a city of churches also, to find a man waiting for apostles and prophets and the gifts of the spirit as enjoyed anciently.

"Suppose that you should hear that away in the west somewhere there was such an organization, with apostles and prophets, pastors and teachers, such as you are waiting for." Then he began telling me about a young man in New York who had been visited by an angel. He gave me the young man's history and I was very much interested in the recital. He told me about a book that had come forth through the instrumentality of this young man. He told me of a church already organized with prophets, apostles, and all the offices appertaining to the Church of Christ, with all the gifts of the spirit enjoyed by the Saints anciently.

We had conversed upon these subjects until midnight but he had not yet told me the name of the young man neither the title of the book. About midnight he mentioned the name of Joseph Smith the translator of the Book of Mormon.

At the mention of this name a curious feeling crept over me. I had heard some reports of this Joseph Smith, not at all to his credit, and that he was an imposter, etc. But did not the Jews call Jesus a glutton and a winebibber, a friend of publicans and sinners? The only question in my mind now were these: Did the church which Mr. Pratt had been telling me of really hold their authority from Jesus Christ as did the apostles of old? And did signs follow the believers?

Mr. Pratt, when taking his leave of me that night, said to me, "Brother Mace, if you are honest, and I believe you are, the Lord will make known to you that we hold this authority." He bade me farewell with this promise. I now awaited the fulfillment of this promise, that the Lord would make known to me that these things were true.

I saw no more of Mr. Pratt for about one month and then it was I went for him to come to my house and administer in my family by the very authority I so much questioned.

One Sunday evening on returning from a religious meeting I found one of our children very sick, a little boy about a year old, and through the night he grew worse. Monday morning the family physician was called in and he pronounced the sickness inflammation of the brain. He used all his skill to arrest the disease in vain; the child grew worse. He told us if water settled on the brain there was no hope. He told us what the indications would be if this was the case. We watched him closely and every symptom he pointed us to appeared to the smallest minute. The child would be thrown into spasms; it would writhe and twist until it was enough to rend the hearts of all who watched its sufferings. The doctor gave him black drops—a concentrated tincture of laudanum—He at first gave one drop, increasing the quantity just sufficient to quiet him. He said had it been given to the child when in health one drop would destroy his life.

We watched the little sufferer as he still grew worse until Wednesday, when my sister Jane, who was present, remarked it was very singular that the child should be kept so long in such terrible suffering. My wife suggested it would be a good time to try Mr. Pratt's religion. I remarked, "If you wish I will go and bring him." The fact was, I was very anxious to do so but did not suggest it for fear of raising opposition.

As it was raining I took my umbrella and immediately started for Mr. Pratt. I had taken the precaution to learn his place of residence, being extremely anxious to call upon him. Mr. Pratt himself answered my knock on the door. I told my errand and he put on his hat and cloak, stepped out under my umbrella and accompanied me home. As we entered the room where the child lay it seemed to cause much confusion. In the room present were my wife, my sister Jane, and Mrs. Dexter. Mr. Pratt wished me to call the house to order. When order was restored he offered a prayer which was in conformity with the doctrines of Jesus Christ as taught in the New Testament, that God was the same God that he was anciently, and that the prayer of faith would save the sick, etc.

When we arose from prayer he said, "Brother Mace, you hold more authority in your family than any other man can, and I want you to lay your hands on this child with me." I did so. He then administered with all confidence in the authority he held and rebuked the disease in the name of Jesus Christ, and said the child should begin to mend in that very hour. My wife asked him if she should give the child any more of the black drops and he replied, "If you have perfect confidence in the administration I would rather you would not, but if you have not perfect confidence you can decrease the quantity gradually." She decreased the drops gradually. [Written in the margin was: Parley told me in Florence in 1856 that this was the only time he had asked a man not a member of the church to lay hands on the sick.]

Before stated I had given Mrs. Dexter an upper room in my house where she could take care of her sick and suffering daughter. She was present during this administration and remarked, "If this child can be healed my daughter can also." My sister Jane, who was also present, ran upstairs to the sick woman and told her there was a man downstairs who put himself in the place of Jesus Christ, that he laid his hands on the little child and rebuked the disease in the name of Jesus Christ and commanded it to depart. The Spirit, and the manner of my sister in giving this information to the sick woman, alarmed her. Upon entering her room Mrs. Dexter found her daughter laboring under great excitement. She was a sensible Bible-reading woman and she explained to her daughter all that had taken place in the room where the sick child lay. This soothed and calmed her as she listened to the words of her mother.

The next morning I went to my shop to work. About ten o'clock my wife sent a messenger to me saying the child was well and playful. I went home and found this was even so. Oh, what joy swelled our hearts as we gazed upon the child so miraculously healed. We had truly found that this man, Parley P. Pratt, did indeed hold the authority to rebuke the disease in the name of Jesus Christ and we gave God thanks.

From the time our little boy, Charles, began to recover, Mrs. Dexter's daughter grew worse and her babe also. The doctor said it was impossible for either to recover. All that night and the next day, Thursday, she still grew worse, and Thursday night it seemed impossible to keep life in her until morning. Next morning Friday Mrs. Dexter sent for Elder Pratt, who brought with him Mr. Elijah Fordham, also an elder. Together they sang a hymn to soft pleasant music as follows: [The text included the hymn, "Now Let us Rejoice."]

After singing, Elder Pratt offered a prayer and then explained the principles of the gospel as he had done on the previous occasion. The sick woman listened attentively and at her request Elders Pratt and Fordham administered to her and also her babe, and they began to mend from that hour. She had not partaken of food for several days, but a short time after the elders left the house she asked her mother for a cold potato and some vinegar. She sat up in the bed and ate half of the potato and lied down again. In a short time she called for the remainder of the potato and ate it. The vinegar did not distress her as formerly; her babe and herself improved rapidly and she was soon able to move about the room. She had been so badly salivated, that if the door stood ajar or if she ate anything sour, her mouth became filled with lumps, and water would run from her mouth, causing her the greatest distress. Consequently, she was very cautious moving about her room, and to the top of the stairs and back, and finding no bad effect follow, she ventured downstairs to our sitting room. She found the changes from one room to another, the doors being ajar, etc., did not hurt her any more.

Elder Pratt was holding meetings about a quarter of a mile distant, and she accompanied her mother to meeting. As she stepped outside the dorm, my sister Jane was passed on the way to her Baptist meeting and chided the young lady for venturing out on such a blustery day. But she went to the meeting and returned rejoicing. She found herself well, no bad effect followed her venture, and she said she found herself stronger at every step. She was healed every whit.

Truly there was great rejoicing in my house, No. 13 Bedford Street. We had witnessed the power of God made manifest and knew for a surety that He had again given authority to man on the earth to administer in the name of Jesus Christ, and could say as was said by one of old, no man can do these miracles except God be with him.

In a short time after these miracles were performed, Elder Pratt appointed a day for baptizing in the East River, about two miles from my home. It was a very wet disagreeable day with snow and rain. The sidewalks were shoe deep with snow and mud, but this did not prevent the young woman from going. She said her feet were wet from the time she started from home until she returned yet she took no cold. There were six persons baptized at that time by Elder Elijah Fordham. They were: my wife, Margaret Mace; Mrs. Dexter and daughter; Theodore Curtis and wife; and Miss Ann Shaffer, who was afterward married to Elder Fordham. I stood upon a block of ice and witnessed the baptisms.

All retired to the house of Brother Cox, who lived nearby, where those who had been baptized changed their clothing and we then returned home. All wondered why I was not then baptized. My reasons for this was that I wanted to see them act on their own volition, not because I set them the example. A few days after this I was baptized in the same place by Elder Parley P. Pratt. I do not remember the month but these things took place in the winter of 1837–1838.

Additional Information: From the following journal account it appears that Mace supervised the framework of the Nauvoo Temple:

"A large number of elders was called at this conference to go on missions, I was of the number but being already engaged to work on the [Nauvoo] temple I was released from the mission. For, while I was working at Mr. Kimballs Iron Foundry, the temple committee found difficulty in getting an experienced hand to frame some masts to hoist the stone onto the walls of the temple so applied to me. I thereupon engaged to do the work of building three masts and cranes to be used for that purpose, which when completed was perfectly satisfactory to the temple committee, I was then engaged by them and the architect William Weeks to draft and superintend the framing of all the timber work of the temple, commencing on the ground and throughout to the top of the tower. This was the most complicated piece of timber work or framing I ever done, and was the most easily accomplished. I was also called to draft and superintend the timber work, the framing etc. of the Nauvoo House, Arsenal and other public buildings. On the temple grounds, I built a saw mill to saw plank and such small timbers as was needed."

Mary A. Noble (1810–1900)

Source: Autobiography (1810–1835). Included in Joseph Bates Noble, typescript, BYU–S.

My father sold his place in Levonia and we moved with his family to Avon, Livingston County. Some year previous to this, my father became acquainted with father Joseph Smith, the father of the Prophet. He frequently would go to Palmyra to see father Smith and his family during this time. Brother Joseph Smith came in possession of the plates that contained the Book of Mormon. As soon as it was noised around that there was a Golden Bible found, for that was what it was called at the time, the minds of the people became excited, and it rose to such a pitch that a mob collected together to search the house of father Joseph Smith to find the records. My father was there at the time and assisted in concealing the plates in a box in a secluded place where no one could find them, although he did not see them. My father soon returned.

At this time I was engaged most of the time in school teaching. The next season I taught in Avon, Livingston County, New York. I taught there two seasons, and there I became acquainted with Joseph B. Noble. I first received introduction with him at Mr. [James] McMillan's house. The first time I ever saw him I felt an attachment for him that I never did any other man from so short an acquaintance.

Previous to this my father purchased a Book of Mormon, the only one in that region of country. I took this book down where I was teaching school. It was the first one they ever saw. There were different opinions respecting the book. Some believed in it, others did not. I lent the book to Mother Wilcox. She was a believer in it, and her son. Mr. Noble was boarding there at this time. He likewise read it and after this the elders came around preaching, first ones I ever saw, with the exception of father Smith and Samuel, that were around preaching here.

Brother Joseph Young and Brother Brigham Young, Father Smith, and Samuel had been to father's before this on business, but when I came to see the two Brother Youngs, I had a testimony in myself that they were servants of the Lord, for they looked different to me than any other men I ever saw. They carried an expression in their countenances that be spoke men of God. From that time they used to call to fathers often in company with others. Father's house was the only one in that region that they visited. I was always edified when in that society, to hear them converse on the subject of Mormonism, for I realized that they were in possession of something that I was not. It was my meditations by day and by night; the principles of the gospel that they held forth on the subject of Mormonism I knew were principles that I had never heard preached by any other people, and I had a testimony within myself that it was the truth of God.

At this time I was teaching school, as I said before, in Avon, Livingston County, and Mr. Noble was boarding at Mr. Knowles, the same place I made my home when I did not go to my father's. My father lived about two miles from there. At this time Mr. Noble was paying attention to Mr. Owles daughter. She was a fine girl. She was my intimate acquaintance. She was also a school teacher. We were frequently in each other's society. She was naturally rather of a proud spirit girl and did not care much about religion, but was naturally very lively, and I was rather different turn. I always had respect for the principles of truth and righteousness and sought the happiness of others as well as my own; I did not much expect at this time ever to be united to Mr. Noble. Still, it would have been a matter of my choice, could I have been permitted to have made it.

But I unbosomed my feelings to no one. I held sacred the feelings of my heart. My mind was employed in school and I attended my own business, and trusted in the Lord, believing he would rule all things for my good, and for the glory of God. I taught school two seasons in the same district. About this time, Mr. [Joseph B.] Noble was baptized into the Mormon Church, as it was then called. His conversation was highly gratifying to me. He was a person of good habit, good principles, and a fine intelligent young man. In his society I was happy.

The next season I taught school in the neighborhood of my fathers. This was 1833, in the fall and winter of the same year. I commenced keeping company with Mr. Noble, and in a year, the spring of 1834, Brother Joseph Smith came from Kirtland, Ohio, to my father's New York estate, Avon, Livingston County. This was the first time I ever beheld a prophet of the Lord, and I can truly say at the first sight that I had a testimony within my bosom that he was a man chosen of God to bring forth a great work in the last days. His society I prized, his conversation was meat and drink to me. The principles that he brought forth bind the testimony that he bore of the truth of the Book of Mormon made a lasting impression upon my mind. While he was there, Sidney Rigdon and Joseph and Brigham Young, Luke and Lyman Johnson, and 12 or 14 of the travelling elders had a council to my father's. I, in company with my sisters, had the pleasure of cooking, and serving the table, and waiting on them, which I considered a privilege and blessing.

Nancy Naomi Alexander Tracy (1816–1902)

Source: Autobiography (1816–1846). Autobiography of Nancy Naomi Alexander Tracy. Typescript, Harold B. Lee Library.

Everything was bright before us. As yet we had not tasted the bitter. Those were happy days. That summer we began to hear rumbles about a gold bible that a gold-digger had dug up. Reports came fast and thick. It made quite an excitement. The newspapers were full of the vilest slander about Joseph Smith, the finder of these gold records. Time passed on in this way for awhile. At last there came sole traveling preachers styling themselves Mormon missionaries. Of course, prejudice was against them.

However, they succeeded in getting a place to hold meeting. I heard of it. It was two miles from where I lived, but out of curiosity I determined to go and see and hear what those horrid creatures looked like and had to say, for I hardly expected they were human from what I had heard. So I got two other woman to go with me and repaired to the place appointed. The house was filled, waiting to see this wonderful man. My astonishment was better felt than described when he appeared tall and sit with piercing black eyes filled with the spirit of God. He gave out a hymn and sang, a few joining him. Then he prayed and such a prayer! He was full to the brim. All eyes were upon him and you could have heard a pin drop. It seemed as though his influence put all prejudice under his feet. He took his text from the Bible, but I have forgotten it. However, I well remember his powerful sermon on the first principles of the Gospel as taught by the Savior and his apostles. O how plain and beautiful and easy to understand. I believed with my whole soul and I could see that I had been preserved from uniting with other creeds and was waiting to hear and told the folks that for the first time I had heard the true Gospel preached by David Patten who had been chosen as an Apostle, ordained and set apart to teach the pure doctrine of our Savior. They laughed at me and cried, "Delusion, false prophets," and so on. But the seed had taken root and I would talk with my husband and was very anxious that he should hear and investigate. So I waited. At last Parley P. Pratt came into the neighborhood, another apostle. So there was a great turnout to hear him. My husband went and his eyes began to be opened. He began reading the Bible. He took his time to investigate. By this time other elders came. There were quite a number who believed and were baptized. As yet we had not joined them, although I had longed to do so.

On the 25th of November, 1833, there came a son to our house to take up his abode and for six weeks I hovered between life and death. By this time there had been a branch organized, and James Blaksley was set apart to preside. He would come and talk of the gifts and blessings of the Gospel, the healing of the sick by the power of faith. But I felt unworthy to claim the blessing because I had not done my duty, but I determined that if the Lord would spare my life, when I was able I would be baptized. So In the spring of 1834, the 10th of May, my husband and myself were baptized with Elder Thomas Dulcher officiating. We were confirmed at the water's edge.

Additional Information: "In March 1836, Nancy and Moses had the privilege of attending the dedication of the Kirtland Temple. She described the Pentecost-like event as 'two of the happiest days of my life.' This experience prepared Nancy spiritually for the sacrifices ahead."

See https://www.lds.org/ensign/2012/03/nancy-naomi-alexander-tracy-faithful-pioneer?lang=eng (04/11/2014).

Benjamin Ashby (1828–1907)

Source: Covers the Period 1828–1847. Photocopy of holograph, Harold B. Lee Library. Autobiography of Benjamin Ashby.

In the year 1839 or 1840 there came to Salem, Erastas Snow, preaching the gospel in its purity, as revealed to Joseph Smith. My father was not a member of any denomination but attended the Universalist Church of which my mother was a member because as I have often heard her say they preached the love of God for his children in contrast to the doctrines of the Orthodox churches that held to the everlasting punishment of all who did not embrace their peculiar dogmas.

Father returned home one Sunday noon, saying he had been to hear a new religion preached by a Mormon in the Masonic Hall and seemed much interested in what he had heard preached he took down the Bible and began to read some of its passages to Mother. She being confined to her bed by the birth of my sister, Mary Jane, in the afternoon and attended the meeting with father and continued to do so with the agreement that I was to attend the Sunday School, it being against mother's principles to allow her children to go from one meeting to another but inasmuch as father went she could not reasonably object. My mind soon became enlightened upon the plan of salvation. I firmly believed in the divinity and sacred character of the Book of Mormon which I read; a copy of which had been lent to father by Brother Snow.

One Sunday, there was some questions in the book from which we studied, concerning the ancient prophets with scriptural texts as answers and some questions that were to be answered by the pupil. One of these was "Is there any prophets in these days," which happened to come to me in turn. To the teacher's surprise, I answered, "Yes, sir." "False prophets I suppose you mean." "No sir, true ones." Who, pray, was his query. Joseph Smith was my answer. He made some reply and passed on to the next. I heard no more of it until about two weeks after when mother called me to her and asked me what I had been saying to my teacher about Joseph Smith. I told her what had occurred. I learned that this testimony had been talked of from the minister down through all that congregation. I was about twelve years old and this was the first time I had the privilege of bearing testimony to the work of God in the latter days.

Mother, as soon as she could go out, attended the meetings in the Masonic Hall and became convinced of the truth of the gospel. One Sunday morning father gave me some money and told me to go to Sexton and give up his pew and shortly after, he and mother were baptized into the church and though they had bore excellent characters all their days they were called crazy, and derided by relatives and friends.

We all continued to attend the meetings of the Saints and a large branch was organized. In December 1842 I was taken sick; mother sent for Brother Snow who came and laid hands upon me as there was to be a baptism the next day. I embraced the opportunity to be baptized. That night there was a great storm and though I had been sick all night and the streets were ankle deep in snow and water I went to the pond, leaning upon the arm of Brother Nickerson, and was baptized and I was healed of my sickness. It cleared up and froze and in the evening I went two miles to a prayer meeting where I was confirmed by Brother Snow and while their hands was on my head, Brother Nickerson said, "Brother Benjamin, upon you we confer the gift of healing and of being healed." My experience through life will testify as to the fulfillment of this blessing given by a servant of God at my confirmation.

Additional Information: "I was in the congregation when the question of succession to the leadership of the church was [?] the people and I [?] and testify that the last time I was [?] the gestures and heard the sound of the voice of Joseph Smith, was when the form, voice and countenance of Brigham Young was transfigured before the congregation so that he appeared like Joseph Smith in every particular. The Lord showed the people that the mantle of Joseph had been bestowed upon Brigham."

See Autobiography of Benjamin Ashby, Harold B. Lee Library.

Harvey Harris Cluff (1836–1916)

Source: Autobiography (1836–1846). Typescript, BYU Harold B. Lee Library.

Father himself served in the army during the war of 1812 and when the hostilities ceased and the army disbanded Father went to Canada where he married Elizabeth Hall and shortly thereafter he returned to his native state and with his wife settled there until they started West. Father being a ship carpenter by trade found employment at the Dover ship yards. About this time considerable excitement prevailed in religious sects throughout the eastern states concerning the "New Bible" brought forth by the Prophet Joseph Smith called the Book of Mormon. The claim went forth throughout all the land, that this young man, only about fifteen years of age, had been visited by God and His son Jesus Christ and by angels and had obtained from the Hill Cumorah gold plates which gave an account of the ancient inhabitants of America and contained the fullness of the gospel as given to that people. As father had become deeply interested in accounts published by explorers of antiques showing that a civilized people once inhabited America, he naturally became imbued with the hope that the new record, would give him the information that he was seeking after.

Father was led to go to Kirtland, Ohio, where the prophet was and see and talk with him. He seemed to have a great desire to hear from the prophets direct a statement of the wonderful visions, and condescensions of heavenly beings. During his journey from new Hampshire he chanced to meet Martin Harris, a convert to the new faith on a canal boat from whom he gained much information which only intensified his anxiety to see the prophet. The meeting with the prophet of God and listening to the inspiring voice of that great man became the greatest epoch in the life of David Cluff. His whole soul was illuminated and he partook of the fruit of the tree of life. His soul was lifted from the dogmas of man made religions and he had a glimpse of the joys within the veil. The study of the antiques of America now developed into satisfactory knowledge. The Book of Mormon and the prophets/statements, dispersed all doubts and poured in flood of knowledge and information that satisfied this student of antiques and built up a faith that never wavered.

The interest and faith in the gospel culminated in moving the family to Kirtland. Father at once enlisted in the cause and became an earnest worker on the Kirtland temple. During the residence of the family in Kirtland, father took a mission to the Eastern states and Canada.

Additional Information: "In 1864 he was called to serve in the Sandwich Islands (Hawaii) along with Elders Lorenzo Snow, Joseph F. Smith, Ezra T. Benson, and Alma L. Smith. It was while landing on the Hawaiian Islands that the boat that the Elders were riding in capsized. All Elders came to the surface except for Elder Lorenzo Snow. When they finally found him, he had drowned. Elder Cluff then writes the following in his journal: 'Finally we were impressed to place our mouth over his and make an effort to inflate his lungs, alternately blowing in and drawing out the air, imitating, as far as possible, the natural process of breathing. This we persevered in until we succeeded in inflating his lungs. After a little, we perceived very faint indications of returning life. A slight wink of the eye, which, until then had been open and death-like, and a very faint rattle in the throat, were the first symptoms of returning vitality. These grew more and more distinct, until consciousness was fully restored.'"

See Eliza R. Snow Smith, *Biography and Family Record of Lorenzo Snow* (1884), 276–79.

Charles Francis Adams (1807–1886)

Source: Book of Abraham Project (www.boap.org).

Tuesday, May 14. Clear. Steamer *Amaranth.* Visit to Quincy [Ill.]

The day was fine—the boat an excellent one, and the company very much better than we have yet had. Among others Captain Bell of the Army was very civil to us. The river does not vary much in its character from what we have seen—As we ascend, we catch glimpses of open country, which is called prairie in this region. In other respects the scene is the same—the same low banks covered with wood, with now and then a rise which is called a bluff. In the course of the morning we stopped at Quincy on the Illinois side—and for the sake of the name, we went up to see it. It is a very pretty place inhabited mainly by New England people. There is an open square in the centre of the town, and from the top of the hotel which is kept by a man who formerly kept the Bromfield House in Boston, we observed a very rich and beautiful prairie country. This was the only town on the river during this day which struck me at all favorably.

As we went on it became very necessary that we should settle upon our course. Quincy [Josiah Quincy, Jr., Adams's travelling companion] wished to stop at Nauvoo, the city of the Mormons and see something of Joe Smith, the prophet. I was passive, as I have always been on this journey. But it became late before we got up and the passengers were full of discouraging tales of the disposition of these Mormons. Had it not been for a certain Doctor Goforth, a living skeleton of a man, I think Quincy would have been discouraged by the darkness and solitude which reigned on the shore. But he urged our landing so much that we finally ordered our things on shore.

Wednesday, May 15. Joe Smith. Visit the Temple.

It was about one o'clock when we got into the very indifferent room which the labours of our tall and thin doctor had procured for us in a house on the bank of the river. For at so late an hour we determined not to attempt to disturb the great prophet himself, although he was the keeper of the tavern. We threw ourselves on the outside of the bed allotted to Quincy and myself and slept until five o'clock, when the daylight roused us. Shortly aferward the carriage of the prophet which had been sent for by the doctor and two other passengers who had stopped with us. There was also on the outside one of the leaders of the sect, who was called General White [Lyman Wight]. The day was cloudy and it soon after set in to rain and rained in showers until night.

At the door of a two-story wooden house with a sign post before it, we stopped and were introduced to the celebrated Joe Smith. A middle-aged man with a shrewd but rather ordinary expression of countenance, unshaved and in clothes neither very choice nor neat. The whole air of the man was that of frank but not coarse vulgarity. He received us civilly and forthwith introduced us into his house, trying one room after another without success as they all appeared to contain occupants. At last we were ushered into one where was a man in bed whom he very abruptly slapped on the shoulder and notified to quit. The awkwardness of this scene was relieved by a call to breakfast, which we all obeyed. The table was amply provided as usual in the Western Country, but without order or delicacy.

Upon our return from the meal we were introduced into another chamber with had been prepared in the interval, and here we sat down and held a long conference with prophet upon himself, his doctrines and his projects. He then took us down into his mother's chamber and showed us four Egyptian mummies stripped and then undertook to explain the contents of a chart or manuscript which he said had been taken from the bosom of one of them. The cool impudence of this imposture amused me very much. "This," said he, "was written by the hand of Abraham and means so and so. If anyone denies it, let him prove the contrary. I say it." Of coarse [course], we were too polite to prove the negative, against a man fortified by revelation.

His mother looked on with attention and aided in the explanation whenever the prophet hesitated, from which I inferred that she was usually made the exponent of the writing to strangers. At the close, he notified us that for this instruction, his mother was in the habit of receiving a quarter of a dollar a piece form them, which sum we paid forthwith. Then came another long conversation, in which a brother of his and some other persons joined, detailing the severe and shocking persecution which they suffered at the time of their cruel expulsion from Missouri four years ago. This is one of the most disgraceful chapters in the dark history of slavery in the United States, and shows that the spirit of intolerance, religious and political, can find a shelter even in the fairest professions of liberty.

We dined at one, and after dinner, at our request, we went up in his carriage to see the stone temple and the font which the prophet is causing to be built. It is a massive edifice on a most commanding site, about half finished. The architecture is original—and curious. It is built by the contribution of one-tenth of labor and goods. The prophet seems to have drawn his ideas largely from the Jewish system. One of the persons who accompanied us from the boat, proved a travelling Methodist preacher, and he by his turn for dispute elicited much amusement to us. This on our return to the tavern took the shape of a specific address to a parcel of the sect who were hanging about the door, half jest, half earnest, which appears to be habitual with Joe. I was not so well able to judge of it as I had been called upstairs to meet a gentleman by the name of Johnson, who was in the employment of the government of the United States and had come here to catch a defaulter supposed to be a lawyer—told me that he had thought it wisest to apply at once to Joe himself, being convinced that without his aid he should not succeed in his object—so well had Joe fenced himself in here from the ordinary course of law, by concessions made to him by the dominant party in the state in consequence of the control he exercises over the elections.

There is a mixture of shrewdness and extravagant self-conceit, of knowledge and ignorance, of wisdom and folly in this whole system of this man that I am somewhat at a loss to find definitions for it. Yet it is undoubted that he has gained followers at home and abroad—and boasts of having twenty-five thousand at Nauvoo and two hundred thousand in the Union. This is an extravagant estimate, but the number must be large. His theological system is very nearly Christian Unitarianism—with the addition of the power of baptism by the priests of adults to remit sin, and of the new hierarchy of which Smith is the chief by divine appointment. After tea, as we expected the steamer to take us off in the night, we returned to the wretched quarter we left in the morning—and bade good bye to the prophet, who accompanied us to them in his carriage. On the whole I was glad I had been [to see Joseph Smith]. Such a man is a study not for himself, but as serving to show what turns the human mind will sometimes take. And hereafter if I should live, I may compare the results of this delusion with the condition in which I saw it and its mountebank apostle.

Josiah Quincy (1802–1882)

Source: Josiah Quincy, *Figures of the Past From the Leaves of Old Journals,* 3rd ed (Boston, 1883), 376–400.

It is by no means improbable that some future textbook, for the use of generations yet unborn, will contain a question something like this: What historical American of the nineteenth century has exerted the most powerful influence upon the destinies of his countrymen? And it is by no means impossible that the answer to that interrogatory may be thus written: Joseph Smith, the Mormon prophet. And the reply, absurd as it doubtless seems to most men now living, may be an obvious commonplace to their descendants. History deals in surprises and paradoxes quite as startling as this. The man who established a religion in this age of free debate, who was and is today accepted by hundreds of thousands as a direct emissary from the Most High,—such a rare human being is not to be disposed of by pelting his memory with unsavory epithets. Fanatic, imposter, charlatan, he may have been; but these hard names furnish no solution to the problem he presents to us. Fanatics and impostors are living and dying every day, and their memory is buried with them; but the wonderful influence which this founder of a religion exerted and still exerts throws him into relief before us, not as a rogue to be criminated, but as a phenomenon to be explained. The most vital questions Americans are asking each other today have to do with this man and what he has left us. Is there any remedy heroic enough to meet the case, yet in accordance with our national doctrines of liberty and toleration, which can be applied to the demoralizing doctrines now advanced by the sect which he created? The possibilities of the Mormon system are unfathomable. Polygamy may be followed by still darker "revelations." Here is a society resting upon foundations which may at any moment be made subversive of every duty which we claim from the citizen. Must it be reached by that last argument which quenched the evil fanaticisms of Mulhausen and Munster? A generation other than mine must deal with these questions. Burning questions they are, which must give a prominent place in the history of the country to that sturdy self-asserter whom I visited at Nauvoo.

Joseph Smith, claiming to be an inspired teacher, faced adversity such as few men have been called to meet, enjoyed a brief season of prosperity such as few men have ever attained, and, finally, forty-three days after I saw him, went cheerfully to a martyr's death. When he surrendered his person to Governor Ford, in order to prevent the shedding of blood, the prophet had a presentiment of what was before him. "I am going like a lamb to the slaughter," he is reported to have said; "but I am calm as a summer's morning. I have a conscience void of offense and shall die innocent." I have no theory to advance respecting this extraordinary man. I shall simply give the facts of my intercourse with him. At some future time they may be found to have some bearing upon the theories of others who are more competent to make them. Ten closely written pages of my journal describe my impressions of Nauvoo, and of its prophet, mayor, general, and judge; but details, necessarily omitted in the diary, went into letters addressed to friends at home, and I shall use both these sources to make my narrative as complete as possible. I happened to visit Joseph Smith in company with a distinguished gentleman, who, if rumor may be trusted, has been as conscientious a journal-writer as was his father. It is not impossible that my record may one day be supplemented by that of my fellow-traveller, the Hon. Charles Francis Adams.

It was on the 25th of April, 1844, that Mr. Adams and myself left Boston for the journey to the West which we had had for some time in contemplation. I omit all account of our adventures— and a very full account of them is before me—until the 14th of May, when we are ascending the clear, sparkling waters of the Upper Mississippi in the little steamboat "Amaranth." With one exception we find our fellow-passengers uninteresting. The exception is Dr. Goforth. A chivalric, yet simple personage is this same doctor, who has served under General Jackson at the battle of New Orleans and is now going to Nauvoo, to promote the election of the just nominated Henry Clay. It is to this gentleman we owe our sight of the city of the Saints, which, strangely enough, we had not intended to visit. Though far from being a Mormon himself, Dr. Goforth told us much that was good and interesting about this strange people. He urged us to see for ourselves the result of the singular political system which had been fastened upon Christianity, and to make the acquaintance of his friend, General Smith, the religious and civil autocrat of the community. "We agreed to stop at Nauvoo," says my journal, "provided some conveyance should be found at the landing which would take us up to General Smith's tavern, and prepared our baggage for this contingency. Owing to various delays, we did not reach the landing till nearly midnight, when our friend, who had jumped on shore the moment the boat stopped, returned with the intelligence that no carriage was to be had, and so we bade him adieu, to go on our way. But, as we still lingered upon the hurricane deck, he shouted that there was a house on the landing, where we could get a good bed. This changed our destiny, and just at the last moment we hurried on shore. Here we found that the "good bed" our friend had promised us was in an old mill, which had been converted into an Irish shanty. However, we made the best of it, and, having dispossessed a cat and a small army of cockroaches of their quarters on the coverlet, we lay down in our dressing-gowns and were soon asleep."

We left our lowly bed in the gray light of the morning, to find the rain descending in torrents and the roads knee-deep in mud. Intelligence of our arrival had in some mysterious manner reached General Smith, and the prophet's own chariot, a comfortable carryall, drawn by two horses, soon made its appearance. It is probable that we owed the alacrity with which we were served to an odd blunder which had combined our names and personalities and set forth that no less a man than ex-President John Quincy Adams had arrived to visit Mr. Joseph Smith. Happily, however, Dr. Goforth, who had got upon the road before us, divided our persons and reduced them to their proper proportions, so that no trace of disappointment was visible in the group of rough-looking Mormons who awaited our descent at the door of the tavern. It was a three-story frame house, set back from the street and surrounded by a white fence, that we had reached after about two miles of the muddiest driving. Pre-eminent among the stragglers by the door stood a man of commanding appearance, clad in the costume of a journeyman carpenter when about his work. He was a hearty, athletic fellow, with blue eyes standing prominently out upon his light complexion, a long nose, and a retreating forehead. He wore striped pantaloons, a linen jacket, which had not lately seen the washtub, and a beard of some three days' growth. This was the founder of the religion which had been preached in every quarter of the earth. As Dr. Goforth introduced us to the prophet, he mentioned the parentage of my companion. "God bless you, to begin with!" said Joseph Smith, raising his hands in the air and letting them descend upon the shoulders of Mr. Adams. The benediction, though evidently sincere, had an odd savor of what may be called official familiarity, such as a crowned head might adopt on receiving the heir presumptive of a friendly court. The greeting to me was cordial—with that sort of cordiality with which the president of a college might welcome a deserving janitor—and a blessing formed no part of it. "And now come, both of you, into the house!" said our host, as, suiting the action to the word, he ushered us across the threshold of his tavern.

A fine-looking man is what the passer-by would instinctively have murmured upon meeting the remarkable individual who had fashioned the mould which was to shape the feelings of so many thousands of his fellow-mortals. But Smith was more than this, and one could not resist the impression that capacity and resource were natural to his stalwart person. I have already mentioned the resemblance he bore to Elisha R. Potter, of Rhode Island, whom I met in Washington in 1826. The likeness was not such as would be recognized in a picture, but rather one that would be felt in a grave emergency. Of all men I have met, these two seemed best endowed with that kingly faculty which directs, as by intrinsic right, the feeble or confused souls who are looking for guidance. This it is just to say with emphasis; for the reader will find so much that is puerile and even shocking in my report of the prophet's conversation that he might never suspect the impression of rugged power that was given by the man. On the right hand, as we entered the house, was a small and very comfortless-looking bar-room; all the more comfortless, perchance, from its being a dry bar-room, as no spirituous liquors were permitted at Nauvoo. In apparent search for more private quarters, the prophet opened the door of a room on the left. He instantly shut it again, but not before I perceived that the obstacle to our entrance was its prior occupancy by a woman, in bed. He then ran upstairs, calling upon us to follow him, and, throwing open a door in the second story, disclosed three Mormons in three beds. This was not satisfactory; neither was the next chamber, which was found, on inspection, to contain two sleeping disciples. The third attempt was somewhat more fortunate, for we had found a room which held but a single bed and a single sleeper. Into this apartment we were invited to enter. Our host immediately proceeded to the bed, and drew the clothes well over the head of its occupant. He then called a man to make a fire, and begged us to sit down.

Smith then began to talk about himself and his people, as, of course, we encouraged him to do. He addressed his words to Mr. Adams oftener than to me, evidently thinking that this gentleman had or was likely to have political influence, which it was desirable to conciliate. Whether by subtle tact or happy accident, he introduced us to Mormonism as a secular institution before stating its monstrous claims as a religious system. Polygamy, it must be remembered, formed no part of the alleged revelations upon which the social life at Nauvoo was based; indeed, the recorded precepts of its prophet were utterly opposed to such a practice, and it is, at least, doubtful whether this barbarism was in any way sanctioned by Smith. Let a man who has so much to answer for be allowed the full benefit of the doubt; and Mormonism, minus the spiritual wife system, had, as it has today, much that was interesting in its secular aspects. Its founder told us what he had accomplished and the terrible persecutions through which he had brought his people. He spoke with bitterness of outrages to which they had been subjected in Missouri, and implied that the wanton barbarities of his lawless enemies must one day be atoned for. He spoke of the industrial results of his autocracy in the holy city we were visiting, and of the extraordinary powers of its charter, obtained through his friend, Governor Ford. The past had shown him that a military organization was necessary. He was now at the head of three thousand men, equipped by the state of Illinois and belonging to its militia, and the Saints were prepared to fight as well as to work. "I decided," said Smith, "that the commander of my troops ought to be a lieutenant-general, and I was, of course, chosen to that position. I sent my certificate of election to Governor Ford, and received in return a commission of lieutenant-general of the Nauvoo Legion and of the militia of the state of Illinois. Now, on examining the Constitution of the United States, I find that an officer must be tried by a court-martial composed of his equals in rank; and as I am the only lieutenant-general in the country, I think they will find it pretty hard to try me."

At this point breakfast was announced, and a substantial meal was served in a long back kitchen. We sat down with about thirty persons, some of them being in their shirt-sleeves, as if just come from work. There was no going out, as the rain still fell in torrents; and so, when we had finished breakfast, the prophet (who had exchanged his working dress for a broadcloth suit while we lingered at the table) proposed to return to the chamber we had quitted, where he would give us his views of theology. The bed had been made during our absence and the fire plentifully replenished. Our party was now increased by the presence of the patriarch, Hiram Smith; Dr. Richards, of Philadelphia, who seemed to be a very modest and respectable Mormon; Dr. Goforth; and a Methodist minister, whose name I have not preserved. No sooner were we seated than there entered some half-dozen leaders of the sect, among whom, I think, were Rigdon and Young; but of their presence I cannot be positive. These men constituted a sort of silent chorus during the expositions of their chief. They fixed a searching, yet furtive gaze upon Mr. Adams and myself, as if eager to discover how we were impressed by what we heard. Of the wild talk that we listened to I have preserved but a few fragments. Smith was well versed in the letter of the scriptures, though he had little comprehension of their spirit. He began by denying the doctrine of the Trinity, and supported his views by the glib recitation of a number of texts. From this he passed to his own claims to special inspiration, quoting with great emphasis the eleventh and twelfth verses of the fourth chapter of Ephesians, which, in his eyes, adumbrated the whole Mormon hierarchy. The degrees and orders of ecclesiastical dignitaries he set forth with great precision, being careful to mention the interesting revelation which placed Joseph Smith supreme above them all. This information was plentifully besprinkled with cant phrases or homely proverbs. "There, I have proved that point as straight as a loon's leg." "The curses of my enemies run off from me like water from a duck's back." Such are the specimens which my journal happens to preserve, but the exposition was constantly garnished with forcible vulgarisms of a similar sort. The prophet referred to his miraculous gift of understanding all languages, and took down a Bible in various tongues, for the purpose of exhibiting his accomplishments in this particular. Our position as guests prevented our testing his powers by a rigid examination, and the rendering of a few familiar texts seemed to be accepted by his followers as a triumphant demonstration of his abilities. It may have been an accident, but I observed that the bulk of his translations were from the Hebrew, which, presumably, his visitors did not understand, rather than from the classical languages, in which they might more easily have caught him tripping.

"And now come with me," said the prophet, "and I will show you the curiosities." So saying, he led the way to a lower room, where sat a venerable and respectable-looking lady. "This is my mother, gentlemen. The curiosities we shall see belong to her. They were purchased with her own money, at a cost of six thousand dollars;" and then, with deep feeling, were added the words, "And that woman was turned out upon the prairie in the dead of night by a mob." There were some pine presses fixed against the wall of the room. These receptacles Smith opened, and disclosed four human bodies, shrunken and black with age. "These are mummies," said the exhibitor. "I want you to look at that little runt of a fellow over there. He was a great man in his day. Why, that was Pharaoh Necho, King of Egypt!" Some parchments inscribed with hieroglyphics were then offered us. They were preserved under glass and handled with great respect. "That is the handwriting of Abraham, the Father of the Faithful," said the prophet. "This is the autograph of Moses, and these lines were written by his brother Aaron. Here we have the earliest account of the creation, from which Moses composed the first book of Genesis." The parchment last referred to showed a rude drawing of a man and woman, and a serpent walking upon a pair of legs. I ventured to doubt the propriety of providing the reptile in question with this unusual means of locomotion.

"Why, that's as plain as a pikestaff," was the rejoinder. "Before the Fall snakes always went about on legs, just like chickens. They were deprived of them, in punishment for their agency in the ruin of man." We were further assured that the prophet was the only mortal who could translate these mysterious writings, and that his power was given by direct inspiration.

It is well known that Joseph Smith was accustomed to make his revelations point to those sturdy business habits which lead to prosperity in this present life. He had little enough of that unmixed spiritual power which flashed out from the spare, neurasthenic body of Andrew Jackson. The prophet's hold upon you seemed to come from the balance and harmony of temperament which reposes upon a large physical basis. No association with the sacred phrases of scripture could keep the inspirations of this man from getting down upon the hard pan of practical affairs. "Verily I say unto you, let my servant, Sidney Gilbert, plant himself in this place and establish a store." So had run one of his revelations, in which no holier spirit than that of commerce is discernible. The exhibition of these August relics concluded with a similar descent into the hard modern world of fact. Monarchs, patriarchs, and parchments were very well in their way; but this was clearly the nineteenth century, when prophets must get a living and provide for their relations. "Gentlemen," said this bourgeois Mohammed, as he closed the cabinets, "those who see these curiosities generally pay my mother a quarter of a dollar."

The clouds had parted when we emerged from the chamber of curiosities, and there was time to see the temple before dinner. General Smith ordered a capacious carriage, and we drove to that beautiful eminence, bounded on three sides by the Mississippi, which was covered by the holy city of Nauvoo. The curve in the river enclosed a position lovely enough to furnish a site for the Utopian communities of Plato or Sir Thomas More; and here was an orderly city, magnificently laid out, and teeming with activity and enterprise. And all the diligent workers, who had reared these handsome stores and comfortable dwellings, bowed in subjection to the man to whose unexampled absurdities we had listened that morning. Not quite unexampled either. For many years I held a trusteeship which required me to be a frequent visitor at the McLean Asylum for the Insane. I had talked with some of its unhappy inmates, victims of the sad but not uncommon delusion that each had received the appointment of vicegerent of the Deity upon earth. It is well known that such unfortunates, if asked to explain their confinement, have a ready reply: "I am sane. The rest of the world is mad, and the majority is against me." It was like a dream to find one's self moving through a prosperous community, where the repulsive claim of one of these pretenders was respectfully acknowledged. It was said that Prince Hamlet had no need to recover his wits when he was despatched to England, for the demented denizens of that island would never detect his infirmity. If the blasphemous assumptions of Smith seemed like the ravings of a lunatic, he had, at least brought them to a market where "all the people were as mad as he." Near the entrance to the temple we passed a workman who was laboring upon a huge sun, which he had chiselled from the solid rock. The countenance was of the Negro type, and it was surrounded by the conventional rays.

"General Smith," said the man, looking up from his task, "is this like the face you saw in vision?"

"Very near it," answered the prophet, "except" (this was added with an air of careful connoisseurship that was quite overpowering)—"except that the nose is just a thought too broad."

The Mormon [Nauvoo] Temple was not fully completed. It was a wonderful structure, altogether indescribable by me. Being, presumably, like something Smith had seen in a vision, it certainly cannot be compared to any ecclesiastical building which may be discerned by the natural eyesight. It was built of limestone, and was partially supported by huge monolithic pillars, each costing, said the prophet, three thousand dollars. Then in the basement was the baptistery, which centered in a mighty tank, surrounded by twelve wooden oxen of colossal size. These animals, we were assured, were temporary. They were to be replaced by stone oxen as fast as they could be made. The Temple, odd and striking as it was, produced no effect that was commensurate with its cost. Perhaps it would have required a genius to have designed anything worthy of that noble site. The city of Nauvoo, with its wide streets sloping gracefully to the farms enclosed on the prairie, seemed to be a better temple to Him who prospers the work of industrious hands than the grotesque structure on the hill, with all its queer carvings of moons and suns. This, however, was by no means the opinion of the man whose fiat had reared the building. In a tone half-way between jest and earnest, and which might have been taken for either at the option of the hearer, the prophet put this inquiry: "Is not here one greater than Solomon, who built a Temple with the treasures of his father David and with the assistance of Huram, King of Tyre? Joseph Smith has built his temple with no one to aid him in the work."

On returning to the tavern, dinner was served in the kitchen where we had breakfasted. The prophet carved at one end of the board, while some twenty persons, Mormons or travellers (the former mostly coatless), were scattered along its sides. At the close of a substantial meal a message was brought to the effect that the United States marshal had arrived and wished to speak to Mr. Adams. This officer, as it turned out, wanted my companion's advice about the capture of some criminal, for whom he had a warrant. The matter was one of some difficulty, for, the prophet being absolute in Nauvoo, no man could be arrested or held without his permission. I do not remember what was the outcome of this interview, which was so protracted that it caused Mr. Adams to miss one of the most notable exhibitions of the day.

"General Smith," said Dr. Goforth, when we had adjourned to the green in front of the tavern, "I think Mr. Quincy would like to hear you preach." "Then I shall be happy to do so," was the obliging reply; and, mounting the broad step which led from the house, the prophet promptly addressed a sermon to the little group about him. Our numbers were constantly increased from the passers in the street, and a most attentive audience of more than a hundred persons soon hung upon every word of the speaker. The text was Mark xvi. 15, and the comments, though rambling and disconnected, were delivered with the fluency and fervor of a camp-meeting orator. The discourse was interrupted several times by the Methodist minister before referred to, who thought it incumbent upon him to question the soundness of certain theological positions maintained by the speaker. One specimen of the sparring which ensued I thought worth setting down. The prophet is asserting that baptism for the remission of sins is essential for salvation. Minister. Stop! What do you say to the case of the penitent thief? Prophet. What do you mean by that? Minister. You know our Savior said to the thief, "This day shalt thou be with me in Paradise," which shows he could not have been baptized before his admission. Prophet. How do you know he wasn't baptized before he became a thief? At this retort the sort of laugh that is provoked by an unexpected hit ran through the audience; but this demonstration of sympathy was rebuked by a severe look from Smith, who went on to say: "But that is not the true answer. In the original Greek, as this gentleman (turning to me) will inform you, the word that has been translated paradise means simply a place of departed spirits. To that place the penitent thief was conveyed, and there, doubtless, he received the baptism necessary for his admission to the heavenly kingdom. " The other objections of his antagonist were parried with a similar adroitness, and in about fifteen minutes the prophet concluded a sermon which it was evident that his disciples had heard with the heartiest satisfaction.

In the afternoon we drove to visit the farms upon the prairie which this enterprising people had enclosed and were cultivating with every appearance of success. On returning, we stopped in a beautiful grove, where there were seats and a platform for speaking. "When the weather permits," said Smith, "we hold our services in this place; but shall cease to do so when the temple is finished." "I suppose none but Mormon preachers are allowed in Nauvoo," said the Methodist minister, who had accompanied our expedition. "On the contrary," replied the prophet, "I shall be very happy to have you address my people next Sunday, and I will insure you a most attentive congregation." "What! Do you mean that I may say anything I please and that you will make no reply?" "You may certainly say anything you please; but I must reserve the right of adding a word or two, if I judge best. I promise to speak of you in the most respectful manner." As we rode back, there was more dispute between the minister and Smith. "Come," said the latter, suddenly slapping his antagonist on the knee, to emphasize the production of a triumphant text, "if you can't argue better than that, you shall say all you want to say to my people, and I will promise to hold my tongue, for there's not a Mormon among them who would need my assistance to answer you." Some back-thrust was evidently required to pay for this; and the minister, soon after, having occasion to allude to some erroneous doctrine which I forget, suddenly exclaimed, "Why, I told my congregation the other Sunday that they might as well believe Joe Smith as such theology as that." "Did you say Joe Smith in a sermon?" inquired the person to whom the title had been applied. "Of course I did. Why not?" The prophet's reply was given with a quiet superiority that was overwhelming: "Considering only the day and the place, it would have been more respectful to have said Lieutenant-General Joseph Smith." Clearly, the worthy minister was no match for the head of the Mormon Church.

I have before me some relics of my visit to Nauvoo. Here is the Book of Mormon, bearing the autograph which its alleged discoverer and translator wrote, at my request; and here are some letters addressed to the same personage, which I came by strangely enough. I took them from a public basket of wastepaper, which was placed for the service of the inmates of the tavern. Three of these abandoned epistles I asked leave to keep as memorials of my visit, and no objection was made to my doing so. The most interesting of these letters is dated "Manchester, August 29, 1842," and comes from an English convert to Mormonism. The man writes four pages of gilt-edged paper to his "beloved brother in the Lord," and sends him by the favor of Elder Snider the following presents: "A hat, a black satin stock with front, and a brooch." He would fain join the prophet in Nauvoo; but the way in blocked by that not-unheard-of obstacle, a mother-in-law, and until this excellent lady "falls asleep" the disciple must deny his eyes the sight of the master's face. The account of himself given by this correspondent shows with what pathetic sincerity the divine commission of Smith was accepted by a class of men which would seem to be intellectually superior to so miserable a delusion. Suppressing the name of the writer, I shall give a portion of this letter, as it furnishes food for reflection, and shows that the secret of the Mormon prophet is not to be fathomed at a glance:—

"I take the liberty of writing a few lines, being assured that you are a man of God and a prophet of the Most High, not only from testimony given by the brethren, but the Spirit itself beareth witness. It is true that mine eyes have not seen and mine ears heard you; but the testimony I have received shows plainly that God does reveal by his Spirit things that the natural man has not seen by his natural eyes. You may perhaps wonder who the individual is that has written this letter. I will tell you, in a few words: My father died about twenty-four years since, leaving my mother a widow with seven children. . . . I remember her teachings well, which were these: Fear God, be strictly honest, and speak the truth. I remember, when about three or four years old, being with her in a shop. I saw a pin on the floor. I picked it up and gave it to her. She told me to give it to the shopman, with a sharp reprimand, showing me that it was a sin to take even a pin. The remembrance of this slight circumstance has followed me from that time to the present. [An account of the writer's conversion to Mormonism follows, after which he goes on thus.] Previously to joining this Church, I was a singer in the Church of England, had eight pounds a year, and a good situation in the week-time at a retail hat shop. My wife's brother told me I was robbing my children of their bread in giving up the eight pounds. I told him I was not dependent on that for bread, and said unto him the Lord could make up the difference. He laughed at me; but, beloved brother, in about one month from the time I left the Church of England my master raised my wages four shillings a week (which was about one shilling per week more than that just sacrificed), and this has continued on ever since, which is now two years this month, for which I thank the Lord, together with many other mercies."

I have quoted enough to show what really good material Smith managed to draw into his net. Were such fish to be caught with Spaulding's tedious romance and a puerile fable of undecipherable gold plates and gigantic spectacles? Not these cheap and wretched properties, but some mastering force of the man who handled them, inspired the devoted missionaries who worked such wonders. The remaining letters, both written a year previous to my visit, came from a certain Chicago attorney, who seems to have been the personal friend as well as the legal adviser of the prophet. With the legal advice come warnings of plots which enemies are preparing, and of the probability that a seizure of his person by secret ambush in contemplated. "They hate you," writes this friendly lawyer, "because they have done evil unto you. . . . My advice to you is not to sleep in your own house, but to have some place to sleep strongly guarded by your own friends, so that you can resist any sudden attempt that might be made to kidnap you in the night. When the Missourians come on this side and burn houses, depend upon it they will not hesitate to make the attempt to carry you away by force. Let me again caution you to be every moment upon your guard." The man to whom this letter was addressed had long been familiar with perils. For fourteen years he was surrounded by vindictive enemies, who lost no opportunity to harass him. He was in danger even when we saw him at the summit of his prosperity, and he was soon to seal his testimony—or, if you will, to expiate his imposture—by death at the hands of dastardly assassins. If these letters go little way toward interpreting the man, they suggest that any hasty interpretation of him is inadequate.

I should not say quite all that struck me about Smith if I did not mention that he seemed to have a keen sense of the humorous aspects of his position. "It seems to me, General," I said, as he was driving us to the river, about sunset, "that you have too much power to be safely trusted to one man." "In your hands or that of any other person," was the reply, "so much power would, no doubt, be dangerous. I am the only man in the world whom it would be safe to trust with it. Remember, I am a prophet!" The last five words were spoken in a rich, comical aside, as if in hearty recognition of the ridiculous sound they might have in the ears of a Gentile. I asked him to test his powers by naming the successful candidate in the approaching presidential election. "Well, I will prophesy that John Tyler will not be the next president, for some things are possible and some things are probable; but Tyler's election is neither the one nor the other." We then went on to talk of politics. Smith recognized the curse and iniquity of slavery, though he opposed the methods of the Abolitionists.

His plan was for the nation to pay for the slaves from the sale of the public lands. "Congress," he said, "should be compelled to take this course, by petitions from all parts of the country; but the petitioners must disclaim all alliance with those who would disturb the rights of property recognized by the Constitution and foment insurrection." It may be worthwhile to remark that Smith's plan was publicly advocated, eleven years later, by one who has mixed so much practical shrewdness with his lofty philosophy. In 1855, when men's minds had been moved to their depths on the question of slavery, Mr. Ralph Waldo Emerson declared that it should be met in accordance "with the interest of the South and with the settled conscience of the North. It is not really a great task, a great fight for this country to accomplish, to buy that property of the planter, as the British nation bought the West Indian slaves." He further says that the "United States will be brought to give every inch of their public lands for a purpose like this." We, who can look back upon the terrible cost of the fratricidal war which put an end to slavery, now say that such a solution of the difficulty would have been worthy a Christian statesman. But if the retired scholar was in advance of his time when he advocated this disposition of the public property in 1855, what shall I say of the political and religious leader who had committed himself, in print, as well as in conversation, to the same course in 1844? If the atmosphere of men's opinions was stirred by such a proposition when war-clouds were discernible in the sky, was it not a statesmanlike word eleven years earlier, when the heavens looked tranquil and beneficent?

General Smith proceeded to unfold still further his views upon politics. He denounced the Missouri Compromise as an unjustifiable concession for the benefit of slavery. It was Henry Clay's bid for the presidency. Dr. Goforth might have spared himself the trouble of coming to Nauvoo to electioneer for a duelist who would fire at John Randolph, but was not brave enough to protect the Saints in their rights as American citizens. Clay had told his people to go to the wilds of Oregon and set up a government of their own. Oh yes, the Saints might go into the wilderness and obtain justice of the Indians, which imbecile, time-serving politicians would not give them in the land of freedom and equality. The prophet then talked of the details of government. He thought that the number of members admitted to the Lower House of the National Legislature should be reduced.

A crowd only darkened counsel and impeded business. A member to every half million of population would be ample. The powers of the President should be increased. He should have authority to put down rebellion in a state, without waiting for the request of any governor; for it might happen that the governor himself would be the leader of the rebels. It is needless to remark how later events showed the executive weakness that Smith pointed out,—a weakness which cost thousands of valuable lives and millions of treasure; but the man mingled Utopian fallacies with his shrewd suggestions. He talked as from a strong mind utterly unenlightened by the teachings of history. Finally, he told us what he would do, were he President of the United States, and went on to mention that he might one day so hold the balance between parties as to render his election to that office by no means unlikely.

Who can wonder that the chair of the National Executive had its place among the visions of this self-reliant man? He had already traversed the roughest part of the way to that coveted position. Born in the lowest ranks of poverty, without book-learning and with the homeliest of all human names, he had made himself at the age of thirty-nine a power upon earth. Of the multitudinous family of Smith, from Adam down (Adam of the "Wealth of Nations," I mean), none had so won human hearts and shaped human lives as this Joseph. His influence, whether for good or for evil, is potent today, and the end is not yet.

I have endeavored to give the details of my visit to the Mormon prophet with absolute accuracy. If the reader does not know just what to make of Joseph Smith, I cannot help him out of the difficulty. I myself stand helpless before the puzzle.

Part Five

The "Golden Bible"

Millions have been touched by the Book of Mormon. This curiosity developed in people's souls to see and read the "Gold Bible" during the 1830s continues today. There have been those that touched the book for the first time and knew it was true. Others have been drawn only by its title, not knowing what to expect, and have been guided to the truth. Such was the case of a small town Vermont high school student that my companion and I had the chance to teach, who was eventually baptized. I'm writing this on Christmas Day, thirty-five years later to the day that we baptized the high school girl into the Church. It was truly the whitest Christmas I have ever experienced. One day, while browsing through the titles on the library shelves of her school, she came across the Book of Mormon. Not knowing what the book was or what it represented, she pulled it from its resting place on the shelf and took it home. Touched by the spirit of the book and desiring to know more, she contacted the only Latter-day Saint family in the area. Funny enough, it happened to be the ward mission leader, who resided in the next town to the south of where she lived. The family brought her to Church and introduced her to us. That particular copy of the Book of Mormon is now responsible for bringing hundreds if not thousands into the Church. She went on to serve a mission, being called to Argentina where she experienced great success and has now seen some of her own children serve missions.

In the upcoming part are eleven journal entries of individuals who knew nothing about the Church other than that they had "heard of a gold bible." Actually, a number of journal entries in previous sections that have stated something along those lines. In most instances, the rumors of "Joe Smith and his Gold Bible" preceded the elder's arrival. Some of these people were affected by the rumors and did not accept the Gospel immediately; however, with others, the moment they read the Book of Mormon, they knew it was true and were baptized.

Philo Dibble provides a fascinating account when he relates how certain men, prejudiced against the Church—and wanting to convince Philo of his folly in having been baptized—told him that "a man that will not lie" (Edward Partridge) had been sent to New York to check out Joseph Smith and his story of the "Golden Bible." If Partridge sends word back that the story was legitimate, then there were others willing to be baptized. However, if he detected fraud in Joseph Smith or his story, then would Philo reconsider? The outcome of the story is interesting. The two journal accounts after Philo's are the accounts of Edward Partridge's daughters, Emily and Eliza, verifying the account given by Philo.

I included the account of John H. Gilbert, the typesetter during the Book of Mormon publication at the Grandin Bookstore in Palmyra, New York. This account, written by him, sheds light on the publishing process and the feelings of those associated with the work.

At the conclusion is an interesting letter from Reverend Diedrich Willers to other clergy about the Book of Mormon. When reading his account, it's relatively easy to pick out the absurdities mixed with some actual facts. The tricks of the devil have never changed. He will present a number of truths if he can slip by one falsehood. The early Saints had to work through such misrepresentations in their search for the truth.

Benjamin F. Johnson (1818–1905)

Source: Autobiography (1818–1846). Benjamin F. Johnson, My Life's Review (Independence, Missouri: Zion's Printing and Publishing Co., 1947), 7–107.

In my earlier years, although but a child, I was often led to wonder at the difference between the present and former religions, and especially in the life and character of their advocates. And in reading of the persecution of our Savior, His apostles, and the prophets, my very soul would become enthused with the wish that I had lived in their day, or that the day of prophets and revelation might come again while I yet lived.

In the year 1829, in our village paper, was published an account of some young man professing to have seen an angel, who had shown and delivered to him golden plates, engraved in a strange language and hid up in the earth, from which he had translated a new Bible, and I could hardly refrain from wishing or hoping it might be so. I think it was the year previous that there was seen at night in the heavens a large ball of light, like fire, which passed from the east to the western horizon. My older brothers who were out hunting coons, saw it and came home to tell of the wonder they had seen. When I asked my mother what its cause or meaning was, she said it was one of the signs of the near approach of the coming of Christ, or the day of judgment. This remained upon my mind a subject of deep thought, and I afterwards learned from those who should know, that this sign was given the night following the day on which the plates were taken from the earth by the Prophet Joseph.

About 1830 my oldest brother, Joel H., sold his farm and mill and moved out to Amherst, in Loraine County, Ohio, soon after my oldest sister, Nancy, was thrown from a horse and her thigh bone was broken close to its hip socket. This to me seemed a terrible calamity, especially as the doctors told us she would remain a cripple for life.

About this time we began to hear more about the "Golden Bible" that had been found by "Joe Smith" the "money digger," etc., etc. My elder brother, David, having gone to visit Joel H. in Amherst, Ohio, had remained there until the next season, in the spring of which the first elders, going from Kirtland to Missouri, stopped and raised up a large branch of the Church into which both of my brothers were baptized. Previous to this, rumors had come from Ohio of the spread of what was called "Campbellism," a new sect, of which Sidney Rigdon was then the chief apostle, and through fear that my brothers would become deluded by the new doctrines, my mother had written a letter of caution to them, which was soon answered to say that they had both joined the "Mormonites" (then so called), believers in the Prophet Joseph Smith and the Book of Mormon or "Golden Bible." This news came upon us almost as a horror and a disgrace. The first news was soon followed by the Book of Mormon, accompanied by a lengthy explanation, on the receipt of which my mother, brother Seth, sister Nancy, and Lyman R. Sherman, with some of the neighbors, all devoted to religion, would meet together secretly to read the Book of Mormon and accompanying letter, or perhaps to deplore the delusion into which my brothers had fallen. But their reading soon led to marveling at the simplicity and purity of what they read, and at the spirit which accompanied it, bearing witness to its truth. After a few days of secrecy I was permitted to meet with them, to hear it read, being then 13 years of age; and in listening, a feeling of the most intense anxiety came over me to learn more. It seemed as if I must hear it all before I could be satisfied; and the principle of faith began to spring up in my heart to believe it. This was in the early fall of 1831. Now a bright hope began to arise in my heart that there really was a living prophet on the earth, and my greatest fear was that it would not prove true.

Later in the fall my brothers came from Ohio to see us and bear their testimony, and were accompanied by Almon W. Babbitt, then not seventeen years of age. They bore a faithful testimony, but neither of them seemed capable of teaching in a public capacity. As a family we were being converted to the truth, when unexpectedly there came to us Elders James Brackinbury and Jabez Durfee. Elder Brackinbury was a capable man and a great reasoner, and the Spirit of the Lord rested mightily upon him, confirming the words we had already received. My mother, and Lyman R. Sherman, my brother-in-law, were soon baptized, shortly followed by the baptism of all my brothers and sisters who had attained their majority. At this time my father was employed upon job work as a canter in Fredonia and not being inclined to accept the gospel, would not permit us minor children to receive our baptism. My mother, brothers, sisters, brother-in-law and neighbors who were now in the church had always been esteemed among the most eminent in religious society, and the news spreading around, the priests began to howl about Faith, Prophets, and Delusions, and to do all possible to turn us away from the truth, calling publicly for "signs," etc., asking why my sister Nancy, who then walked upon crutches, was not healed? But upon the subject of her being healed I have written more full in "Faith Promoting Series."

Additional Information: Lyman Sherman is mentioned in the above account by Benjamin Johnson. Lyman holds the distinction of the only person in this dispensation selected to the Apostleship, but never notified of this calling. He passed away before he was informed of the call.

See Lyndon W. Cook, "Lyman Sherman—Man of God, Would-be Apostle," *BYU Studies* Vol. 19, (Fall 1978), 121–24.

William Farrington Cahoon (1813–1897)

Source: Autobiography (1813–1878) Reynolds Cahoon and His Stalwart Sons (Salt Lake City, Utah): Paragon Press 1960.

My father, Reynolds Cahoon, was the son of William Cahoon Jr. and Mehitable Hodge. William Jr. was son of William Sr. whose forefathers came to America from Scotland and settled in Rhode Island and from thence scattered abroad in different parts of the land and I have no record of them. My father was born April 3, 1790 at Cambridge, Washington County, New York. He married December 11, 1810 in New Port, New York, to Thirza Stiles, daughter of Daniel Olds Stiles, son of John Stiles. They were married by Honorable John Stiles. Reynolds moved to Harpersfield, Ohio, then a new country and began farming in the year 1811. . . .

In the winter of 1812 my father Reynolds was called by the government of the United States to go to Buffalo, New York to assist in driving the British from Buffalo, who had crossed Lake Erie from Canada and burned the city. Upon arriving at Erie, they found that the British had crossed back over the lake and he was released and returned home. . . . Reynolds lived in Harpersfield about twelve years. Five children were born at this place.

In the year 1825 he moved about thirty miles farther west near the town of Kirtland and went into the business of tanning leather and making shoes. In this business, he was quite prosperous and accumulated considerable amounts of property.

During this time, a great stir was created over what was known as the "Golden Bible," or Book of Mormon. He [Reynolds Cahoon] soon became satisfied that the book was of divine origin, and that God had commenced this great and marvelous work as was spoken of by the inspired men of former days. He soon went and was baptized, 12 October [probably November] 1830 and confirmed a member of the Church of Jesus Christ of Latter-day Saints. He was baptized by Parley P. Pratt, one of the four elders who had been appointed by revelation to go to the western boundaries of the United States, preaching by the way. He was ordained an elder by Sidney Rigdon and went on a mission calling the people to repent and be baptized. He was ordained a `High Priest' by Lyman Wight. His missionary companion was Samuel Smith, Joseph's brother.

Additional Information: This is the same William Cahoon who was Joseph Smith's home teacher during the Kirtland years of the Church. William's first visit to the Prophet and his family is too lengthy to share here, but it's worth a read. You can find the account in the book *Joseph Smith's Kirtland* by Karl Ricks Anderson (Deseret Book, 1989, 120–21). His father Reynolds, that William refers to in this account, is also the same individual that delivered Emma's letter, begging the Prophet to come back to Nauvoo at the time Joseph, Porter Rockwell, and others were going to flee to the west, just prior to the Prophet's martyrdom.

See Berrett, William E., *The Restored Church* (Salt Lake City: Deseret Book, 1977), 189.

Philo Dibble (1806–1895)

Source: "Early Scenes in Church History," *Four Faith Promoting Classics* (Salt Lake City: Bookcraft, 1968), 74–96.

My wife having some property in Ohio, we sold our possessions in Connecticut and removed to that part. While crossing Lake Erie from Buffalo to Fairport we encountered a terrible storm, and our destruction seemed imminent, but through an overruling Providence we were saved and landed safely. We passed through Chardon, Ohio, and located three miles west of that city, at a place called King Street, which was within five miles of Kirtland. I there purchased a farm and entered into the business of buying and selling wild lands.

One morning I was standing at my gate when two men drove up in a two-horse wagon, and asked me to get in and go home with them, about quarter of a mile distant. On the way, one asked me if I had heard the news, and informed me that four men had come to Kirtland with a golden Bible and one of them had seen an angel. They laughed and ridiculed the idea, but I did not feel inclined to make light of such a subject. I made no reply, but thought that if angels had administered to the children of men again I was glad of it; I was afraid, however, it was not true. On my return home I told my wife what I had heard.

The next day I was intending to go fifty miles south to the town of Suffield, Ohio, to pay some taxes, but my wife thinking that one or two days would not make much difference about that, proposed that we should hunt up those strange men in Kirtland.

The next morning I took my wife, another man and his wife, and started for Kirtland. When we arrived there, the men we were seeking had gone to the town of Mayfield, but were to return to Kirtland the next day. The following morning I hitched up my carriage and again drove to Kirtland, one of my neighbors accompanying us with his team and family. On arriving there, we were introduced to Oliver Cowdery, Ziba Peterson, Peter Whitmer, Jr., and Parley P. Pratt. I remained with them all day, and became convinced that they were sincere in their professions. I asked Oliver what repentance consisted of, and he replied, "Forsaking sin and yielding obedience to the gospel!"

That evening he preached at Brother Isaac Morley's, and bore his testimony to the administration of an angel at noonday. He then dwelt upon the subjects of repentance and baptism and the bestowal of the Holy Ghost, and promised that all who embraced these principles with honesty of heart should receive a testimony. He also requested all who wished to be baptized to make it manifest by arising. Five persons, among whom were William Cahoon and myself, arose. I then made preparations for baptism by borrowing a suit of clothes. My wife thought I was too hasty, and said if I would wait awhile perhaps she would go along with me. She was a Baptist by persuasion. I paid no heed to her, but went forthwith and was baptized by Parley P. Pratt. This was on the 16th of October [probably November], 1830. When I came out of the water, I knew that I had been born of water and of the spirit, for my mind was illuminated with the Holy Ghost.

I spent that evening at Dr. F. [Frederick] G. Williams'. While in bed that night I felt what appeared to be a hand upon my left shoulder and a sensation like fibers of fire immediately enveloped my body. It passed from my right shoulder across my breast to my left shoulder, it then struck me on my collar bone and went to the pit of my stomach, after which it left me. I was enveloped in a heavenly influence, and could not sleep for joy.

The next morning I started home a happy man. All my neighbors were anxious to know the result of my visit to Kirtland, and I was visited by two Campbellite preachers, named respectively Scott and Williams, one of whom remarked, "Mr. Dibble, I understand you have joined the 'Mormons.' What reason have you to believe they have the truth?"

I told them, "The scriptures point to such a work, which should come forth."

He then asked me where I found it. I took the Bible and opened it where it speaks of truth springing out of the earth and righteousness looking down from above. He read it and handed it to the other preacher. They made no comments.

I bore my testimony to them of what I had received, and Mr. Scott said, "I don't doubt, Mr. Dibble, that you have received all you say, because you are honest, but they are impostors."

I then asked Mr. Scott if he believed the Lord would bless the labors of a false prophet, to which they did not stop to reply but left, and told the people it was no use talking to me.

One of my neighbors came to me and said, "We have sent a man down to [New] York State to find out the truth of this work, and he is a man who will not lie. If he returns and says it is false, will you believe him?"

I told him I would believe the truth, and asked him if that man (whose name was Edward Partridge) should come back and say it was false if he would believe him.

He replied, "Yes; for he is a man who would not lie for his right arm!"

I then added, "If he says it is true, will you then believe him?" to which he reluctantly replied that he would.

Shortly after this, however, when Brother [Edward] Partridge wrote back and said that he had been baptized, and was then preaching the gospel, this man shunned me, and for a long time afterwards gave me no chance to talk with him. But when we met, I asked him what he thought of Brother Partridge, and he replied that he was honest, but had been deceived.

Additional Information: In 1838, Philo Dibble participated in and was shot during the Battle of Crooked River. He would later be miraculously healed by Newel Knight and remain a faithful member of the Church.

See *Church History In the Fulness of Times* (Salt Lake City: The Church of Jesus Christ of Latter-day Saints, 1989), 136.

Emily Partridge Young (1824–1899)

Source: Autobiography. Typescript, BYU Harold B. Lee Library.

I think I must have had a rummaging disposition for I remember every nook and corner of the house, store, shop and from garret to cellar, inside and out. I remember the orchard that was in another block, and the pasture land that was down in the woods where we would go in a wagon to gather chestnuts and butternuts. I remember we had plenty to eat and wear and would sometimes ride in a spring wagon and I wore the sweetest pink calico dress that ever was, and little yellow shoes. Harriet had a pink dress too but not as pretty as mine (as I thought.) Well I think my father must have been almost a rich man when I look back and consider the amount of property he owned. But when "Mormonism" came, our home went (whether it was sold or not, I do not know.) And I have never had such a home since. It was some time in the year 1830 that four elders came to Ohio. Their names were Parley P. Pratt, Oliver Cowdery, Peter Whitmer, and Ziba Peterson. My mother soon believed the gospel after she heard it; and was baptized by Parley P. Pratt. My father was not so ready to believe at first, and told them he thought they were impostors when Brother Oliver Cowdery said he was thankful there was a God in heaven who knew the hearts of all men.

What they said must have made considerable impression on his mind, for he sent to them after they were gone to Kirtland, to purchase a Book of Mormon. And then he concluded to take a trip to New York and see the Prophet for himself. And this is what Brother Joseph says of him (in his history):

"It was in December 1830, that Elder Sidney Rigdon came to inquire of the Lord, and with him came that man of whom I will hereafter speak more fully, named Edward Partridge. He was a pattern of piety, and one of the Lord's great men, known by his steadfastness and patient endurance to the end." Brother Joseph baptized him in the Seneca River on 11 December 1830.

He then went to visit his relatives, who reside in Pittsfield, Massachusetts, anxious that they should hear the joyful tidings that so filled his heart with gladness. He thought they had only to hear, to believe it. But, oh! how disappointed he was when they rejected him with his joyful news. They pronounced him crazy, and one of his sisters ordered him out of her house, and said "she never wanted to see him again." What a bitter spirit lays hold of the unbelievers as soon as the truth is presented to them, and those that profess the most religion are the most uncharitable. When my father returned to New York, his parents sent his youngest brother to accompany him, they thinking him deranged and not capable of taking care of himself. But this brother, after he arrived in Painesville, received the gospel and was baptized. His name was James Harvey Partridge. They reached home about the beginning of February 1831.

From New York, home, my father traveled in company with the Prophet who was moving his family to Kirtland, which had been appointed a gathering place for the Saints. After his arrival home, his old and most intimate friends that had been so anxious for him to go and find out the truth of the reports about "Mormonism" because of his honesty and superior judgment, pronounced him crazy when he declared the Book of Mormon true.

After my parents had joined the Church they were seized with the spirit of gathering, as everybody is, as soon as they are baptized. My father bought a house and lot in Kirtland, but he never had the privilege of living there as you will see.

Eliza Marie Partridge Smith Lyman (1820–1885)

Source: Eliza Marie Partridge Smith Lyman, "Life and Journal of Eliza Marie Partridge (Smith) Lyman." Typescript, BYU Harold B. Lee Library.

I was born in Painesville, Geauga County, Ohio. My parents' names were Edward and Lydia Clisbee Partridge. At a very early age I was sent to school where I acquired a very good common education. At the age of eight years my parents went on a visit to their friends' in Massachusetts taking me and my sister Caroline (then a babe), with them. The other children, my sisters Harriet and Emily, were left in [the] charge of my Aunt Phebe Lee. We went to my grandfather Partridge's in Pittsfield, Berkshire County, Massachusetts, where they left me while they went to visit my mother's friends in the eastern part of the state. They returned in a short time bringing my mother's sister Elsey with them.

Although I was very young yet, I remember many things that I saw on this journey. My grandfather's nice brick house, and the cider mill, the orchard and the farm are all plain in my memory; also the cities that we passed through and the Erie Canal with its locks and the roaring of the Niagara Falls in the distance, the crossing of the lake, my sickness while crossing and many other things are still fresh in my mind. I do not remember anything more worthy of note except that I was sent to school until I was about 13 years of age or a short time before this when the Book of Mormon was shown to my father. He did not accept it at first as being what it was represented to be, but after making a journey to New York where the Prophet Joseph Smith lived, and making inquiry of those in the Church and also of those out, he became convinced that the Lord had commenced to set up his kingdom on the earth and embraced the opportunity of becoming a member of the Church of Jesus Christ of Latter-day Saints and was ordained to the office of a bishop, there having been none ordained in this dispensation until that time.

Tamma Durfee (1813–1885)

Source: Written by Tamma Durfee Miner for the Relief Society Jubilee Box of the Utah Stake Relief Society. Opened in May 1930 and given to Frances Carter (Clark) Knight.

My father's name was Edmund Durfee, he was born in Rhode Island on the 3rd October 1788 of Dutch decent. My mother's name was Magdalena "Lana" Pickle and she was born 6 June 1788. Her father and mother were from Holland. I was born 6 March 1813 in Lennox, Madison County, New York and lived there until I was about nine years old when we moved to Amboy, Oswego County. Father bought some land, built him a house, made a small farm, and worked at his trade that was mostly carpenter and millwright. We lived there until the first of June 1830, father bought more land. There were lots of maple trees. Then father wanted to go West so he sold his sugar bush and farm and everything started for the south of Ohio. We went through Camden Village to the canal, went on the canal to Buffalo, we went to Briggles (Ruggles) in Huron County. Father bought land and went to work to make a home, and the next winter in 1831 we heard about the Mormons and the "Gold Bible." The next spring Solomon Hancock came preaching about Joseph Smith and said that the Lord and the Angel Moroni had revealed them to Joseph Smith. Solomon Hancock joined in with us the Methodists and Campbellites, and he would preach in our meeting-house. We would go to hear him and many were astonished at his message for it was so much different from what it had been reported.

This was sometime in April 1831, and my father Edmond Durfee was baptized about the middle of May and my mother and sister. Martha and brother, Edmund were baptized about the first of June by Solomon Hancock. I believed it the first time I heard him preach, that the Book of Mormon was true.

I was a Mormon in belief but was not baptized until December 1831 and will tell you the reason why I was not baptized. I was keeping company with a good young man, as I thought, and I was told that he had said that he would not have a Mormon for a wife. So I waited until after I was married. I went to the Mormon meetings and sometimes to the Methodists until 9 August 1831 when I was married to Albert Miner. He was born in Jefferson County, New

York on 31 March 1809 and was the son of Azel Miner and Sylvia Monson. We got along first rate and we went to meetings sometimes to one place and sometimes to the Mormons until December 1831, when my father was going on a mission to the State of New York and he baptized me before going on his mission. Albert Miner's mother, brothers and sisters had a great deal to say about the Mormons as they did not believe in the Book of Mormon. But he told them, "the more they had to say, the sooner he would be baptized". He waited until the first of February 1832 when they cut a hole in the ice and baptized him.

Additional Information: Her first husband, Albert Miner, is listed as a bodyguard to the Prophet Joseph Smith in Kirtland.

See http://www.findagrave.com/cgi-bin/fg.cgi?page=gr&GRid=62167 (04/11/2014).

Orson Hyde (1805–1878)

Source: Autobiography (1805–1842) in The Latter-day Saints' Millennial Star 26 (1864):742–44, 760–61, 774–76, 790–92.

About this time some vague reports came in the newspapers that a "golden bible" had been dug out of a rock in the state of New York. It was treated, however, as a hoax. But on reading the report, I remarked as follows—"Who knows but that this 'golden bible' may break up all our religion, and change its whole features and bearing?" Nothing more was heard of it for a long time in that section.

Not long after this, the Campbellite doctrine began to be preached in Mentor and in Kirtland. Elder S. [Sidney] Rigdon was its chief advocate there. Being forcibly struck with the doctrine of immersion or baptism for the remission of sins, and many other important items of doctrine which were advocated by this new sect, and which were passed over by the Methodists as not essential, I left the Methodists and became a convert to this new faith [Mormonism].

Additional Information: Ordained to the original Quorum of the Twelve in February 1835, Orson would travel to Palestine and dedicate the land for the return of the Jews.

William Hyde (1818–1874)

Source: Autobiography (1818–1846). Journal, BYU Harold B. Lee Library.

In the year 1830 or 1831 he [referring to his father, Heman Hyde] began to hear something concerning the Book of Mormon, and the setting up of the kingdom of god on the earth in the last days. The little information that we gained upon this subject, until the elders came preaching, was through Warren A. Cowdery whose farm joined with our farm. Warren A. obtained from his brother, Oliver, at an early date some of the proof sheets to the Book of Mormon, some of which we had the privilege of perusing, and we did not peruse any faster than we believed.

In the year 1833 elders were preaching in different parts of the country. Sectarianism was also playing a heavy part, as there were revivals on all sides, and the motto with priestcraft seemed to be, now or never. Early in the year 1834 Joseph Smith and Parley P. Pratt came to my father's house. They preached two or three times in the neighborhood, and conversed much in private. Before they left my oldest brother was baptized and went the same year to Missouri with Joseph Smith and many others in what was called the Zion's Camp. On the 7th of April, 1834, my father and myself were baptized, and soon after all the family were numbered in the Church of Jesus Christ of Latter-day Saints.

Additional Information: William would eventually move to Kirtland with his family. Of the Kirtland Temple dedication he states in his journal, "This was, by far, the best meeting I had ever attended. The gifts of the gospel were enjoyed in a marvelous manner, and angels administered unto many."

See http://wk77.net/family/h/hyde_heman_1788/heman_and_polly/heman_and_polly.pdf (04/11/2014).

Marinda M. [N] Hyde (1815–1886)

Source: Autobiography (1818–1868). Cited in Edward W. Tullidge, *The Women of Mormondom*: New York, 1877.

In February of 1818, my father, in company with several families from the same place, emigrated to Hiram, Portage County, Ohio. In the winter of 1831, Ezra Booth, a Methodist minister, procured a copy of the Book of Mormon and brought it to my father's house. They sat up all night reading it, and were very much exercised over it. As soon as they heard that Joseph Smith had arrived in Kirtland, Mr. Booth and wife and my father and mother went immediately to see him. They were convinced and baptized before they returned. They invited the prophet and Elder Rigdon to accompany them home, which they did, and preached several times to crowded congregations, baptizing quite a number. I was baptized in April following [1831].

Lyman Omer Littlefield (1819–c1890)

Source: Autobiography (1819–1848). Lyman Omer Littlefield, *Reminiscences of Latter-day Saints* (Logan, Utah): The Utah Journal Co., 1888.

Lyman Omer Littlefield, who has undertaken in this little volume to give publicity to many incidents connected with the experience of the Saints, is the second son of Waldo Littlefield and Mercy Higgins. His grandfather, Josiah Littlefield, fought through the war of 1812, for which service he drew a pension during the latter years of his life. He is a native of the state of New York, township of Verona, Oneida County, and first breathed the vital spark of life November 22, 1819. Counting up the years, it is easily determined that he is now nearing the "three score and ten," which so frequently fixes the limit of human life.

When his mind wanders back over the vista of the past to call up the time and place where he first heard a rumor of anything pertaining to the strange people now having a world-wide fame as Mormons, or, more properly, Latter-day Saints, the focus of his mind concentrates upon a spot in dear old Verona which was his home by virtue of its being the abode of his parents. In that neighborhood he made his infantile debut upon this terrestrial globe and there is laid the scene of his earliest recollections. But that halcyon period is ended now. The actors are scattered upon the wide globe, and those then so devoted in their friendships would be strangers now if chance were to bring them together. But, at such meeting, did some fortuitous chance reveal the parties' names, the intuitive powers would be instantaneous in throwing off feelings of restraint and prompting enquiries into the fortunes of each since the days of childhood had gone down forever in the great whirlpool of time.

A golden bible—the rumor said—had been taken out of the earth in the western portion of New York State by a young man named Joseph Smith, who said an angel of the Lord had revealed it to him: that it purported to give an account of a great and enlightened nation of people, then extinct, from whom the American Indians were descendants. This strange rumor became the topic of much talk and wonderment through that part of the country.

Soon after hearing this rumor it was my lot to turn my back upon the hallowed scenes of that natal home—scenes still dear in memory—as my parents removed to Michigan, settling near the town of Pontiac, in Oakland county. Not long after our location there, two Mormon Elders came to our neighborhood and held meetings. Of course we knew they were followers of Joseph Smith, whom rumor had associated with the golden Bible matter concerning which we had heard in the state of New York. Naturally enough we felt a curiosity to see these strange men and hear more concerning their new religion.

My parents were members of the Methodist Church and did not wish to exchange that faith for another; but they went to hear what these strangers had to say. Their little son Lyman was permitted to bear them company. It was winter and of course a sleigh was our mode of conveyance. Their place of holding meeting was in a log schoolhouse built in the edge of some timber and as we turned from the main road to drive near we knew that meeting had commenced, for we heard the speaker in a full and animated tone of voice enunciating his doctrines. It is said in the scriptures: "Blessed are they who know the joyful sound;" so the writer must just then have been one of the favored, for at the very first sound of Jared Carter's voice—for it was he who was speaking—a strange, unaccountable feeling came over me, and before hearing one word pronounced by him, there was something connected with the tone of his voice that convinced me he was a man of God and was telling the truth. The writer went in that meeting prepared to believe all the speaker said, and your humble friend has been a believer in what many call Mormonism from that hour.

After attending one or two more meetings and reading the Book of Mormon all she could, my mother was fully convinced of the truth of the gospel. My father did not believe so readily, but after a few weeks he, too, was convinced and my parents became members of the Church of Jesus Christ of Latter-day Saints—they being baptized by immersion for the remission of sins and having hands laid upon them for the reception of the Holy Ghost. Quite a number of people in that vicinity embraced the new faith and a branch of the Church was organized and presided over by Elder Samuel Bent.

Noah Packard (1796–1860)

Source: Autobiography (1796-c.1860). Typescript, BYU Harold B. Lee Library.

This brings me down to the 35th year of my age, during which time neither I nor my wife had ever made any profession of religion; yet a member of the Baptist Church who lived neighbor to us, thought we were good enough to join their Church and requested me to do so; but my answer to him was that if I knew that I was the best Christian there was upon the face of the earth, I would not join any church under heaven, and that there was something wrong and that the sects of the day were not right and that they would go to meeting and put on a long face on the Sabbath, and on the next day would go home and cheat their neighbors and that such a religion I did not believe in. Notwithstanding this, I had a reverence and love for all good people having been in my youth, religiously instructed by my parents.

My father never joined any church although he prayed daily in his family. My mother belonged to the Congregational Church.

In the year 1831 a rumor was in circulation that a gold Bible had been dug out of the earth; and hearing the preachers of the day rail out against it, I believed the words of the Savior were about to be fulfilled in regard to false prophets and teachers arising in the last days, who, if it were possible would deceive the very elect. In the fall of this same year a man by the name of William Jolly and family moved into the neighborhood; who I was informed, were believers in the gold Bible. I felt in my heart to pity them, and told my wife we would go and make them a visit; accordingly as soon as they commenced conversation on the subject of religion, quoting the words of the Savior in regard to false prophets and teachers in the last days; on hearing this, Mrs. Jolly went and placed a stand in the middle of the floor and put a candle and a large family Bible upon it and said, "Now to the law and testimony." When she immediately turned to the passages of scripture I had quoted and read them, and applied them to the sects long extinct upon the earth, which I could not refute. I immediately commenced searching the Bible and found that in the last days God would set His hand the second time to gather Israel from all the earth.

About this time Mrs. Jolly presented the Book of Mormon to me and asked me if I would read it; I told her I would, and took it and carried it home and placing the book against my forehead asked secretly the Lord if that work was His, He would make it manifest to me. I then opened the book and commenced reading aloud that my wife might also hear it. We read it through and I commenced reading it the second time and the Lord poured out His spirit upon me and the scriptures were opened to our understanding, and we were convinced that the Book of Mormon was a true record of the Aborigines of America containing the fullness of the gospel of Jesus Christ which was to come forth at the time of the restitution of the house of Israel.

Accordingly I and my wife were baptized in the town of Parkman by Parley P. Pratt and were confirmed in the Church of Jesus Christ of Latter-day Saints, under his hands and Hyrum Smith's hands, the day I am unable to state, but think it was between the first and fifth of June 1832. Between this time and January following I went to Kirtland and was ordained a priest under the hands of Joseph Smith, the Prophet, and Sidney Rigdon.

Additional Information: Noah only held the office of priest when he left to serve his first mission to the eastern states.

See http://josephsmithpapers.org/person/noah-packard (04/11/2014).

John H. Gilbert (1802–1895)

Source: *Recollections of John H. Gilbert* [Regarding printing of the Book of Mormon], 8 September 1892, Palmyra, New York Typescript, BYU Harold B. Lee Library.

I am a practical printer by trade. I have been a resident of Palmyra, New York, since about the year 1824, and during all that time have done some typesetting each year. I was aged ninety years on the 13th day of April 1892, and on that day I went to the office of the Palmyra Courier and set a stickful of type.

My recollection of past events, and especially of the matters connected with the printing of the "Mormon Bible" [Book of Mormon], is very accurate and faithful, and I have made the following memorandum at request, to accompany the photographs of "Mormon Hill," which have been made for the purpose of exhibits at the World's Fair in 1893.

In the forepart of June, 1829, Mr. E. [Egbert] B. Grandin, the printer of the Wayne Sentinel, came to me and said he wanted I should assist him in estimating the cost of printing 5,000 copies of a book that Martin Harris wanted to get printed, which was called the "Mormon Bible." It was the second application of Harris to Grandin to do the job—Harris assuring Grandin that the book would be printed in Rochester if he declined the job again.

Harris proposed to have Grandin do the job, if he would, as it would be quite expensive to keep a man in Rochester during the printing of the book, who would have to visit Palmyra two or three times a week for manuscript, etc. Mr. Grandin consented to do the job if his terms were accepted.

A few pages of the manuscript were submitted as a specimen of the whole, and it was said there would be about 500 pages.

The size of the page was agreed upon, and an estimate of the number of ems in a page, which would be 1,000, and that a page of manuscript would make more than a page of printed matter, which proved to be correct.

The contract was to print, and bind with leather, 5,000 copies for $3,000. Mr. Grandin got a new font of small pica, on which the body of the work was printed.

When the printer was ready to commence work, [Martin] Harris was notified, and Hyrum Smith brought the first installment of manuscript, of 24 pages, closely written on common foolscap paper—he had it under his vest, and vest and coat closely buttoned over it. At night [Hyrum] Smith came and got the manuscript, and with the same precaution carried it away. The next morning with the same watchfulness, he brought it again, and at night took it away. This was kept up for several days. The title page was first set up, and after proof was read and corrected, several copies were printed for Harris and his friends. On the second day—[Martin] Harris and [Hyrum] Smith being in the office—I called their attention to a grammatical error, and asked whether I should correct it? [Martin] Harris consulted with [Hyrum] Smith a short time, and turned to me and said, "The Old Testament is ungrammatical, set it as it is written."

After working a few days, I said to [Hyrum] Smith on his handing me the manuscript in the morning, "Mr. [Hyrum] Smith, if you would leave this manuscript with me, I would take it home with me at night and read and punctuate it, and I could get along faster in the daytime, for now I have frequently to stop and read half a page to find how to punctuate it." His reply was, "We are commanded not to leave it." A few mornings after this, when [Hyrum] Smith handed me the manuscript, he said to me, "If you will give your word that this manuscript shall be returned to us when you get through with it, I will leave it with you." I assured Smith that it should be returned all right when I got through with it. For two or three nights I took it home with me and read it, and punctuated it with a lead pencil. This will account for the punctuation marks in pencil, which is referred to in the Mormon Report, an extract from which will be found below.

Martin Harris, Hyrum Smith and Oliver Cowdery, were very frequent visitors to the office during the printing of the Mormon Bible [Book of Mormon]. The manuscript was supposed to be in the handwriting of [Oliver] Cowdery. Every chapter, if I remember correctly, was one solid paragraph, without a punctuation mark, from beginning to end.

Names of persons and places were generally capitalized, but sentences had no end. The character or short "&" was used almost invariably where the word "and" occurred, except at the end of a chapter. I punctuated it to make it read as I supposed the author intended, and but very little punctuation was altered in proofreading. The Bible [Book of Mormon] was printed sixteen pages at a time, so that one sheet of paper made two copies of sixteen pages each, requiring 2,000 sheets of paper for each form of sixteen pages. There were thirty-seven forms of sixteen pages each—570 pages in all.

The work was commenced in August 1829, and finished in March 1830—seven months. Mr. J. H. Bortles and myself did the presswork until December taking nearly three days to each form.

In December Mr. Grandin hired a journeyman pressman, Thomas McAuley, or "Whistling Tom," as he was called in the office, and he and Bortles did the balance of the presswork. The Bible [Book of Mormon] was printed on a "Smith" Press, single pull, and old-fashioned "Balls" or "Niggerheads" were used—composition rollers not having come into use in small printing offices.

The printing was done in the third story of the west end of "Exchange Row," and the binding by Mr. Howard, in the second story; the lower story being used as a bookstore, by Mr. Grandin, and now—1892—by Mr. M. Story as a dry goods store.

[Oliver] Cowdery held and looked over the manuscript when most of the proofs were read. Martin Harris once or twice, and Hyrum Smith once, Grandin supposing these men could read their own writing as well, if not better, than anyone else; and if there are any discrepancies between the Palmyra edition and the manuscript these men should be held responsible.

Joseph Smith, Jr., had nothing to do whatever with the printing or furnishing copy for the printers, being but once in the office during the printing of the Bible [Book of Mormon], and then not over fifteen or twenty minutes.

Hyrum Smith was a common laborer, and worked for anyone as he was called on.

[Oliver] Cowdery taught school winters—so it was said—but what he did summers, I do not know.

Martin Harris was a farmer, owning a good farm, of about 150 acres, about a mile north of Palmyra Village, and had money at interest. Martin—as everybody called him—was considered by his neighbors a very honest man; but on the subject of Mormonism, he was said to be crazy. Martin was the main spoke in the wheel of Mormonism in its start in Palmyra, and I may say, the only spoke. In the fall of 1827, he told us what wonderful discoveries Jo [Joseph] Smith had made, and of his finding plates in a hill in the town of Manchester (three miles south of Palmyra),—also found with the plates a large pair of "spectacles," by putting which on his nose and looking at the plates, the spectacles turned the hieroglyphics into good English. The question might be asked here whether Jo [Joseph] or the spectacles was the translator?

Sometime in 1828, Martin Harris, who had been furnished by someone with what he said was a facsimile of the hieroglyphics of one of the plates started for New York. On his way he stopped at Albany and called on Lieutenant Governor Bradish—with what success I do not know. He proceeded to New York, and called on Professor C. Anthon, made known his business and presented his hieroglyphics.

This is what the professor said in regard to them—1834—"The paper in question was, in fact, a singular scroll.

"It consisted of all kinds of singular characters, disposed in columns, and had evidently been prepared by some person who had before him, at the time, a book containing various alphabets; Greek and Hebrew letters, crosses and flourishes, Roman letters inverted or placed sidewise, arranged and placed in perpendicular columns, and the whole ended in a rude delineation of a circle, divided into various compartments, arched with various strange marks, and evidently copied after the Mexican Calendar, given by Humboldt, but copied in such a way as not to betray the source whence it was derived. I am thus particular as to the contents of the paper, inasmuch as I have frequently conversed with my friends on the subject since the Mormon excitement began, and well remember that the paper contained anything else but "Egyptian Hieroglyphics."

Martin [Harris] returned from this trip east satisfied that "Joseph" was a "little smarter than Professor Anthon."

Martin was something of a prophet—he frequently said that "Jackson would be the last president that we would have; and that all persons who did not embrace Mormonism in two years' time would be stricken off the face of the earth." He said that Palmyra was to be the New Jerusalem, and that her streets were to be paved with gold.

Martin was in the office when I finished setting up the testimony of the Three Witnesses— ([Martin] Harris—[Oliver] Cowdery and [David] Whitmer). I said to him, "Martin, did you see those plates with your naked eyes?" Martin looked down for an instant, raised his eyes up, and said, "No, I saw them with a spiritual eye."

Diedrich Willers (1830)

Source: D. Michael Quinn, trans. and ed., "The First Months of Mormonism: A Contemporary View by Rev. Diedrich Willers," *New York History* 54 (July 1973):317–33.

1830 Letter of Rev. Diedrich Willers

Reverend Brethren

The greatest fraud of our time in the realm of religion is certainly Joseph Smith, the alleged translator of a book entitled: "The Book of Mormon, an account written by the hand of Mormon upon plates taken from the plates of Nephi wherefore it is an abridgment of the record of the people of Nephi and also of the Lamanites written to the Lamanites which are a remnant of the house of Isreal [Israel] and also to Jew and Gentile written by way of commandment and also by the spirit of prophesy and of revelation.

"Written and sealed up and hid up unto the Lord that they might not be destroyed to come forth by the gift and power of God unto the interpretation thereof; sealed by the hand of Moroni and hid up unto the Lord, to come forth in due time by the way of Gentile the interpretation thereof by the gift of God an abridgment taken from the book of Esther [Ether]—also which is a record of the people of Jared which were scattered at the time the Lord confounded the language of the people when they were building a tower to get to heaven which is to shew unto the remnant of the house of Isreal [Israel] how great things the Lord has done for their fathers and that they may know the covenants of the Lord that they are not cast off forever and also to the convincing of the Jew and Gentile that Jesus is the Christ the eternal God manifesting himself unto all nations. And now if there be fault it be the mistake of men wherefore condemn not the things of God that ye may be found spotless at the judgment seat of Christ."

The publication of the above work of deception stems from a speculation which is intended to benefit the financial interests of the publisher and those who are allied with him.

Like deceivers of earlier centuries, this man claims to associate with spirits and angels. Because the plates from which the original was translated, according to the allegation, were of gold, in the region hereabouts this book is known by the title "The Golden Book."

Since this work was printed in this region, I want to inform you of the following, according to the most credible reports:

1) The history of the origin of the book.

In the month of July [in 1829], Joseph Smith made his appearance in Seneca County, in the neighborhood of Waterloo, about six miles from my hometown. There a certain David Whitmer claimed to have seen an angel of the Lord, so Smith proceeded to his house, in order to complete the translation of the above work himself. According to the reports, only there could he work—where men who have had association with the other would also reside. This is the eleventh place where he had worked on the translation of his work and where men saw angels.

He asserted that the angel of the Lord appeared to him and made it known that in the neighborhood of Palmyra there were golden plates in the earth, upon which was described the doings of a Jewish prophet's family, associated with many not yet fulfilled prophecies. The angel indicated that the Lord destined him to translate these things into English from the ancient language, that under these plates were hidden spectacles, without which he could not translate these plates, that by using these spectacles, he (Smith) would be in a position to read these ancient languages, which he had never studied, and that the Holy Ghost would reveal to him the translation in the English language. Therefore, he (Smith) proceeded to Manchester township, Ontario County, and found everything as described, the plates buried next to the spectacles in the earth, and soon he completed the translation of this work.

Upon receiving this report, I hurried immediately to Whitmer's house to see this man, in order to learn the actual source of this story and to find out how it might be possible to nip this work in the bud. However, I received the reply from Whitmer's father that Smith had already departed to take his translation to press. I tried to expose the clumsy deception to this man, and he was silent about Smith's pretension, which is such that it is not worthy of refutation.

Since last year all of the neighboring congregations have been frequently and earnestly warned to beware of this so-called Golden Book [Book of Mormon] and not to buy any. The above-named Smith, however, found his followers. The security had been given to the printer for the payment of his work, and about 10,000 copies of the book have been printed, which are supposed to be sold for

$1.75 each. Already in this region more have been sold than one would have expected, and the unbelieving and godless vermin have now gone to Pennsylvania in order to scatter their books among the public. The author has already been frequently challenged to demonstrate his inspiration, as did the Apostles, through genuine miracles. Naturally he cannot perform such. His followers, however, claim that through their preachers devils have been cast out recently. It goes without saying that this is allowed only in the presence of their own followers. The dear Savior has already pronounced their judgment for such false exorcists. Matthew 7:22–23.

2) Various weighty volumes could be written against the contents of this book which consists of 588 pages. The style is so insipid and wretched that even men of mediocre intelligence can recognize it. It is nothing more than a tempting work of man. I have read only a little of it and would wish to be excused from this effort, but it is the express request of my congregations which have obtained it for me so that I could read it.

The first two books are called the book of Nephi and describe the family of a so-called prophet Lehi (about whom the Bible tells us nothing) and his four sons Laman, Lemuel, Sam, and Nephi. They are represented as descendants of Joseph who lived during the reign of Zedekiah, King of Judah. It is said that Lehi saw God in the heavens which had been opened unto him. (John 1:18; 4:24). This Lehi (elevated to the status of a prophet by man) prophesies concerning John the Baptist, that he would baptize at Bethabara and that the Messiah should be baptized by him. The author must not yet have learned that prophecies deal with future things, and that something which happened 1,800 years ago can no longer be a prophecy in this year, because it deals with the past. Nephi (the created prophet) even affirmed that in his own time he had seen in the heavens Mary the mother of the Savior with the child Jesus in her arms. Such false prophecies contrast with the prophecies throughout the Bible: 1) that they make prophecies about things which have already occurred, 2) that they have too much clarity which God according to his wisdom reserved for the bible prophecies, so that either men, as they seek to fulfill these same prophecies, do not give the honor of the fulfillment to themselves, which belongs alone to God the highest, or men try to subvert them, and thereby induce the Almighty to perform miracles where natural means would have sufficed.

According to God's command, this prophet's family departed Jerusalem so that they would not experience the coming destruction of Jerusalem by Nebukednezzar [Nebuchadnezzar], and to live for awhile in the desert. Shortly after, Nephi and his brothers travel again back to Jerusalem and bring Ishmael and his family back to their father Lehi. Ishmael, Abraham's son, however, must have been 1,800 years old by the time of King Zedekiah. The Bible certainly would not have concealed so great an age from us, since it established Methuselah as the oldest man. It says much more about Ishmael (Genesis 23), that he died when 137 years old and was gathered to his people. According to the history of the world, the Arabians in the 13th Century were the discoverers of the compass needle, but according to Nephi's book, God himself gave this family a compass in order to lead them across a great sea to the promised land.

As a punishment, God is supposed to have given the Lamanites a black skin, because they did not want to follow the Nephites. Prior to this they had been white and delightsome (as Asiatics). According to this assumption the origin of the Blacks would come from Laman, one of Nephi's brothers whom God had given a black skin because of his godlessness, and yet so many reasons exist to conclude that the origin of the Blacks came from Ham the son of Noah.

According to page 65 of the Book of Mormon, human reproduction was a result of the Fall; consequently, if Adam and Eve had not sinned, according to this principle, they would have had no children. The author in his blindness must have never read Genesis 1:28. Moreover, he maintains that if the Fall had not occurred, the animal creations would have been [illegible] and that they would have remained in their original condition, thus incapable of propagating themselves. The last refutation in Genesis 1:22 concerns the everlasting life of animals. The holy scriptures describe the death of man as a result of the Fall, and it is recognized that without the Fall the body of man would have remained in immortality. Never, however, do the holy scriptures mislead one to conclude that the death of animals resulted from the Fall.

In chapter 8 of the book of Moroni, a letter of his father Mormon is presented. To begin with, he writes that the Holy Ghost instructed him that children were wholesome, needing no baptism (Romans 3:12) and that those who claim that child baptism is necessary were filled with bitter gall and were without faith, love, and hope; and those who believe in child baptism must be consigned to hell. The holy scriptures, however, never prescribe damnation for belief in any kind of baptism, but instead for disbelief. (Mark 16:16). The scriptures also never assert that faith, love, and hope are fruits of the baptism of adults, but instead maintain that they are the fruits of the gospel and of the Holy Ghost (John 20:31; Romans 10:17; Galatians 5:22). When he writes that infant baptism invalidates the Atonement of Christ, then the Apostle Paul makes him (Mormon) a false teacher (Romans 6:3), who writes that everyone who is baptized unto Jesus Christ is baptized unto his death.

I have read only about 100 pages in the Book of Mormon. The author, now established as a prophet through the transmission of his nonexistent plates, wants to elevate his book to the status of a canonical work through which the Spirit of God is revealed to men. Even with this he is not satisfied, but introduces a second Bible, and thereby expects it to be acknowledged that the Word of God is not complete. Moreover, he threatens damnation upon all who do not believe in his false bible. We must with the Apostle Paul await this curse upon such: Galatians 1:6–8.

3) What the ultimate object of this book concerns is its self-condemnation. The reprobate Jewish people are supposed to receive mercy once more and become part of the Church of Christ, and the Gentiles likewise are to be grafted into the true church. There are teachings which we have in the true Bible and we need no new Bible in addition. Such superfluous revelations conflict with the wisdom of God which has done nothing unnecessary. In all of His ways there has been the grandest design which has been achieved by the shortest means.

4) The effects of this book already extend upon members of various Christian persuasions. Some members of the Lutheran, Reformed, Presbyterian, and Baptist congregations have given this book their approval, have been baptized by immersion, and formed their own sect. Because they baptize by immersion they are winning over many members of the Baptist Church (including General as well as Particular Baptists), first because of their teachings about the universal grace of God and lastly because of their agreement in attitude toward the proper subject of holy baptism.

This upstart sect calls itself the True Followers of Christ; however, because they believe in the Book of Mormon, they bear the name Mormonites. For the past several Sundays many people of both sexes have been immersed by them, and so many during the week that their numbers in the region hereabouts may amount to at least 100 persons. They have their own preachers whom I know, Oliver Cowdery by description and David Whitmer (the so-called angel-viewer) personally. Their sect, however, numbers still other preachers, unknown to me. The Book of Mormon, from which they all preach every Sunday, must be regarded by the converts as not only a symbolic book but even more as a second Bible to be used for godly instruction. Most of their present adherents were apparently General Baptists.

By itself this new sect may not astound the Christian Church. Past centuries have also had their religious monstrosities, but where are they now? Where are the sects of Nicolaites, Ebionites, Nasoreans, Montanites, Paulicians, and such others, which the Christian churches call fables. They have dissolved into the ocean of the past and have been given the stamp of oblivion. The Mormonites, and hopefully soon, will also share that fate. Most of their preachers have gone to Pennsylvania in order to make converts to their doctrines and also to carry a quantity of books to sell.

And so I am, your brother, commissioned by the Zion Congregation, imploring you to warn with the utmost urgency the residents of the Union, wherever our Magazine of the Reformed Church is read, against these new doctrines and against the purchase of these books.

In conclusion I will add the testimony of these unbelieving and godless men:

The Testimony of Three Witnesses

Be it known unto all nations, kindreds, tongues and people, unto whom this work shall come, that we, through the grace of God the Father, and; our Lord Jesus Christ have seen the plates which contain this record, which is a record of the people of Nephi, and also of the Lamanites, his brethren and also a record of the people of Jared which came from the tower, of which has been spoken, and we also know that they have been translated by the gift and power of God, for his voice has declared it unto us, wherefore we know of a surety that the work is true, and we also testify that we have seen the engravings which are upon the plates, and they have been shewn unto us by the power of God, and not of man, and we declare with words of soberness, that an angel of God came down from heaven, and he brought and laid before our eyes, that we beheld and saw the plates, and the engravings thereon and we know that it is by the grace of God the Father, and our Lord Jesus Christ, that we beheld and bear record that these things are true; and it is marvellous in our eyes. Nevertheless the voice of the Lord commanded us, that we should bear record of it; wherefore to be obedient of God, we bear testimony of these things, and we know that if we are faithful in Christ, we shall rid our garments of the blood of all men, and be found spotless before the judgment seat of Christ, and shall dwell with him eternally in the heavens, and the honor be to the Father, and to the Son, and to the Holy Ghost, which is one God. Amen.

(Signed) Oliver Cowdery, David Whitmer, Martin Harris.

And Also the Testimony of Eight Witnesses.

Be it known unto all nations, kindreds, tongues and people, unto whom this work shall come that Joseph Smith, Jr., the author and proprietor of this work, has shewn unto us the plates of which has been spoken, which have the appearance of gold; and as many of the leaves as the said Smith has translated, we did handle with our hands; and we also saw the engravings thereon, all of which has the appearance of ancient work and of curious workmanship and this we bear record, with words of soberness, that the said Smith has shewn unto us, for we have seen and hefted, and know of a surety that the said Smith has got the plates of which we have spoken, and we give our names unto the world to witness unto the world that which we have seen: and we lie not, God bearing witness of it.—Christian Whitmer, Jacob W., Peter W., Jr., John W., Hiram Page, Joseph Smith, Sen., Hyrum Smith, Samuel H. Smith.

I am acquainted with the Whitmers. During the past nine years, they were followers of the Methodists, Reformers, Presbyterians, Mennonites, and Baptists, and are unstable, spineless men; moreover, they are gullible to the highest degree and even believe in witches. Hiram Page is likewise full of superstition, and the Smiths are probably the close relations of Joseph Smith, Jr., author of the Book of Mormon.

With deep respect and love,

D. W.

Reverend L. Mayer and D. Young

York

Part Six

"Do You Want to See a Picture of My Horse?"

Not everyone, at the unfolding of this last dispensation took the leap of faith and entered the water of baptism the moment they heard their first sermon preached, or when they read the Book of Mormon for the first time. Truth be told, rarely does it happen that way today either. I spoke to literally thousands of people on my mission and on only two occasions did I have someone ask me to be baptized before being offered the invite. I found that most people took three to six months to convert, and that's okay. We are still relatively new as far as mainstream religions go and not everyone understands the basic LDS beliefs, which must be taught and *understood* before baptism.

Changing religion greatly affects a person's life, especially in the case of the LDS Church. It's a decision that can take time, especially if the Spirit is silent. For some, the search is no more complicated than trying to decide between two brands of peanut butter on the grocery store shelf, whereas for others the decision is far more intricate. Some are easily guided by the Spirit, while others must engage in a detailed study of the Church and its philosophies. Again, that's okay. Brigham Young, Warren Foote, John Corrill, and my uncle (as a modern-day example) are such individuals that required a detailed search. Brigham Young took over two years, Warren Foote longer still, and my own uncle even longer than that.

My mother joined the Church when she was nineteen. After she joined, my grandmother also united herself. My mother's brother was a medical doctor, a man of science, and as such had to mull the beliefs of the Church over in his mind for quite some time. Not because his mind was numb to spiritual things, but rather that's the way he learned and the only way it was going to make sense to him. He was taught by many pairs of missionaries; however, one day a very humble missionary broke the ice with my uncle when he stated, "Do you want to see a picture of my horse?" Where other missionaries had failed, this one succeeded in making that important connection.

In the upcoming section are the investigative searches of John Corrill, Warren Foote, and Ebenezer Robinson. The length of the conversion process does not guarantee complete conversion, as was the case with Corrill and Robinson both. With time, they left the Church and never came back.

Foote is a curious study. Of the individuals in this part, he took by far the longest. What's interesting, he knew early in the investigative process that the Church was true, but he couldn't bring himself to be baptized. Once in, though, he was as loyal a Saint as could be found.

John Corrill (1794–1843)

Source: *History of the Mormons* (1839): St. Louis, 1839.

Sometime in the fall of 1830, Oliver Cowdery, Parley P. Pratt, Peter Whitmer and Tiba [Ziba] Peterson, came through the county of Ashtabula, Ohio, where I then resided, on their way westward. They professed to be special messengers of the Living God, sent to preach the Gospel in its purity, as it was anciently preached by the Apostles. They had with them a new revelation, which they said had been translated from certain golden plates that had been deposited in a hill, (anciently called Cumorah,) in the township of Manchester, Ontario County, New York. They were deposited about 1400 years since by one Moroni, under the direction of Heaven, with a promise that in the Lord's own due time, they should be brought forth, for the special benefit of the remnant of his people, the house of Israel, through Joseph, of Egypt, as well as for the salvation of the Gentiles upon this continent. This soon became the topic of conversation in that section of the country, and excited the curiosity of the people,—at first, more to inquiry than otherwise, as these messengers stopped in the place only one night.

In the course of two or three days, the book of Mormon, (the Golden Bible, as the people then termed it, on account of its having been translated from the Golden plates,) was presented to me for perusal. I looked at it, examined the testimony of the witnesses at the last end of it, read promiscuously a few pages, and made up my mind that it was published for speculation. In my feelings and remarks I branded the "messengers" with the title of impostors, and thought I would not trouble myself any more about them. But I shortly heard that these messengers had stopped in Kirtland, about thirty miles distant, among a society of people called Campbellites, at whose head stood Elder Sidney Rigden [Rigdon], a noted preacher of that order. With this news I was at first much pleased; for, from my former acquaintance with that society, I knew that they were well versed in the Scriptures, and I supposed that, without fail, they would confound the impostors, convince them of their folly, and send them home again. But, to my astonishment, in a short time I heard that they had converted the majority of the society, together with Elder Rigden, [Rigdon] to their faith. What does this mean, thought I? Are Elder Rigden [Rigdon] and these men such fools as to be so duped by those impostors? I became much excited in my feelings; for in that society were several men for whom I had formed the most favorable opinion, and for whom I felt the greatest veneration and respect. By the advice of a neighbor whose feelings were similar to mine I concluded to pay them a visit, with a determination if I could, to persuade Elder Rigden [Rigdon] to go home with me, on a preaching visit; for I thought, if I could get him away from them until his mind became settled, he might be saved from their imposition. But before I arrived at his residence, I heard that he had embraced their faith, and had been baptized by them. On receiving this news, my feelings became much embittered, and I felt more and more determined in my opposition. But when within a short distance of their residence, I was met by a respectable gentleman, (whose name I forget,) who tried to check my violence, and cautioned me not to go there with prejudiced feelings, but to weigh the matter carefully. I said very little to him in reply, but resumed my journey. On arriving at the place, I found the society under a high state of religious excitement, well pleased with their new religion, enjoying as they supposed, the gift and power of the Holy Ghost. I felt indignant, and sought an argument with Oliver Cowdery, who refused. Tiba [Ziba] Peterson then took the ground, and we contended a short time.

After supper I was invited to see Elder Rigden [Rigdon]. I requested to converse with him on the subject of his new religion. He observed that he was now beyond the land of contention, and had got into the land of peace. I proceeded to ask him if the scriptures were not sufficient for our salvation, and what we wanted with another revelation. He answered that the scriptures informed us of perilous and distressing times, great judgments that should come in the last days, and destructions upon the wicked; and now God had sent along his servants to inform us of the time, that we might repent and be prepared against it, and if we rejected them, it would be with us as it was with the people of Sodom and Gomorrah, who rejected the words of Lot. With this he refused to talk any more upon the subject. I then tried others, and found them of the same spirit. I could make no impression on them. The next day, I started home with my heart full of serious reflections. I thought of Solomon's words,—"that he is a fool who judges a matter before he hears it;" that perhaps it might be well enough to investigate the matter;

investigation could certainly do me no harm. The ancients rejected the prophets and apostles through a hasty spirit, and the people of Borea were said to be more noble than the people of Thesalonica [Thessalonica], because they "searched the scriptures daily, whether these things were so. Therefore many of them believed."—Acts, xvii. Now, it is not impossible, thought I, but that ere I am aware of it, I may be found fighting against God; perhaps I had better stop and reflect on the subject a little; weigh the matter more closely, and compare this new doctrine with the Scriptures; and if it does not agree with the Scriptures, I shall certainly know that it is not of God. Two or three weeks were spent in reading the Book of Mormon, comparing it with the scriptures, and in reflecting and conversing with others upon the subject. Scarcely a day passed but I heard of some evil report against the new sect. These reports I need not relate.

Suffice it to say, that every thing bad was reported against them, as I thought, that could be invented by man. I was always careful, however, to inquire after the author, and the truth or ground-work of his statement, and always found these reports to be without foundation. Apprehending there might be some truth in them, I went to Kirtland to see for myself, and whilst there, watched every movement with a jealous eye. I attended several meetings, one of which was the laying on of hands for the gift of the Holy Ghost, which, I thought, would give me a good opportunity to detect their hypocrisy. The meeting lasted all night, and such a meeting I never attended before. They administered the sacrament, and laid on hands, after which I heard them prophesy and speak in tongues unknown to me. Persons in the room, who took no part with them, declared, from the knowledge they had of the Indian languages, that the tongues spoken were regular Indian dialects, which I was also informed, on inquiry, the persons who spoke had never learned. I watched closely and examined carefully, every movement of the meeting, and after exhausting all my powers to find the deception, I was obliged to acknowledge, in my own mind that the meeting had been inspired by some supernatural agency. The next day I returned home, satisfied that the evil reports were not true, and spent about six weeks more in the further investigation of the subject.

I shall now proceed to set forth the faith and principal doctrines peculiar to the church that presented themselves to my view; and I would remark, in advance, that I always believed the Bible, (the Old and New Testament,) to be true. The whole course of my investigation was predicated upon that fact, and I felt safe in embracing anything that corresponded with the scriptures. The following were the subjects of my investigations:

1st. On the subject of prophets, prophesying, and the gift of revelation, in modern times.

2nd. The Book of Mormon and its origin.

3rd. The singularity of the hiding up, preservation, and coming forth of the same.

4th. Its contents.

5th. The doctrine of the gospel.

6th. The work of gathering.

7th. The morality and effects of the new religion.

I will treat each of these points in distinct chapters. . . .

Chapter II

Investigation—Prophets and Revelations—God the same in all ages—References to Scripture—Conclusion.

1st. On the subject of prophets, prophesying, and the gifts of Revelation in modern times.

It was objected, and I admitted, that we had no such things in our day. But what is the reason that we are not to look for them? They certainly were expected in ancient times, and were received. Has God changed? Are the scriptures false? Has the plan of salvation been altered? Or have we departed from God, transgressed his laws, changed the ordinances and broken the everlasting covenant, as the prophet said?—(Isa. xxiv. 5. Mal. iii. 7.) Or has the time come, spoken of by the Apostle, when men would not endure sound doctrine, but turn their ears from truth, give heed to fables, and heap up to themselves teachers having itching ears, having a form of Godliness, but denying the power.—(2 Tim. iv. 3, 4, and iii. 5.)

I found, on searching the scriptures, that from the commencement of time, through every age, God continued to send prophets to the people, and always when God had a message for the people, he chose a special messenger to send it by, and it was always headed with a "thus said the Lord." This was certainly the case in the days of Enoch, Noah, Abraham, Moses, and so on down to the apostles, and Jeremiah declares that the Lord sent them daily.—(Jer. vii. 25.) Now, if God did these things formerly, why not now? If he supplied every other age and people with prophets and special messengers, why not this? Many such reflections passed through my mind. But I was told that the prophets continued until the Saviour [Savior] came, but since that we have no need of them. On searching the New Testament, I found that the Church had prophets in it after Christ as well as before, and the apostle said that God had placed them in it for its benefit.—(1 Cor. xii. Eph. iv. 11, 12.) And the Apostle Peter, in explaining the prophecy of Joel, said, "And it shall come to pass in the last days," (saith God) "I will pour out of my spirit upon all flesh; and your sons and your daughters shall prophesy, and your young men shall see visions, and your old men shall dream dreams, and on my servants and on my handmaidens, I will pour out, in those days of my spirit, and they shall prophesy."—(Acts ii. 17–20)

Instead, therefore, of there being no prophets after Christ, it looked to me as if God meant there should be many; for the assertions are positive, "that your sons and your daughters shall prophesy," and this should be in the last days. Now, if the last days are past and gone, then we may give up looking for prophets; but if not, then the promise stands good for more prophets; and if God made this promise and did actually place prophets in his church, as the apostles say he did, I ask by what authority have they been taken out; or who has had authority, since the apostles, to alter or change the order which they established in the Church, and certainly prophets constituted a part of that order.

Thus I reasoned, and became satisfied, that it was just as consistent to look for prophets in this age as in any other. As to the person of Joseph Smith, Jr., he might as well be a prophet as anyone else, but it was said of him that he was a money hunter, and a bad man before he was called to be a prophet. So it was said of Moses, that he murdered a man, hid him in the sand, and ran away from justice, and while in this state God called him to be a prophet.—(Exod. ii. 11–25 & xii. 1–18.) As to the gift of prophecy and revelation, it is well known to every man who is acquainted with his Bible, that God always endowed his prophets with the gift of prophecy, and through them revealed his will. As, however, God never called a servant without having something for him to do, the question was what did he want with Smith? What great work had he to perform? This leads me to my second proposition.

Chapter III

Book of Mormon, the production of Smith—Witnesses—Bible, the production of many generations. The Book of Mormon and its origin.

This was the first production of Smith after his call to the prophetic office. As to the origin of the book, I made very diligent inquiry, and from all I could learn, I became satisfied that Smith was the author, and I never have been able to trace it to any other source. As to its being a revelation from God, eleven persons besides Smith bore positive testimony of its truth. After getting acquainted with them, I was unable to impeach their testimony, and consequently thought that it was as consistent to give credit to them as to credit the writings of the New Testament, when I had never seen the authors nor the original copy. As the Bible, (although we see it bound in one volume) was made up of many detached parts of revelation given from time to time, as God saw proper, through the space of four thousand years, for the special benefit of those to whom it was given, I thought it was no more than reasonable that we should also receive additional revelation for our special benefit; for this was according to his promise, to give line upon line, precept upon precept here a little and there a little.—(Isa. xxviii. 9, 10.)

Chapter IV

Account of the Golden Plates, and the finding of them—Smith chastened by an Angel—his wickedness—Plates obtained and translated—the Language—Martin Harris—Characters shown—Urim and Thummim—Translation published—Plates shown to witnesses—Church organized—Reflections—Scriptures not complete—Word of God sealed and hid—Ezekiel's two Records.

The singularity of the hiding up, preservation, and coming forth of the Book.

The simple story as related by others was this. Sometime in A. D. 1825, as nearly as I can recollect, Smith was informed by an angel, that there was a valuable record concealed in the earth, and the time had now arrived for it to be brought forth and published to the world. After being warned several times, he went to the spot and found the record engraved on leaves or plates of gold, fastened together by rings passing through one edge of all the leaves, on which they would turn as you opened them. The plates, as near as I can remember, were said to be about six by eight inches square, and very thin. This book was carefully enclosed in a stone box, provided for that purpose, which Smith broke open. After he obtained the plates, and before he left the place, he began to contemplate the vast riches that he would acquire by their means. While thus thinking and contemplating upon the subject, the angel hid the plates from his view, and chastised him for his wickedness in acting contrary to the commandment; for the purposes in the salvation of his people, that the Lord gave him access to the plates; but as he thought to become rich and aggrandize himself, therefore he should not obtain the plates any more till he repented of his folly. A year or more elapsed before he obtained the plates again, which I think he did in A. D. 1827; after which, through much difficulty, on account of persecution and poverty, he translated it by degrees, with the assistance of Oliver Cowdery and others, who wrote as he dictated. If I remember right, the language in which it was written on the plates, was the reformed Egyptian. And Martin Harris, who contributed much towards the publication of the book, drew off several of the characters on paper, took them to the learned in New York, to see if they could be translated, but was requested to bring them the plates, which Smith was forbidden to do of the Lord, but was commanded to translate them himself, which he did, by the help of what he calls the Urim and Thummim, two stones set in a bow, and furnished by an angel for that purpose.

After finishing the translation, the plates and stones of Urim and Thummim were again taken and concealed by the angel for a wise purpose, and the translation published to the world in the winter of A. D. 1829 and '30.

In the course of the translation, these plates were shown to eleven persons, by the special command of God; three of whom had it manifested and shown to them by an angel from heaven, who declared the truth of the book, and the other eight saw the plates and handled them; and all were commanded to bear testimony to the world, of the truth of what they had seen and handled, which they did, and published their testimony in the end of the book.

On the sixth day of April, A. D. 1830, they organized the first church in the state of New York, consisting of six members only.

This tale, simple as it is, formed a new subject of contemplation for me. As to the preservation of the record, if the plates were pure gold, of course they would remain pure any length of time, and as to the language, it might as well be reformed Egyptian as any other language, if it had to be translated by the power of God.

I searched the scriptures again to see if God had ever concealed or hid up his word, or commanded his servants to do so for a wise purpose. I always thought before, that we had all the scripture that we ever should have, and that the Bible was complete; but on searching the scriptures, I found to my surprise, that they, in many instances, refer to books for information that they do not contain; nor are they anywhere to be found,—such as the Book of Jasher, of the wars of the Lord—of Nathan the Prophet—of Shemaiah the Prophet, of Goed the Seer, and of Iddo the Seer, etc.—(1 Chron. xxix. 29; 2 Chron. ix. 29, and xii. 15.) and many others which I need not mention at this time. This satisfied me at once, that there was much of the word of God that we had not got, and still are referred to it for further information; therefore, the scriptures are not complete without it. Neither could the knowledge of God cover the earth as waters do the sea, without receiving more knowledge or revelation from God. I also found that Habakkuk, (ii. 2, 3,) was commanded to write the vision and make it plain upon tables; for, at the end of the appointed time, it should speak and not lie, and though it tarry, yet we must wait for it, for surely it would come. And Daniel, (xii. 4, 9,) was commanded to shut up the words and seal the book, which was to remain so till the time of the end. And John, the Revelator, was commanded to seal up the words of the seven thunders. And old King David declares, that truth shall spring out of the earth, (Ps. lxxxv. 11) Isaiah, (xxix. 11, 12,) said that all their visions should become the words of a sealed book, that should be delivered to the learned to be read, but they not being able, it should be read by the unlearned, whereupon the Lord would proceed to do a marvelous work, etc. And Ezekiel, (xxxvii. 15–21,) plainly shows, that two records should be written, one for the house of Judah and his companions, and another for the house of Joseph and his companions, and these two records should be brought together for the purpose of bringing about the gathering of all the tribes of Israel, etc.

Chapter V

Contents of the Book of Mormon—the object of bringing it forth—Offspring of Joseph—Blessings of Jacob—Reflections.

I then proceeded to examine the contents of the Book of Mormon, which I found to contain an account of the posterity of Joseph, who was sold into Egypt. It gives the history of their journey from Jerusalem across the ocean to this land, and their settlement here, with their manners, customs, wars, and more especially their religion, which was the same as existed among the Jews, both under the law of Moses, (which they brought with them) and also the gospel, after Christ, in its purity. This looked to me very much like the record of Joseph in the hand of Ephadins, (kept by his seed) that should be joined to the record of Judah (our Bible) for the restoration of the house of Israel, according to the prophecy of Ezekiel, as quoted above. For it also contains many promises of great things that should take place in the last days, for which purpose it has come forth, such as the preaching of the gospel in its purity, setting up the true church of Christ, and establishing the regular orders of priesthoods in it as the ancients had them, and to bring about the great work of gathering the saints and the house of Israel—making preparations for and ushering in the great Millennial, building up the New Jerusalem, etc., as spoken by the prophets.

As to the seed of Joseph, I found in the scripture a curious blessing pronounced upon them by Jacob his father. It reads thus: "Joseph is a fruitful bough, even a fruitful bough by a well, whose branches run over the wall—The blessings of thy father have prevailed above the blessing of my progenitors, unto the utmost bounds of the everlasting hills, these shall be upon the head of Joseph," etc.—(Gen. xlix. 22, 26.)

Now, we know, that Abraham and Isaac were Jacob's progenitors and they had the land of Canaan promised to them and their seed for an everlasting possession; but Joseph's blessing prevailed above, or exceeded theirs; he was to have an inheritance, somewhere of course, that far exceeded the land of Canaan; it was to extend to the utmost bounds of the everlasting hills. Now, when and where did they ever receive it? According to the Book of Mormon they received it upon this continent. And if so, we discover the fulfillment of the promise made to Ephraim and Manassah, that they should become a multitude of nations in the midst of the earth.—Gen. viii. 11, 20.

Chapter VI

The Gospel—Promises of God—Belief in their Fulfillment—Want of Faith. The doctrines of the gospel.

On this subject the Mormons believe in the same God, and in the same Saviour [Savior], and the same gospel that other professors do; and they believe as firmly in the scripture of the Old and New Testaments as any other people. They look upon their new revelations only as bringing about the fulfillment of the Bible. The main difference between them and other professors on the gospel is, that they believe rather more firmly in the promises of God, especially those that require great faith for their fulfillment, than others do. Where the scriptures hold out fair promises to the believers, they believe those promises will be fulfilled, just in proportion to their faith. Hence, when the Savior commanded the apostles to go into all the world and preach the gospel to every creature, and gave them a promise that these signs shall follow them that believed; in his name they shall cast out devils, heal the sick, etc.,—(Mark xvi. 15, 18.) they believe to be good to all that believe, whether in this age or any other. There are many promises of this kind, which, perhaps, are not noticed so particularly by others as the Mormons. I will name two or three. The Saviour [Savior] says, "Verily, verily I say unto you, he that believeth on me the works that I do he shall do also, and greater works than these shall he do—And whatsoever ye shall ask in my name, that will I do, that the Father may be glorified in the Son; if ye shall ask anything in my name I will do it."—(John xiv. 12–14.) Again: "Is any among you sick, let him call for the elders of the Church, and let them pray over him, anointing him with oil in the name of the Lord—And the prayer of faith shall save the sick."—James v. 13, 14.

These promises, the Mormons believe, are plain and sure, and the only reason why Christians do not enjoy them is, because they are wanting in faith. Much more might be quoted, but I will pass to the next topic.

Chapter VII

The Gathering—Prophets quoted—Power of God to be manifested in the fulfillment of Prophecy—Many to be called and sent of God—Conclusions. The work of the gathering.

On searching the Scriptures, I found that much was said on the subject, though it was little noticed generally. The thirty-seventh chapter of Ezekiel speaks very clearly; but it is too lengthy to quote here. Suffice it to say, that it promises to gather the Israelites from every place where they have been scattered; and that they and their children and their children's children shall inherit the land of Israel forever. Isaiah, ii. 2, 3, and Mich. iv. 1, 2, make similar promises. Isaiah, xi. 11, 16, also speaks of the same, together with the promises of working great miracles for their safe return, such as drying the tongue of the Egyptian sea, and smiting the river (Nile) in the seven streams thereof, and casting up a highway as it was to Israel in the days that he came up out of the land of Egypt.

When, how, where, and by whom shall this great work be accomplished, unless God calls, qualifies, and sends forth men endowed with power to do it; for the house of Israel is scattered to all parts of the earth, and who shall know who they are, and where to find them, and how to gather them, unless God reveals it to, and send them for that purpose? But this he has promised to do; for Jeremiah says that the Lord will send many fishers, and many hunters, and they shall fish them and hunt them from every mountain and hill, and from the holes of the rocks in every land, whither they have been driven, and bring them again into the land that he gave to their fathers.—(Jer. xvi. 14, 16.) Not only is the house of Israel to be gathered; but God hath purposed in the dispensation of the fullness of times, he will gather all things whether in heaven or in earth.—Eph. i. 9, 10.

Thence, after considering all these scriptural declarations, and many others that might be named, I came to the conclusion that it was not unreasonable to believe that there was to be a gathering in the last days.

Chapter VIII

New Religion compared with the Bible—Mode of admission into the Church—Effects.

The morality and effects of the new religion.

I found that the Book of Mormon taught all the morality, piety, virtue, honesty, righteousness and Godliness that the Bible did, and even condemned the whoredoms of David, Solomon and others, and strictly enjoined family and secret prayer, and too, in great faith, that our prayers may be answered; and, in order to be admitted into the Church a person must manifest faith in Christ, and a hearty repentance of their sins. Baptism, by immersion, they believed was for the remission of sins; and the laying on of hands for the gift of the Holy Ghost, they think will be attended with signs following, just in proportion to the faith and righteousness of the believer.

Chapter IX

Join the Church—Cowdery goes to the West—Singular behavior of some of the younger members—Ordained an Elder—Smith's arrival at Kirtland—Appointment of a Bishop—The new Revelation called the Law—an outline of its Contents—Start for the West—Return to Kirtland.

I have thus given a brief account of the investigation I went through in relation to these different subjects. Although I was not fully satisfied, yet viewing this religion to be much nearer the religion of the Bible than any other I could find, I concluded to join the Church, with this determination, that if ever I found it to be a deception, I would leave it. There are other doctrines and discipline of the Church which I shall mention in their proper place, but will now resume my history. During the fall and winter of A.D. 1830 and 1831, Kirtland was continually crowded. Persons came from all quarters inquiring after the new religion. [Oliver] Cowdery and his company left in the fall [November 1831] for the west, to find the spot, as some said, for the temple and place of gathering.

Additional Information: John would eventually leave the Church (excommunicated in 1839) and not return. It was Joseph Smith that assigned Corrill, then a counselor in the Jackson County bishopric, the task of writing a history of the Church. This history also became his history, stating the reasons why he left the Church.

Warren Foote (1817–1903)

Source: Autobiography (1817–1846). Typescript, BYU Harold B. Lee Library.

In my infancy I took a severe cold which settled on my lungs and a severe attack of the lung fever was the consequence. My lungs ever since have been weak. I was of a sober turn of mind and often prayed to God in secret. I learned all the branches of education as taught in the Common Schools in that day. I read the Bible a great deal and was very fond of reading histories. Some time about the month of Feb. 1830, my Father borrowed a Book of Mormon (which went by the name of Golden Bible) which I read through. I, like my Father, believed it to be a true record. My mother and two youngest sisters being members of the Presbyterian Church, I was sent to the Sunday school taught by that church. I had to learn ten verses in the New Testament and repeat them every sabbath. Our teacher would comment on these verses and try to explain them to us. His comments were never very satisfactory to me. I read in the gospels about the great miracles that were performed by Jesus and his disciples, and wondered why the same miracles were not wrought in our day.

My health being very poor, many thought that I would not live to manhood. I often prayed to the Lord in secret to spare me life that I might one day become a preacher of the gospel. I could not believe in the gospel as taught by any of the sects. I often went to the Methodist revival meetings to see them jump and hear them shout and sing, and when they all got to praying, shouting and singing at once it was fun to me to hear them, I could not see any thing in such proceedings, like the gospel as taught by the ancient apostles of Christ. I read in their teachings that God was not the author of confusion, also that the house of God is the house of order etc.

In the year 1831 my Father sold his place in Dryden, and in March, 1832, moved with his family to Greenwood, Steuben County, New York, distant one hundred miles from Dryden. After we came to this place my health was much better and I got able to do considerable work. In the spring of 1833 I borrowed a Book of Mormon, of Uncle Josiah Richardson, and read it through. I had by this time read the Bible three times through by course, and could bring almost any passage of scripture to my mind. In the fall of the same year two men by the name of Landon and Orton who professed to be elders of the Church of Latter Day Saints, came to my Father's house. I paid strict attention to their conversation with Father, setting forth the principles of the gospel as taught by the Latter Day Saints. Being familiar with the scriptures, I saw at once that these principles accorded with those taught by Christ and his apostles. On the following Sunday, Landon preached in our school house. While on the road to this meeting I had very serious reflections on the principles of the gospel. I believed that I was going to hear the truth from these men. Landon's subject was the gathering of Israel in the last days. He seemed to have the prophecies of Isaiah, Jeremiah, Ezekiel and other prophets, all on his tongue's end, and proved conclusively that the children of Israel would be gathered back to the land of their forefathers in the last days. He said nothing about the first principles of the gospel. On their departure they invited Father and some others to visit them at Geneseo, Livingston County, distant from Greenwood 40 miles.

In November, Father and three of the neighbors went to Geneseo to learn more of the doctrine as taught by the Latter Day Saints. On arriving there, they found that Landon and Orton and several others had been excommunicated from the branch of the church at Geneseo; and Elder John Murdock was presiding there instead of Landon. Landon and others had been cut off from the church for rejecting the vision concerning the three glories etc, as recorded in the Book of Doctrine and Covenants [D&C 76].

After being further instructed in the first principles of the gospel, Father was baptized and, procuring a Book of Mormon returned home. During the following winter I made the Bible and Book of Mormon my particular study; I could now begin to understand the words of the prophets with regard to Israel and the setting up of the Kingdom of God in the last days, and the preparatory work for the coming of our Savior. I could begin to comprehend these things in a very small degree. In the spring of 1834, Elders John Murdock, and Orson Pratt came to my father's house, and taught the principles of the gospel more perfectly. In the evening after their arrival Elder Murdock gave a very interesting account of the peculiar manners and customs of the Missourians, which made a great deal of laughter amongst us young folks; and I remember that Elder Pratt in his evening prayer prayed the Lord to forgive us for our much laughter.

They preached a few times, and baptized one or two (who afterward apostatized) and then went on their journey. About Feb. 1835, Elders John Gould and Babcock came to Greenwood, and preached a short time. My Father, having been once an Elder, had been preaching some during the winter, and some were believing. Elder Gould baptized a few, and a branch of the church was organized, and Father was appointed Presiding Elder. They now held regular meetings, which I generally attended. My brothers David and George attended occasionally but George soon became a convert to Methodism, and joined that sect. He became bitterly opposed to the Latter Day Saints, believing all the lies about Joseph Smith which were put in circulation by the ministers of his church. My brother-in-law who lived within a few rods of Father's house, belonged to the Methodist and the Circuit preachers, generally put up with him. I have repeatedly heard one of them tell the stories then in circulation about Joe Smith, one especially with regard to his attempt to walk on the water, which story ran about like this: "On a certain occasion, J. Smith proclaimed that he would perform a miracle the next Sabbath, by walking on the water. Accordingly he went to work and fixed some planks on some posts, just under the water of a pond. After all things were arranged, some fellows went in the night, and sawed his plank nearly in two. When Sunday came, a multitude came to gather to witness the miracle. When the hour appointed arrived, 'Joe Smith' walked boldly into the water, and on reaching the middle of his last plank, down he went, and came nearly being drowned, before he could be got out." I have heard that Methodist Priest relate that story to my brother-in-law, and sister, and chuckle over it, as though it was a splendid joke on "Joe Smith," and that story was sufficient to burst up "Mormonism."

I could relate other stories, but this will serve for a sample; to show what foolish lies the first members of the church had to contend with. My brother-in-law and sister, and brother George professed to believe these lies, for surely their pious "ministers could not lie." My bother David had served his time learning the cabinet trade in Dryden, and when Father moved to Greenwood, he came as far as Bath, the county seat of Steuben County and worked at journeyman work. Here he became acquainted with Mary Bidwell whom he married. He soon after came to Greenwood and set up his trade. George and I worked in the shop with him. After George joined the Methodist he would sometimes get to talking to me about the "Mormons," as they were called, rehearsing some of the lies he had heard. I would then quote scripture from the Bible and prove to him the truth of "Mormonism," and by comparing Methodism with the gospel, as preached by the ancient apostles, showed to him the inconsistencies and foolishness of the creed of his church. He would sometimes get almost fighting mad. I had a great deal the advantage of him for I had studied the scriptures a great deal, but he had but little knowledge of what was in the Bible, having never read it much. Previous to his joining the Methodist he had cared very little about any book.

During our arguments David would sit and laugh, when he saw how nicely I would confound George with the scripture. At that time he cared nothing for religion of any kind. I was always a particular favorite of his. During the summer of 1835, several elders visited Greenwood, among whom was George A. Smith. The branch now numbered about twenty members, among whom were my sisters Almira and Clarissa. Not being able to labor much, I spent a good portion of my time reading the Bible, Book of Mormon, and Doctrine and Covenants. I was fully satisfied that the doctrine taught by the Latter Day Saints was in very deed the gospel of Christ. I prayed much in secret, and I believe that I was fully as firm in the faith as any of the members of the church although I had not been baptized. In fact I had never had a doubt from the first time I read the Book of Mormon.

The following winter I spent my time in studying grammar and arithmetic at home. I mastered all the sums in Daybell's Arithmetic. In the spring of 1836, the most of the Saints in Greenwood removed, some to Kirtland, and some to Missouri. My father and sister Almira went to Kirtland. George went to work for a man in Lima, Livingston County (N.Y.). This left but three of us at home. My mother, Clarissa, and myself. I spent the summer doing the chores, gardening etc. Father returned from Kirtland in the Fall, and I took him to Livingston County, where he intended to stay during the winter, and brought George home with me. We concluded to go to school this winter and accordingly went to work and got up our winter's wood, and attended strictly to our studies.

Father had subscribed for the Messenger and Advocate, printed in Kirtland, and had them sent to this place, by which means we often got intelligence from that place. Father came home early in the spring of 1837, intending to visit Kirtland again. Being anxious to see that country, and especially the prophet Joseph Smith, I concluded to go with him. My brothers David and George, believing that they could find a better country than Greenwood, concluded to go and look at Michigan, and prepared to accompany us as far as we went. There were four other persons who were going west, who joined with us, in hiring a man to take us to Buffalo. I will here say, that after the school closed to which George and I went, the people wished to continue it a month longer, so they hired me to teach it, by which means I obtained money to bear my expenses on this journey.

On the 8th day of May 1837 we started on our journey in a snow storm which continued until about ten o'clock. It then cleared up and was very fine. We traveled 31 miles and stayed over night at K. Nous. Tavern, near Danville Livingston County. The next day it rained. We crossed the Genessee River at Jones' Bridge and stayed over night in the town of Perry. I will now copy from my journal kept during the journey.

13th. The rest of our company being somewhat anxious to see the Prophet Joseph, and the Temple, concluded to accompany Father, and myself to Kirtland. We hired a man to take us to that place for $5.00—distant 12 miles. We arrived there about noon. In the afternoon we went into the [Kirtland] Temple, and saw the mummies and the records which were found with them (we went to the prophet's house to see him. This is the first I saw him, and shook hands with him). Joseph Smith Sen. explained them to us, and said the records were the writings of Abraham & Joseph, Jacob's son. Some of the writing was in black, and some in red. He said that the writing in red, was pertaining to the Priesthood. We were also shown through the Temple. I stayed over night at Lyman Johnson's, where I found my sister Almira. She was working for Mrs. Johnson. I was glad to find her enjoying a good degree of health, as she had not been able to do but little for several years previous to leaving Greenwood. Oh how pleasant it is to meet with our kindred in distant lands, and among strangers. It cheers our hearts, and brings vividly to mind the pleasant associations, of our childhood, while under the parental roof.

14th. I felt quite unwell this morning, which made me think some of home. I took leave of my brothers, who continued their journey to Michigan. In the afternoon I went to the Temple, to meeting, and heard Hyrum Smith preach. After meeting, Father and I went home with Uncle Josiah Richardson, who lives about five miles from Kirtland.

21st. We went to meeting and heard Sidney Rigdon preach. After meeting we went home with Uncle Josiah Richardson.

[Oct.] 17th. Kirtland is situated on a branch of Chagrin River nine miles from Painesville. It is a rough, broken country. The buildings are generally small, and there is but one that can be called handsome that is the Temple. It is built of stone with a hard finish on the outside. It contains two rooms for worship, one above the other, and it is intended to have both finished in the same style. Besides these, there are some rooms in the attic for schools etc. We went from this place to Chester, (which place joins Kirtland on the south,) where we intended to stop for the winter; but we got disappointed in getting the house that Father had engaged for us before he went to Greenwood. Rodman Clark, a member of the Church of Latter Day Saints offered us a room in his house until we could find a place. We accepted of the offer.

May 1st. [1838] George started for his home in Michigan. I went with him to Willoughby, and stayed over night with David. I will here say that David, and his wife had both embraced Methodism in Willoughby. Although my brothers had had the gospel plainly taught to them, they rejected it, and took up with sectarianism, which was a cause of much sorrow to my father. George had persuaded David to move to Michigan this spring, and another great cause of sorrow was that my mother had concluded to go with him, instead of going to Missouri with Father. This caused me to feel very sorrowful also. She would not embrace the gospel.

20th. I went to Willoughby in company with my nephew, Harrison Ferguson to bid by Mother goodbye. She had gone to David's to go with him to Michigan as has been stated. It makes me feel very sad, as I never expect to see her again in the flesh. Oh, that my mother, and brothers and sisters, could see as I see, and understand the scriptures as I do, that we might not be separated, but journey together in this probation—for I most assuredly believe the Book of Mormon to be authentic, and that Joseph Smith is a prophet of God, although I have not yet been baptized. But we must all act upon our own agency. They choose to reject the gospel, and go to Michigan, but I choose to go with my Father to Missouri where God has commanded his people to gather together to serve him. I returned home in the afternoon, very thoughtful.

26th. [May 1838] All being in readiness we started for far off Missouri about noon. Father's family now consists of my sister Almira, myself and Sister Clarissa, and her husband George Gates. They were married I think in March or April. There are three other families in company with us, namely, Stephen Markham, Abel Lamb, and Jefferson Dimick. We have one team apiece, and we are all dependent on S. Markham for expenses, and teams. We met with some accidents this afternoon. In going up a little hill. Elder Lamb's horses stopped, and let the wagon run backward off a dugway and upset the wagon, with his wife, and four children. She struck on a fence, and hurt her back, but not seriously. I was walking a short distance behind the wagon when the accident occurred. We soon got it righted up again, and had not gone far before the kingbolt of another wagon broke. They fixed it so as to get as far as Russell Center, where they got it mended. We drove a mile south of the village, and pitched our tents, and put on our wagon covers. Mr. Markham had some trouble with some fellows, who said that he owed them, but the truth is, they are persecuting him because he is a "Mormon". Many who left Kirtland had to steal away privately because of persecution. Their persecutors would swear out writs of attachments, and follow them, and attach their teams or goods, they would then have to stop and have a trial or pay an unjust demand; and sometimes both. Samuel Smith, a brother of the Prophet Joseph, had to secrete himself at Father's house a short time, to evade his pursuers. Mr. Markham put $116.00 into my hands for safe keeping, until he could get rid of his persecutors.

[June, 1838] 17th. Sunday again. Yesterday we got in company with four more teams from Kirtland. We all stopped in one place for the purpose of holding a meeting. They obtained a private house for the purpose, and Elder Sherwood preached. After meeting, they arranged some of the affairs in our camp. Instead of having three to preside, they chose Mr. David Dort and three to assist him as counselors. As there had been much envying, strife and contention in camp, they thought it best to have a general settling up, and confessions. There were considerable wrangling, but they succeeded in getting things fixed up by twelve o'clock at night. Not being a member of the church, of course I had nothing to say. I had tried to mind my own business thus far, and not meddle with theirs. But being a disinterested spectator I had many curious reflections. I thought some of them acted like children, in their pouting spells, and could not help to say in my heart, O! the folly and weakness of mankind, how full of selfishness.

September 6th. [1838] I went up to Far West. The militia of this county, who were all "Mormons" had been ordered to meet at this place, to take measures to defend themselves against the mob; who were still actively engaged in spreading false reports, to incite the Missourians, to arise and drive the "Mormons" from the state. The report was, that they had set this day to begin their driving. Their place of operations at this time is in Daviess County, joining Caldwell on the north, and which is very thinly settled. They were not yet bold enough to attack Caldwell County. A few of the mob gathered at Millport, on Grand River, but did not do any damage. The militia at Far West, were ordered not to leave that under penalty of the law, but to hold themselves as minutemen, and be ready at a moments warning, armed and equipped to repel the mob. Far West is situated on a high rolling prairie between Shoal Creek on the north, and Goose Creek on the south, which empties into Shoal Creek a short distance east of Far West. The houses are very scattering, and small, being chiefly built of hewed logs. The basement for the Temple is dug, and the corner stones were laid the 4th of July last. The town contains one printing press, one tavern, and a few small stores, and groceries. It will be a beautiful city, if it is every built up, as it is intended to be. The soil is excellent.

The following is from my Mother, who was living with David.

Ypsilanti Feb. 11th 1839.

Dear Husband and Children.

It gave me much joy to hear from you, to learn that your lives are all spared, and that you enjoy a good degree of health. That is more than I expected to hear, from the accounts in the papers, which you must know has caused me many a sorrowful hour by day, and by night. But I strove to give up, and be reconciled to Him, who rules all things. When the last was wrote you, I had a bad cold, it came on me when Charles was sick, it kept increasing with a violent cough, until I did not know but what it would be the means of ending my days. I got some medicine that helped my cough immediately, but I have been in a feeble state of health all winter, but not so bad but what I have done considerable sewing, and helped Harry some about house. It is better now than it has been before, since I was first taken. I have thought many a time that I should be glad if I was with you, but since the war broke out I have thought that I would be better off here. You have often told about that being a place of safety; and I thought at the time; little did you know about a place of safety, in this world.

Warren says that he is not a Mormon, but he is just as he always was. I can say pretty much the same. I do not know that my mind is changed much as to Mormonism. I talk of going to William Ferguson's in the spring. Warren as to your coming after me, I think you had better not; if I can get any way to go without. You will want all you can earn.

My Dear Son, I want to see you very much, and all the rest: but if we are not permitted to see each other again in this world, I would exhort you to put your trust in God, that you may not be deceived by the works of men. As for the Mormons, you must see that they have failed in many things; and I think that you are all disappointed by going there. I hope that you all will try to do the best you can. I know you must have trouble and trials. Give my respects to Sister and Brother Richardson, Franklin and Caroline Allen, and all other friends there. From your Mother; Irene Foote.

May 27th. [1841] I have worked some on the farm for Father and Isaac Ferguson, and some of the time not doing any thing on account of poor health. But I am now getting better. There has been a great revival of religion among the sects here and many profess to have got religion. I attended many of their meetings; but have seen too much of such nonsense, to have their threatening of hellfire etc. to have any effect on me. I cannot see any religion of the Bible in it. I read that God's house is the house of order; but these revival meetings are nothing but disorder and confusion. The ancient Apostles said, "Repent and be baptized for the remission of your sins and through the laying on of hands ye shall receive the Holy Ghost." But these preachers say, "Come to the anxious seat and we will pray for you, and you will get religion. No matter about baptism that is nonessential." I have read the scriptures too much to be deceived with such stuff. O may my mind ever be opened to understand the scriptures, and may I ever be led in the right way. Today and tomorrow I have to work on the young men under Albert Foster, a new convert who has lately got religion. His religion makes him act very foolish.

September 5th. [1841] I attended the Dunkard's Soup meeting. They had two large iron kettles fixed in a furnace in which they boiled beef and made soup. Bread was also furnished, and bread and soup was free to all. I attended their baptism as there were some to be baptized. They went down into the water, and the administrator immersed the candidate forward, that is face downward, first in the name of the Father, then secondly in the name of the Son and thirdly in the name of the Holy Ghost, plunging them under the water three successive times. At night they administered the ordinance of washing of feet. They had preaching both forenoon and afternoon. I stayed all night at a neighboring house in company with Moses Clawson and Ebenezer Clawson cousins.

October 1st. [1841] We started out about 2 o'clock in the morning—drove 10 miles and stopped and got breakfast. About sunrise it began to rain as we were passing through Carthage. This place is 18 miles from Nauvoo and is the county seat of Hancock County. It rained all day, and we did not get to Nauvoo until 10 o'clock at night. We stopped with Aunt Lowly Richardson, E. Allen's wife's mother, and my father's sister.

2nd. Conference commenced today. After meeting a deposit was made in the southeast corner stone of the Nauvoo House. A square hole had been chiseled in the large corner stone like a box. Any one had the privilege of putting in any little memento they wished to. I was standing very near the corner stone when Joseph Smith came up with the manuscript of the Book of Mormon and said that he wanted to put that in there, as he had had trouble enough with it. It was the size of common foolscap paper and about three inches thick. There were also deposited the Book of Doctrine and Covenants, a five cent piece, a ten [cent], a 25 [cent] and a 50 [cent] and a one dollar all American coin. A close fitting cover of stone had been prepared and was laid in cement and the wall built over it. The day was clear and cool.

3rd. [October 1841] Sunday. The weather is very pleasant. A large congregation assembled this forenoon. Joseph Smith preached on the subject of baptism for the dead. Among a great many other things, he said that the Saints could be baptized for any of their dead relatives, or friends, who had not been murderers. Such could not be baptized for. The Lord had other ways of dealing with murderers.

4th. This is the last day of conference. There has been a great deal of business transacted with regard to Church matters; and much good teaching. This afternoon as Joseph Smith was talking; all at once his countenance brightened up and he said, "Verily thus saith the Lord, Let there not be another general conference held until it is held in mine house."

6th. We started for home. The weather continues very pleasant.

March 17th. [1842] I have had a severe spell of sickness and have just got able to ride out a little. I am reduced to a mere skeleton, but thank God, and a kind Father and Mother, and my sister Almira, who watched over me day and night, I still live. After I was taken sick on Thursday night the 26th of last month I was deranged the most of the time. Sometimes I thought that I was a bundle of chair rounds bound up with a chord and was in great trouble for fear that some one would break the chord and let me fall to pieces. At other times I fancied that I was something else. When any one would speak to me I would come to my right minued [?] in this state until Saturday morning, when the disease seemed to settle on me for a long spell of sickness. It was the inflammation on my lungs. I now became very stupid—did not notice anything much, until Friday the 4th of March, I began to revive a little and for the first time began to realize my situation. I had not partaken of any food since I was taken sick. My reflections were these. "I have been a firm believer in the gospel as taught by the Latter Day Saints, ever since I first heard it. I have written many letters to my brothers and kinfolks proving from the scriptures that the gospel taught by the Saints was true, then why should I not step forward myself and be baptized for the remission of my sins that I may receive the Holy Ghost through the laying on of hands, and thereby obtain a knowledge for myself, and become more useful in building up the Kingdom of God on the earth." After these reflections, I made a covenant with God in my own mind, that if He would spare my life, I would serve Him the remainder of my days according to the best of my abilities.

I sent for two of the elders to administer to me by anointing me with oil and laying on of hands. The Lord heard our prayer and I began to amend. I was near dropping into the grave. Many who came in to see me thought that I would not recover. My father was very anxious for me, and exercised great faith in my behalf. His only hope among his sons was centered on me, to continue the work, that he had begun, after he had passed behind the veil. What then must have been his joy when I yielded myself up to the will of God. He knew that I had ever been a firm believer in the gospel, but at times had been fearful that I would be led astray through the influence of my young associates who did not believe in it. But these associates never had any influence over me to that effect. The fact is I believe that the principles of the gospel of Christ was born in me. I never needed any preaching to convince me of the truth of them. I believed the Bible and hence could not help but believe the gospel when I heard it. I now feel determined to be baptized as soon as I get strength sufficient, which I think will not be long as I am gaining fast.

24th. [March 1842] This is the day that I have appointed to go down into the waters of baptism and thereby fulfill the covenant I made to the Lord when I was near death's door. The meeting was at Elder Jacob Myers house about one mile from Father's. I walked down there and in company with Amos Kimmins, Franklin Allen, and his wife, Samuel Myers, and Lovina Myers, was baptized by Daniel A. Miller, President of this branch, between five and six o'clock P.M. The foregoing named persons, had been baptized before, and now felt to renew their covenants. As it was concluded to have an evening meeting I thought that I would stay to it. The wind blew up from the north very cool and in going home, I took cold.

Additional Information: Throughout his life Warren worked in many professions: farmer (he even kept his own bees), stage driver, school teacher, miller, postmaster, Justice of the Peace, a major in the Mormon Militia, civic leader. See http://wchsutah.org/people/warren-foote.php (04/11/2014).

And, as opposed to the Church as his mother was, she did eventually join, shortly before her death. His mother's name was Irene Lane Foote. She was the sister to the Methodist circuit minister, George Lane. It was this same George Lane that was one of the principle ministers responsible in creating the religious excitement at the time Joseph Smith was searching for the truth. It's also this same minister, according to Joseph's younger brother William, that caused Joseph to turn the Smith family Bible to James 1:5. This, more than anything, explains her antagonism to the Church for so many years.

Ebenezer Robinson (1816–1891)

Source: *The Return* 1–3 (1888–1890).

In May, 1835, went to Kirtland, Ohio, and obtained a situation in the Latter-day Saints' Church printing office, which was conducted under the firm name, of F. G. Williams and Company. The firm consisted of Joseph Smith, Jr., F. [Frederick] G. Williams and Oliver Cowdery. We engaged to work by the month and be boarded by our employers. When we went there we had no faith in their religion, as it was everywhere spoken against, but as we wrote to one of our sisters residing in the state of New York, we considered "Mormon money as good as anybody's money," and were very glad to secure the situation.

We boarded the first two months in the family of Oliver Cowdery, the second two months in the family of F. [Frederick] G. Williams, and the third two months in the family of Joseph Smith, Jr. We found them all very pious, good Christian people, asking a blessing at the table and all attended to family worship morning and evening. This we was glad to see, as we had been accustomed to it from our earliest childhood in our father's home.

We had made a profession of religion when about fifteen years of age, but had not joined any church, as we could not find any that taught the gospel as we read it in the new testament scriptures, and had so stated to our friends when importuned to join their church. We had been raised a Baptist of the strictest order of the sect, both parents belonging to that church, and a brother and two sisters having recently united with it, and one brother united with the Methodist church. We had also been importuned by a young friend belonging to the Presbyterian church, to join that church, our reply was, "they all had some parts of the gospel, but none had it all, and we would not join any church until we found one that had it all." We believe in faith and repentance and baptism by immersion, and the enjoyment of the gifts and blessings promised by our Savior as recorded in the last chapter of Mark; and a consistent daily walk as portrayed by our Savior in his Sermon on the Mount. We found a people there who, to our surprise, taught them all; and, to our understanding, practiced them.

The members of the Church there in that day all seemed to love one another, and take a deep interest in each other's welfare, and it was a pleasure to be with them. It seemed to us that if they met several times a day they would always greet each other with a hearty shake of the hand, and a "God bless you," and all seemed anxious to live according to the teachings of Christ.

All the other hands in the printing office were members of the Church, but none of them ever made any attempt at proselyting us. On one occasion when boarding at Joseph Smith's, he said to us, "When you are baptized I want to baptize you," on another occasion, as we were walking together after dinner, from his house to the printing office, he said to us, "you will help me build Zion, won't you?" do not recollect of making any reply at either time.

Our prejudices were such when we first went there, that when the elders coming into the office and speaking of their success in the ministry which they attributed to the power of truth, as presented by them, we remember to have momentarily stopped from our work, and of mentally saying: "Truth, what do you know about truth." It was not long, however, until we became satisfied we were with a people who not only taught, but more perfectly practiced the gospel lessons, than any people we had ever before known, and we began earnestly to look into the matter. Then for a short time, felt an anxiety to believe the old Calvinistic doctrine of election and reprobation in which we had been reared; reasoning thus, if that doctrine be true, and we should lead ever so pious, self-denying a life and be a reprobate, we would be consigned to the pit; whereas, on the other hand, if we were elected to be saved we could lead ever so free and easy a life and yet have salvation. But our heart revolted at the thought, and we dismissed it from our mind.

After having conclusively settled in our mind that the Calvinistic doctrine of election was not a safe one to risk the salvation of our soul upon, we then went to work in earnest, searching the scriptures, and praying fervently to our Heavenly Father to be pleased to show us the truth as it was with him, as it was the truth, and the truth only, that we wanted.

It was not long until our Heavenly Father condescended to manifest to us clearly, by his peaceful spirit, that the gospel, as set forth in the New Testament scriptures and Book of Mormon, which was taught by this people, was true. Straightway, upon receiving this testimony, we felt an intense desire to be baptized, but told no one our feelings.

At dinner that day, (October 16, 1835) Joseph Smith, Jr., finished his meal a little before the others at the table, and went and stood in the doorway (the door being open, it being a warm pleasant day), with his back to the door jamb, when we arose and went and stood before him, and looking him in the face said, "Do you know what I want?" when he replied, "No, without it is to go into the waters of Jordan." We told him that was what we wanted, when he said he would attend to it that afternoon. We then went to the printing office together, he to his council room which adjoined the room where we worked, and we to our work in the printing office. We worked until well on to the evening, feeling very anxious all the time, for it seemed that we could not live overnight without being baptized; after enduring it as long as we could, went to the door of their room, and gently opened it, (a thing we had never presumed to do before).

As soon as Mr. Smith saw us he said, "Yes, yes, brethren, Brother Robinson wishes to be baptized, we will adjourn and attend to that."

We repaired to the water, (the Chagrin River which flows through Kirtland) and, after a season of prayer, Brother Joseph Smith, Jr., baptized us by immersion, and as we arose from the water it seemed that everything we had on left us, and we came up a new creature, when we shouted aloud, "Glory to God." Our heart was full to overflowing, and we felt that we had born again in very deed, both of water and of the spirit.

In going up from the water Brother Joseph Smith said to the brethren, "I am not afraid of Brother Robinson ever denying the faith." We thank our Heavenly Father that a doubt of the truth of the glorious gospel of our Lord and Savior, Jesus Christ, which we then obeyed, has never found lodgement in this poor heart from that day to this (April 25, 1889), for one single moment. Our soul rejoices in it still, and we trust it will, by his grace assisting us, while our Heavenly Father gives us breath.

Additional Information: Ebenezer remained in the Church for some time, serving several missions. But with the death of the Prophet Joseph Smith, he united himself to Sidney Ridgon's Church of Christ in Pittsburgh, acting as Rigdon's counselor. He edited *The Messenger and Advocate of the Church of Christ.* With time though, he separated himself from Rigdon and joined the RLDS Church in 1855. But then, in 1863, he joined himself with David Whitmer's Church of Christ.

Part Seven

Misunderstanding Mormonism

For those that have been touched by the spirit of gospel principles and the power of the Book of Mormon—in any century since the re-establishment of The Church—whatever the opposition to the cause has had to say has gone largely unnoticed. These people realize what the presidents of the Church have taught: that those who spread lies and half-truths will have their day in the sun and then will be forgotten. The growth of the Church is proof of this. Opposition was intense in the early years of the Church, but yet, since day one, the Church has never looked back as far as growth.

In what year did the Church experience its greatest growth percentage? I don't think many would have to mull this over much to realize that 1830–1831 had, by far, the most significant percentage increase: 3111%. Today we continue to add two to three percent per year, which translates into a million additional Saints every three to four years. I don't doubt that anti-Mormon literature has had its effect, but it's a drop in the ocean in comparison to those that have accepted membership in the Lord's Church. And in certain ways, anti-Mormon literature has actually helped the cause in some instances. There was a time when Elder John Taylor expressed delight when a printer in Wales released the revelations in the Doctrine and Covenants. This saved him the time and cost associated with such a venture. On another occasion, when John Taylor was editing an LDS paper in New York City, a Bible society contacted him, making known their intensions to spread Bibles to the "Godless Mormons" throughout Utah Territory. Elder Taylor was all for the plan, his only demand was that the Bibles have good bindings.

The upcoming section includes the journal accounts of Sarah Studevant Leavitt and Anson Call, among others. Sarah Leavitt was all for the Gospel when it was first introduced to her; however, I include her account here because of her observation of what the papers of the day were saying about the Latter-day Saints. Anson Call didn't accept the Gospel with open arms as Sarah did, even though he knew it was the truth. After a spiritual manifestation he did join. But why did he hesitate? It likely had to do with the bad press that the Church was attracting at the time.

Concluding this part are two newspaper accounts of what the Saints could expect to read. One is by Truman Coe, written in 1835, and the other by William West, which was written in 1837. The stated intent of both articles is to educate those under the delusion of the Mormon faith. Again, I included these articles in this work to give an indication of what early Saints like Anson Call had to filter through in their conversion processes.

Sarah Studevant Leavitt (1798–1878)

Source: Autobiography (1798–c.1847). *History of Sarah Studevant Leavitt*, ed. Juanita L. Pulsipher, 1919.

I was born in the town of Lime, county of Grafton, New Hampshire [date torn off] and am now 76 years, seven months and 15 days old [September 4, 1798]. My father was Lemuel Studevant and my mother was Priscilla Tompson. My parents were very strict with their children, being descendants of the old pilgrims. They taught them every principle of truth and honor as they understood it themselves. They taught them to pray and read the Bible for themselves. My father had many books that treated on the principle of man's salvation and many stories that were very interesting and I took great pleasure in reading them. He was Dean of the Presbyterian Church. For years his house was open to all denominations, so his children had the privilege of hearing the interesting religious conversations, but as I had the privilege of reading the Bible for myself, I found that none of them understood the Bible as I did. I knew of no other way to understand it only as it read. The apostle said, "Though we or angels from heaven preach any other gospel than that which we preach, let him be accursed," and it was very evident to my understanding that they all came short of preaching the doctrine that Paul preached, but I was confident we should have the faith.

From childhood I was seriously impressed and desired very much to be saved from that awful hell I heard so much about. I believed in the words of the Savior, that said, "Ask and you shall receive." I prayed much and my prayers were sometimes answered immediately; this was before I made any pretensions to having any religion. When I was 18 years old, the Lord sent me a good husband. We were married at my father's house, March 6, 1817, in the town of Barton, county of Orleans, state of Vermont. The next June we moved to Canada, 15 miles from the Vermont line, into a very wicked place. They would swear and drink and play cards on Sunday and steal and do any wicked act their master, the devil, would lead them to. This was very different from what I was brought up to. My father would never suffer any profane language in his house. The next February I had a daughter born. She lived only 12 days. There were some things very strange connected with the birth of this child, which I do not think best to write, but I shall never forget, which I never shall know the meaning of until the first resurrection, when I shall clasp it again in my arms.

The next January I had another daughter born. When she was about six months old, I had a vision of the damned spirits in hell, so that I was filled with horror more than I was able to bear, but I cried to the Lord day and night until I got an answer of peace and a promise that I should be saved in the Kingdom of God that satisfied me. That promise has been with me through all the changing scenes of life ever since.

When I was getting ready for bed one night, I had put my babe into the bed with its father and it was crying. I dropped down to take off my shoes and stockings; I had one stocking in my hand. There was a light dropped down on the floor before me. I stepped back and there was another under my feet. The first was in the shape of a half moon and full of little black spots. The last was about an inch long and about a quarter of an inch wide. I brushed them with the stocking that was in my hand and put my hand over one of them to see if it would shine on my hand. This I did to satisfy others; as for myself, I knew that the lights were something that could not be accounted for and for some purpose. I did not know what until I heard the gospel preached in its purity. The first was an emblem of all the religions then on the earth. The half moon that was cut off was the spiritual gifts promised after baptism. The black spots were the defects you will find in every church throughout the whole world. The last light was the gospel preached by the angel flying through the midst of heaven and it was the same year and the same season of the year and I don't know but the same day that the Lord brought the glad news of salvation to Joseph Smith. It must have been a stirring time among the heavenly hosts, the windows of heaven having so long been closed against all communication with the earth, being suddenly thrown open. Angels were wending their way to earth with such a glorious message—a message that concerns everyone, both in heaven and earth. I passed through all this and not a neighbor knew anything of it, although I prayed so loud that my husband was afraid they would all hear me.

After this, there were two of his aunts who came in and commenced talking about being slighted in not being invited to a quilting. I had no relish for any such talk and said nothing. They saw that I made no comment. Being astonished that I was so still, they asked me what I thought about it. I told them I didn't know or care anything about it, and all I cared for was to know and do the will of God. This turned the conversation in the right direction. My telling my experience to these women and the effect it had on their minds was probably of much good, as they spread the news through the neighborhood. The result was, the whole neighborhood was convinced that the manner in which they had spent their time was wrong and instead of taking the name of God in vain, they cried to him for mercy. In short, the whole course of their former lives was abandoned. There were some exceptions, for the leopard cannot change his spots; how then, can men do good that are accustomed to do evil, so says the prophet.

But there was a minister who came from the states and formed a church, called the Baptist, which I joined because I wanted to be baptized by immersion. I had been sprinkled when an infant, but as I said before, I did not believe in any church on earth, but was looking forward to a time when the knowledge of God would cover the earth, and that glorious time is rolling, all glory to the Lord. I lived very watchful and prayerful, never neglecting my prayers, for I felt that I was entitled to no blessing unless I asked for them and I think so yet.

We took a Freewill Baptist paper that I thought always told the truth, but there were a number of columns in this paper concerning a new sect. It had a prophet that pretended he talked with God. They had built a thing they called a meetinghouse, a huge mass of rock and wood, on the shores of Lake Cryenth (I am not sure of the spelling of this word) to make the blue waters of the lake blush for shame. In this Joe would go talk, he said, with the Lord and come out and tell them what the Lord said. But if I should go on and tell all the lies in that paper, how they healed the sick and managed their affairs, it would be too much for me. If you ever read the Arabian Night tales you might guess of what importance they were, for I could compare them to nothing else. No person of common sense would believe a word of it, and yet they wrote it for truth, thinking that would hinder Mormonism from spreading. But in this the devil overshot himself for they were too big lies for anyone to believe.

But I will go on with my experience. I had a place that I went every day for secret prayers. My mind would be carried away in prayer so that I knew nothing of what was going on around me. It seemed like a cloud was resting down over my head. And if that cloud would break there was an angel that had a message for me or some new light. If the cloud would break, there would be something new and strange revealed. I did not know that it concerned anyone but myself. Soon after this one of my husband's sisters came in and after spending a short time in the house, she asked me to take a walk with her. She had heard the gospel preached by a Mormon and believed it and been baptized. She commenced and related the whole of Joseph's vision and what the Angel Moroni had said the mission he had called him to. It came to my mind in a moment that this was the message that was behind that cloud, for me and not for me only, but for the whole world, and I considered it of more importance than anything I had ever heard before, for it brought back the ancient order of things and laid a foundation that could be built upon that was permanent; a foundation made by Him that laid the foundation of the earth, even the Almighty God; and he commanded his people to build up the kingdom of God upon the foundation he had laid, and notwithstanding the heathen raged and Satan mustered all his forces against the work; it has gone onward and upward for more than 40 years, and will continue until the work is finished.

I read the Book of Mormon, the Doctrine and Covenants, and all the writings I could get from the Latter-day Saints. It was the book of Doctrine and Covenants that confirmed my faith in the work. I knew that no man, nor set of men, that could make such a book or would dare try from any wisdom that man possessed. I knew it was the word of God and a revelation from heaven and received it as such. I sought with my whole heart a knowledge of the truth and obtained a knowledge that never has nor never will leave me.

The next thing was to gather with the Saints. I was pondering over in my heart how it was possible for such a journey with what means we could muster. We had a good farm, but could not get much for it, but the voice of the Spirit said, "Come out of Babylon, O my people, that you be not partakers of her plagues." From the time the voice spoke so loud, clear and plain to my understanding, I knew the way would be open for us to gather with the Saints. For the Lord never gives a commandment to man but what he gives them a chance to obey. From this time we set out in earnest and were ready to start with the rest of the company July 20, 1835. The company was made up of the Leavitt family, Mother Sarah Shannon Leavitt and her children, consisting of 23 souls. Franklin Chamberlain, her oldest son-in-law, took the lead. He did not belong to the Church, but his wife did.

We had a prosperous journey of 800 miles to Kirtland, Ohio. I had no chance to be baptized and join the Church until I got there. My daughter, Louisa, and myself and some others were baptized at this place and were confirmed.

Additional Information: "Sarah had a beautiful way with words. Listen to the following: 'To write the love of God … would drain the ocean, though the sea was ink, and the earth paper and every stick a pen and every man a scribe. When I try to praise Him in beauty, honor and magnify the name of God, I find I have no language at my command that will do justice to the case, but when I lay aside this weak, frail body I expect to praise Him in beauty and holiness.'"

See *History of Sarah Studevant Leavitt*, ed. Juanita Leavitt Pulsipher (1969), 29.

John Murdock (1792–1871)

Source: Journal (1792–1864). Typescript, BYU Harold B. Lee Library.

Being thirty years old. In my travelling I came to this place this year where I abode nine years; and now I took an active part in carrying on meetings with the Baptists for awhile. But some misunderstanding taking place between me and some of the members, and finding they held so strongly to Calvinistic Doctrine which I did not believe, and finding their walk not to agree with their profession, I withdrew myself from them and stood about two years aloof from all religious sects and my wife in company with me; (for I had married my wife Julia being the eldest daughter of Orice and Phebe Clapp of Mentor of Geauga County, Ohio. She was born February 23rd, A.D. 1796. We were married December 14th, 1823, I being 31 years old and she being 27 years old; she bore me six children as follows: Orrice C., December 24th, 1824. John R., September 13th, 1825. Phebe, March 10th, 1828. An infant we buried September 1829. Joseph S. and Julia, April 30th A.D. 1831 and my wife died six hours after their birth, and Joseph Smith, the Prophet, took my two infants to bring up) during which time I frequently attended Methodist meetings and was frequently invited to preach to them. I did so and always spoke according to the light I had; and when I did not please them I would have to be silent among them awhile; and I could not agree with them.

I kept searching the scriptures and looking to find a people that lived according to them, but could not find such a people. At length word came to me that a people had risen up that were baptizing for the remission of sins, and promised any person remission of sins that would be baptized and that they had caught a whole Baptist Church in Mentor, and they would receive a drunkard or any profane person. I reasoned with myself on the subject and said it was impossible that they should have caught that whole Baptist Church in such a gross error all at one haul; but said I, they have found something in the scriptures that the rest of the religious world does not have any understanding of, and I sat me down with my Bible in my hand and opened to the 3rd chapter of John's testimony and read the words of the Savior, "Except a man be born again he cannot see the Kingdom of Heaven; and, again, except a man be born of water and the Spirit he cannot enter into the Kingdom of Heaven." I queried what it was to be born of water. I concluded being born of the Spirit was to receive the gift of the Holy Ghost, but to be born of water I did not understand. I said the evangelist does not make it plain and I must see what the practice of the Apostles were [was] in receiving members into the Church; and that will explain the being born of water.

Accordingly, I turned to the 2nd chapter of Acts of the Apostles and found after Peter had preached Jesus and him crucified, the truth pricked them in the heart, and I concluded they were born again, so they could [see] the Kingdom of Heaven and desired to know how to get into it agreeing with 1st Peter, 1st chapter, 23rd verse—being born again not of corrupting deeds but of incorruptible, by the word of God which liveth and abideth forever. They were born of the word and the word showed them the Kingdom of Heaven, and they cried out to know what they should do that they might enter into the Kingdom of Heaven. Peter told them to repent and be baptized, everyone, in the name of Jesus Christ for the remission of sins; this was being born of water, I thought, and ye shall receive the gift of the Holy Ghost; and this was being born of the Spirit; I thought, and I was so sensibly struck with the truth that I said to my wife Julia, "Here is a truth that the religious world has not seen." I read it to her and she saw it and embraced it with me. I then read the Acts of the Apostles through and found many facts agreeing with the idea; also other parts of scripture agreeing therewith.

About two weeks after, my wife's brother, Thomas Clapp, came to see us being armed with many passages of scriptures to convince me of the late discovered truth; for he was among the late converts, at Mentor. I sat and heard his story, and found him to be precisely in the same tract with myself, and understood the scriptures I did; which was the doctrine of the new sect, known by the Campbellites. It caused me to rejoice believing that I had at last found a people that believed the scriptures as they had. I was much engaged about this time searching the scriptures and many times after retiring to my bed, my mind would be exercised to that degree, that it would not be satisfied till I would get up, light my candle, and read my Bible an hour or two, and then I would go to my bed and sleep sweetly.

I, finding the people called the Campbellites, so well agreeing with my feelings, and they professed to be in search of truth as I was, therefore I united with them. I think it was in the year A.D. 1827. Elder Sidney Rigdon was one of the leaders in this part of the country; and I believe that he, with many others were honestly seeking for truth, for awhile; but when the truth came, because it did not come as they wanted, they rejected it. I continued a member with them, about 3 years, I think; but at length finding their principal leader, Alex [Alexander] Campbell, with many others, denying the gift and power of the Holy Ghost, I began to think of looking [for] me a new home. I had firmly became [become] convinced that all the sects were out of the way; so much so that I asked Brother B. Covey, supposing all the different churches to be out of the way, as we believe they are, and we find the ancient manner of building up the Church according to the scriptures, as we believe we have (for by reading we found the ancient manner of building up the Church was by baptizing for the remission of sins and laying on hands for the gift of the Holy Ghost.) Where is the man to commence the work of baptizing? Or where shall he get his authority? Can he go to those who are out of the way and obtain authority? I told him no. If they are out of the way as we believe; they have lost all authority, and I said to him, the only way the authority can be obtained is, the Lord must either send an angel to baptize the first man, or he must give a special command to someone to baptize another.

About one month after this interview with Brother Covey, word came to me that four men had arrived at Kirtland from the state of New York, who were preaching, baptizing, and building up the church after the ancient order; it was one Sunday morning as I was going to attend an appointment to preach, that I was informed on this; I was also told that Elder Rigdon, with many others of the Campbellite Church, were baptized by them. I replied to my informer that it was an insinuation of the devil but I was immediately checked in my feelings, and I made no more harsh expressions respecting them. I attended my appointment and got along with my meeting as easy as I could and went home, and went to reading my Bible and frequently heard of the new preachers until Thursday the same week. I went to see for myself, a distance of about twenty miles. I heard the sayings of many people by the way, some for the new preachers, and some against, but I observed the Spirit that stimulated those for, and those against. I met Squire Waldo, who was a Campbellite [who?] was bitterly opposed. He tried to have me take another road, and not go to Kirtland, but I told him I was of age, and the case was an important one, of life, and death, existing between me and my God, and I must act for myself, for no one can act for me. I rode about three miles further and met another man of the same order, I had about the same kind of discourse with him and passed on.

And arrived at father Isaac Morley's about dark, and was soon introduced to those four men from New York, and presented with the Book of Mormon; I now said within myself, I have items placed before me that will prove to me whether it be of God or not viz: four men professing to be servants of the most high God, authorized to preach the gospel, and practice the ordinances thereof, and build up the Church after the ancient order; and having a book professing to have come forth by the power of God, containing the fullness of the gospel; I said if it be so their walk will agree with their profession, and the Holy Ghost will attend their ministration of the ordinances, and the Book of Mormon will contain the same plan of salvation as the Bible. I was sensible that such a work must come forth, but the question with me was, are these men that are to commence the work. I did not ask a sign of them by working a miracle, by healing a sick man, by raising a dead man, or, by casting out a devil; only I desired to know whether the Spirit would attend their ministration if the Book of Mormon was not true, neither if they were not sent forth by God. Accordingly, that night was held the first confirmation meeting that was held in Ohio. And I said within myself it is a good time for me. For thought I, this night must prove it to be true, or false; I did not find out respecting the meeting till about ten o'clock at night. And at that time they had all left but three men; and I found they wanted to go to the meeting, and did not want those in, that had not been baptized. I said to them go, for if you wish to be alone, I do not blame you. The case is one of importance. They went and I stayed alone, and read the Book of Mormon.

During the evening previous to the meeting, a Nathan Goodwell, a Campbellite came and conversed with Elder Oliver Cowdery for he was the principal one of the four, and I watched the Spirit of each one of them in their conversation, and I found that Goodwell bore down with warmth, whereas Cowdery wished not for contention, and endeavored to evade controversy, and I, seeing this, spake to Goodwell as follows, saying, Brother Goodwell I have come to Kirtland, not to contend either for or against these men, for I do not know whether they are true or false, but I have come to see what they have brought. I want to converse with you if you are willing. I said I had some questions to ask you. He said he would try to answer them.

1st, Do you not think that you and I are possessed of the form of godliness? He replied, yes. I said, you and I agree on that point.

2nd, Do you think we have the power of godliness? He stammered at the question, but concluded we had. I told him that I doubted it. But, said I, we will try it by the word, as follows. Mark 16th chapter, 14th verse, to the end of the chapter, "Afterward he appeared unto the eleven as they sat at meat, and upbraided them with their unbelief and hardness of heart, because they believed not them which had seen him after he was risen. And he said unto them, Go ye unto all the world, and preach the gospel to every creature. He that believeth and is baptized shall be saved; but he that believeth not shall be damned. And these signs shall follow them that believe; In my name shall they cast out devils; they shall speak with new tongues; They shall take up serpents; and if they drink any deadly thing, it shall not hurt them: they shall lay hands on the sick and they shall recover. So then after the Lord had spoken unto them, he was received up into heaven, and sat on the right hand of God. And they went forth, and preached everywhere, the Lord working with them, and confirming the word with signs following. Amen."

Luke 24th chapter, 49th verse. "And, behold, I send the promise of my Father upon you: but tarry ye in the city of Jerusalem, until ye be endued with power from on high." Acts 1st chapter, 8th verse, "But ye shall receive power, after that the Holy Ghost is come upon you: and ye shall be witnesses unto me both in Jerusalem and in all Judaea, and in Samaria, and unto the uttermost part of the earth." Verse 12th. "Then returned they unto Jerusalem, from the mount called Olivet, which is from Jerusalem a sabbath day's journey. And when they were come in, they went into an upper room, where abode both Peter, James, John, Andrew, Philip, Thomas, Bartholemew, Matthew, James, the son of Alpheus, Simon Zelotes and Judas, the brother of James. These all contained with one accord in prayer, and supplication with the women, and Mary, the mother of Jesus, and with his brethren." Chapter 2nd, verse 1st [through 5th]. "And when the day of Pentecost was fully come, they were all with one accord in one place. And suddenly there came a sound from heaven, as of a rushing mighty wind, and it filled all the house where they were sitting. And there appeared unto them cloven tongues like as of fire, and it sat upon each of them. And they were all filled with the Holy Ghost, and began to speak with other tongues, as the Spirit gave them utterance. And there were dwelling in Jerusalem Jews, devout men, out of every nation under heaven. Now when this was noised abroad the multitude came together, and were confounded because that every man heard them repeat in his own language; and they were all amazed and marvelled, saying one to another, Behold, are not all these which speak Galilaeans and now hear we every man, in our own tongue, wherein we were born."

Matthew, 28th chapter and Mark 16th chapter, say the Apostles were to preach the gospel to every creature in all the world. Luke 24th chapter, 49th verse and Acts 1st chapter, 8th verse say they were to receive power to do so, after the Holy Ghost was come upon them, and the power of the Holy Ghost, on the servant of God, is the power of godliness, for there is no man but a godly man that can profess that power with God. The history says they tarried in Jerusalem, and were engaged in prayer, till the day of Pentecost was fully come, at which time the Holy Ghost came on them, and it qualified them to preach the gospel and hear testimony to every creature which they could not do, till they received power of God to speak in other tongues. Paul said the churches which he had built up among the gentiles were not behind in any of these gifts of God.

And in 2nd Timothy, 3rd chapter, 5th verse, that in the last days men should arise, having a form of godliness but denying the power thereof and he says from such turn away. Now in denying the power of godliness they will deny the gift of tongues and other gifts by the power of the Holy Ghost, and as for myself, I mean to turn away from them. He was confused, and could not answer.

I read till it was late and went into Father Morley's chamber to bed and had not been long in bed, before they returned, and some half dozen or more came into the same house, and as soon as they came into the house, although I was in bed up [in the] chamber, the spirit of the Lord rested on me, witnessing to me of the truth of the work. I could no longer rest in bed but got up and went down and found Elder Rigdon among the number, and he said to me I might go back to bed, for he would not talk to me that night, but I sat in a chair and conversed with them, and I found they appeared very tender in their feelings and I retired to bed again. I could not help secretly rejoicing on the occasion. The next morning I conversed with about half a dozen men separately who had been confirmed in the meetinghouse the night before. I found their testimony agreed on the subject that there was a manifestation of the spirit attended the ministration of the ordinance of laying on hands, and I found the items placed before me, that I before noticed, all testified that it was of God.

About ten o'clock that morning, being November 5th, 1830, I told the servants of the Lord that I was ready to walk with them into the water of baptism. Accordingly, Elder P. [Parley] P. Pratt baptized me in the Chagrin River and the spirit of the Lord sensibly attended the ministration, and I came out of the water rejoicing and singing praises to God, and the Lamb. An impression sensibly rested on my mind that cannot, by me, be forgotten. It appeared to me that notwithstanding all the profession of religion that I had previously made and all that I had done, that by my act of now being baptized I had just escaped a horrible pit of destruction. This was the third time I had been immersed, but I never before felt the authority of the ordinance, but I felt it this time and felt as though my sins were forgiven. I continued with the brethren till Sunday at which time they preached in Mayfield and baptized a number, and on Sunday evening they confirmed about thirty. I was one of the number. Elder Oliver Cowdery was administrator. I was also ordained an elder; and it was truly a time of the outpouring of the spirit. I know the spirit rested on me as it never did before and others said they saw the Lord and had visions.

Additional Information: John Murdock mentions in this account his brother-in-law, Thomas Clapp and his wife Julia Clapp. The land that the Columbus Ohio Temple is constructed on belonged to Abner Clapp, the uncle of both Julia and Thomas.

See Chad S. Hawkins, *The First 100 Temples* (Eagle Gate: Salt Lake City, 2001), 164.

Joel Hills Johnson (1802–1882)

Source: Autobiography (1802–1868). Typescript, Church Archives and BYU Harold B. Lee Library (excerpts).

In the year 1829 I invented a machine for striking shingles from a block at one blow, being the original inventor of this principle. I sold many rights which helped me considerable, but being honest myself and supposing everyone else to be the same, I soon was swindled out of the largest part of my rights, and being highly disappointed and discouraged on account of my misfortunes, I concluded to leave the home of my youth and seek an asylum among strangers. Accordingly in the fall of 1830 I left home for the state of Ohio, and after traveling the state mostly over to find a location for my family, I found an old acquaintance of my boyhood in the town of Amherst, Lorain County, by the name of John Clay, who invited me to move my family in to his house and join him in building a saw mill. I accordingly entered company with him and went to work. I sent for my family who arrived in the month of January. By the first of April, 1831, we had a saw mill nearly half completed.

About this time there was considerable excitement about the Mormons at Kirtland where there had been a branch of the church built up, and Joseph Smith had arrived at that place and held a conference and was sending out elders through the country; and many evil reports were in circulation concerning them which most of the people believed to be true. I obtained the Book of Mormon and read it. Some was filled with prejudice on account of the evil reports in circulation that I returned it before I had read it through. But soon there arrived two Mormon elders in the neighborhood by the names of Harvey Whitlock and Edson Fuller who preached upon the first principles of the Gospel, treating upon faith, repentance, and baptism for the remission of sins with the laying on of hands for the gift of the Holy Ghost, with signs following the believer, etc. This preaching filled me with astonishment, it being the first discourse that I had ever heard that corresponded with the New Testament. But when they spoke of the Book of Mormon, they made it equal to the Bible. But my prejudice was so great against the book, that I would not receive their testimony. I heard them twice and concluded to stay at home, but they continued preaching in the vicinity and soon commenced baptizing. In a few days Lyman Wright, Samuel H. Smith, and others came to their assistance, and in a few weeks they baptized about fifty in the vicinity.

All this time I had kept at home except for the first two meetings. My wife, who had always been a strong Methodist, had a desire at this time to attend their meetings which were held every day, and I gave my consent, for I never would abridge one's liberty in religious matters. She attended several meetings and began to believe in the work, and myself having searched the Bible daily while staying at home, began to think that work might possibly be true. I therefore concluded to adhere to the advice of Paul "to prove all things and hold fast the good." I accordingly came to the conclusion to take my Bible in hand and attend all their meetings and investigate and subject thoroughly with prayer for Divine direction which I did for several days, comparing their preachings with the scriptures which brought me to the following conclusions: Firstly, that as all Protestant sects had sprung from the Church of Rome, they have no more authority to administer in the ordinances of the Church of Christ than the Church of Rome had, and if she was the mother of harlots, they must consequently be her daughters; therefore, none of them could be called the Church of Christ. Secondly, that a supernatural power did attend the Mormon Church, and it had risen independent of all denominations; therefore, its origin must be from Heaven or Hell. Thirdly, that it is unreasonable to suppose that God would suffer the devil to bring forth a work with the gifts and blessings of the ancient Church of Christ corresponding with that which he has promised to bring forth in the last days for the gathering of the House of Israel and by that means lead astray all the honest men of the earth. And fourthly, that as the principles taught in the Book of Mormon corresponded with the Bible and doctrine of the Church was the same that was taught by Christ and his apostles with signs following the believer, I concluded that the work was of God and embraced with all my heart and soul, and was baptized on the first day of June 1831, by Elder Sylvester Smith. My wife had been baptized a few days previous.

Additional Information: Joel H. Johnson actually wrote the text to the hymn, "High on a Mountain Top."

Anson Call (1810–1890)

Source: Autobiography (1838–1839). Typescript, BYU Harold B. Lee Library.

My father joined the Church of Latter-day Saints in 1831. My father and family belonged to the Methodist Church. He was baptized by John Murdock. Elders frequently preached in our town, Brigham Young, John P. Greene, Almon W. Babbitt and others.

Their preaching created much excitement in our town but had little effect for nearly three years. It was a constant annoyance to my feelings. I became dissatisfied with all denominations and myself. In the elders' passing through our country, they frequently stopped at my house, and in discussing with them the principles of the gospel, they would cuff me about like an old pair of boots. I came to the conclusion that the reason for my being handled so easily was because I did not understand the Bible and the Book of Mormon.

I resolved to prepare myself for the conflict by investigating the two books. I accordingly furnished myself with the Book of Mormon. I then commenced the Book of Mormon and the Bible, compared the two and read my Bible from Genesis right through, praying and searching diligently for six months. When I finished the two books I became a firm believer in the Book of Mormon. I was then taught by the spirit to obey the principles of the gospel. My feelings were not known by any but my wife. I was proud and haughty and to obey the gospel was worse than death. I labored under those feelings for three months, becoming at times almost insane.

To be called a Mormon, I thought, was more than I could endure. I lamented that my lot was cast in this dispensation. My dreams and my meditations made me miserable. I at last covenanted before the Lord that if he would give me confidence to face the world in Mormonism, I would be baptized for the remission of my sins; before I arose from my knees the horrors of my mind were cleared; I feared no man, no set of men.

The next day I went to the Methodist meeting and declared unto them the truth of Mormonism. I told them I should obey it as soon as I could get to Kirtland. I accordingly went immediately there and was baptized by William Smith, Joseph's brother. My wife accompanied me. I was confirmed in the Kirtland Temple by David Whitmer.

I immediately returned to Madison and was then prepared to tell my Methodist brethren many things they were strangers to. I improved every opportunity in their meetings, class meetings not excepted. There were my brothers, my mother and my schoolmates. I was much desirous that they should obey the gospel with me.

Additional Information: Joseph Smith prophesied to Anson Call, during the summer of 1842, that Anson would go with the Saints to the Rocky Mountains and would be instrumental in establishing numerous settlements in the west. Anson fulfilled this prophesy during his life. He was influential in establishing a number of settlements in central and southern Utah as well as in Nevada.

See https://www.lds.org/ensign/2001/07/anson-call-man-of-action?lang=eng (04/11/2014).

Truman Coe

Source: "Mormonism," *The Ohio Observer* (Hudson), 11 August 1836.

Dear Sir: Having been for the last four years located in Kirtland, on the Western Reserve, I have thought proper to make some communication to the public in relation to the Mormons, a sect of Religious Fanatics, who are collected in this town. This service I have considered as due to the cause of humanity, as well as to the cause of truth and righteousness. What I have to communicate shall be said in the spirit of candor and Christian charity.

Mormonism, it is well known, originated with Joseph Smith in the town of Manchester, adjoining Palmyra, in the state of New York. Smith had previously been noted among his acquaintances as a kind of Juggler, and had been employed in digging after money. He was believed by the ignorant to possess the power of second sight, by looking through a certain stone in his possession. He relates that when he was 17 years of age, while seeking after the Lord he had a nocturnal vision, and a wonderful display of celestial glory. An angel descended and warned him that God was about to make an astonishing revelation to the world, and then directed him to go to such a place, and after prying up a stone he should find a number of plates of the color of gold inscribed with hieroglyphics, and under them a breastplate, and under that a transparent stone or stones which was the Urim and Thummim mentioned by Moses. The vision and the command were repeated four times that night and once on the following day. He went as directed by the angel, and pried up the stone under which he discovered the plates shining like gold, and when he saw them his cupidity was excited, and he hoped to make himself rich by the discovery, although thus highly favored by the Lord. But for his sordid and unworthy motive, when he attempted to seize hold of the plates, they eluded his grasp and vanished, and he was obliged to go home without them. It was not till four years had elapsed, till he had humbled himself and prayed and cast away his selfishness that he obtained a new revelation and went and obtained the plates.

The manner of translation was as wonderful as the discovery. By putting his finger on one of the characters and imploring divine aid, then looking through the Urim and Thummim, he would see the import written in plain English on a screen placed before him. After delivering this, he would again proceed in the same manner and obtain the meaning of the next character, and so on till he came to a part of the plates which were sealed up, and there was commanded to desist: and he says he has a promise from God that in due time he will enable him to translate the remainder. This is the relation as given by Smith. A man by the name of [Martin] Harris, of a visionary turn of mind, assisted in the translation, and afterwards Oliver Cowdery. By the aid of Harris's property, the book was printed; and it is affirmed by the people of that neighborhood, that at first his motives were entirely mercenary,—a mere money speculation. The book thus produced, is called by them The Book of Mormon; and is pretended to be of the same Divine Inspiration and authority as the Bible. The Mormons came in Kirtland about six years ago; being taught by their leaders that this was one of the stakes of Zion—the eastern borders of the promised land. Not long after their arrival in Kirtland, a revelation was obtained that the seat and center of Zion was in Jackson county, in the western part of Missouri; and thither a multitude of them repaired, with Smith at their head. Soon after they were routed and expelled from the county by the infidels, and many of them returned to Kirtland. There they have been gathering their converts from various parts of the United States, until their present number probably amounts to upwards of one thousand: besides the transient companies of pilgrims who come here from the east to inquire the way to Zion, and then pass on to Missouri.

They have built a huge stone [Kirtland] temple in this town, fifty feet high, and 60 by 80 on the ground, at an expense of $40,000. On the front is this inscription, "The House of the Lord, built by the Latter-day Saints." The lower story is the place of worship, the middle for the school of the prophets, and the upper for an academical school; a distinguished professor of Hebrew is their teacher. He is now giving his second course, with about one hundred in each class.

While I am exposing these palpable impositions of the apostles of Mormonism, candor obliges me to say, that many of the common people are industrious, good neighbors, very sincerely deceived, and possibly very sincere Christians. They seem to delight in the duty of prayer, and the services of devotion, and their zeal goes far beyond any thing seen among sober Christians. Some are enterprising and intelligent, conversant with the bible, and fond of reading: and here,

I apprehend, many who have heard of them only by common report, are mistaken; supposing them all to be ignorant and degraded, and beneath the notice of all respectable people. The prevalence of religious delusion is not to be attributed so much to mere ignorance, as to the structure and prejudices and pernicious habits of the mind, a predisposition to be captivated with anything that is new or wonderful.

It is furthermore proper to notice that this religious sect have been slandered, and belied, and persecuted beyond measure. We entirely disapprove of those violent measures which have been taken with them in Missouri and some other places; 1st, because it is an outrage upon inalienable rights—all men justly claiming to be protected in the enjoyment of life, liberty, and the pursuit of happiness; and 2nd, because it is unwise; persecution being the most effectual way to build up fanatics in error and delusion. But since there is a certain class in every community who are predisposed to embrace any wild delusion which chances to meet them, and since many such have already been deceived and lured away to Kirtland and to Zion and have been disappointed and distressed, and reduced to poverty and want; and, moreover, since there are now many converts abroad who are looking to this place with longing eyes, as to a land flowing with milk and honey, and expecting, when they find the means of getting here, to bid farewell to all earthly sorrow, we think the world have a right to know the state of things among them. Many of them live in extreme indigence. They suffer accumulated evils by crowding a multitude of poor people together, when, by a wider distribution, they might have better means of supplying their wants. Some of them are wealthy, and they have purchased 3 or 4000 acres of land in different parts of this town. A grotesque assemblage of hovels and shanties and small houses have been thrown up wherever they could find a footing; but very few of all these cabins would be accounted fit for human habitations.

About the first of May, 1834, a company [Zion's Camp] of armed men from this place, about 100 in number, by command of Joseph, commenced a crusade to Missouri, to expel the infidels of Zion, and to reinstate their brethren into their possessions; at the same time he assured them by a revelation from heaven, that the expedition would succeed and the object be attained. When these gallant knights-errand arrived in Missouri, they were met by some of the constituted authorities and warned to desist; and Joseph very prudently had a revelation that the war was at an end. After spending the hottest part of the season on this long tedious pilgrimage of 2000 miles, having suffered great hardships, and numbers having been swept off by the cholera, they returned in straggling companies to Kirtland. Those of them who remained here during the campaign, were required to work one day in each week on the temple; and the poor females were instructed to part with even the necessaries of life in aid of the same object. They looked forward to the completion of the Temple as a Grand Era, when Christ would descend and dwell among them, and commence his reign on earth. These burdens are severely felt by the poor people among them, and can only be sustained by the unconquerable strength of their faith.

Last summer a man came to Kirtland and brought among the Mormons four Egyptian mummies. The exhibition exactly struck their fancy. All the Mormons flocked to see the wonderful sight; and Joseph deciphered some of the hieroglyphics, and made known in writing the name and character and antiquity of some of the mummies; this was an additional proof of his divine inspiration. The man continued with them a week; and then a command was given them to purchase the whole, which they did for $2400. The mummies were soon sent out for exhibition by one of their apostles, but being unsuccessful, he brought them back to Kirtland, and threw them aside. There is reason to believe, that many who come here with high expectations, have met with sore disappointment. They expected to find everything in apostolic order; but instead of this, they have found a whiskey selling tavern, a pugnacious prophet, and an inhospitable people. Some poor, families, after long journeys to see this Promised Land, have met with a cold repulse; have been compelled to sleep out of doors, and to remain in a community the most unfavorable to get a livelihood, and under a spiritual hierarchy, who bind heavy burdens grievous to be borne, but will not touch them with one of their fingers.

The Mormons to a man all abhor priests, and priestcraft, and societies, and the whole system of religious institutions among established churches; and yet they themselves are the most obsequious and abject slaves to the spiritual rule of their leaders. All their affairs, small and great, are directed by special revelation. By a miserable attempt to ape the language and style of scripture, they clothe their commands with the authority of heaven; and the people have nothing to do but to hear and obey. If the prophet demands their money for the Lord's treasury, he can have it by uttering a Thus saith the Lord. By these sacrifices, they give what among selfish men would be called a pretty good proof of sincerity at least. Thus it happens, that those who complain loudest of priestcraft, are the most woefully priestridden of all men.

In regard to their religious sentiments, the fundamental principle of Mormonism is, that God continues to hold intercourse with the saints on earth by visions and revelations, as freely and familiarly as he has done in any age of the world. That the true church have the same power to cast out devils, to speak with new tongues, to take up serpents, to drink poison unhurt, and to recover the sick by laying on of hands. They make great use of the declaration of our Savior in Mark xvi. 17, 18, and strenuously contend that the promise applies to all that believe in every age.

They contend that the God worshipped by the Presbyterians and all other sectarians is no better than a wooden god. They believe that the true God is a material being, composed of body and parts; and that when the Creator formed Adam in his own image, he made him about the size and shape of God himself. They believe in the final restoration of all men except apostate Mormons. They blaspheme against the Holy Ghost, and can never have forgiveness, neither in this world, neither in the world to come. Their avowed object is to restore Christianity to its primeval purity. In the true style of fanaticism they regard themselves as the exclusive favorites of heaven; and the whole religious world as natural brute beasts that know nothing. After the example of our Savior they have recently ordained and commissioned twelve apostles and seventy elders, to go throughout this heathen country and to give a final call to repent and be baptized and believe in Mormonism before the wicked are cut off. The people of this region are viewed by them as standing in the place of Chorasm and Bethsaida, and Capernaum, unwilling to believe, in spite of all the mighty works they have tried to perform. They are habitually pretending to speak in tongues, and to the working of miracles, but nobody can have any evidence of these wonders but those who have Mormon eyes and Mormon ears.

When they first came to Kirtland, Mr. Rigdon joined them, and a few families followed in his train; but otherwise of the former inhabitants, scarce a single conversion has happened since. The fact is that the people are well assured that all their pretensions to miraculous gifts of every kind, are a sheer imposition. But whenever any miracle fails, they have a convenient salve at hand to account for the failure; that is the want of faith: a most impudent and officious intruder, always ready at hand to nullify all their pious efforts, and to render them weak and feeble as other men. Instances frequently occur which may serve as examples of their power of healing. A young man lying on a bed of sickness, sent after Smith and his elders to come and heal him. After praying over him, anointing him with oil in the name of the Lord, he commanded the disease to depart; pronounced him healed, and ordered him to rise and walk. Stimulated by the circumstances and by high expectation, the youth rose up and attempted to walk; but presently becoming faint, by the help of bystanders he betook himself to the bed again, and grew worse. They of course imputed his sudden relapse to the failure of his faith. He then sent for the regular physician, and by faithful means he recovered. Another late instance was a young woman lying at the point of death with the measles. The elders were called to lay hands on her in like manner; and very soon afterwards she was a corpse. The prophet has undergone repeated trials before the church, and has made frequent confessions; and among the faithful, this is accounted as additional proof of his humility and divine inspiration. They only class his failings with those recorded of the ancient prophets. But the faith of many among them has failed, and they have had honesty enough to confess it. They have opened their eyes—the delusion has vanished, and they have been astonished at their besotted infatuation. Frequent depredations have happened among them, and it has sometimes required the art and assiduity of all their prophets and priests and elders to keep the whole babel from tumbling down together.

It is difficult to foretell how long it will take this gust of Fanaticism to spend itself, and die away, and sink to the oblivion of the 100 others which have gone before it. Situated as we are, we have need of patience; and we often realize the truth of Solomon, that "Though you should bray a fool in a mortar with a pestle, yet will not his folly depart from him."

On the whole, the vice of Mormonism must be accounted one of the most palpable and wide-spreading delusions which this country has ever seen; and nothing can equal the zeal of their leaders in its propagation. The completion of the [Kirtland] temple, according to the pattern shown to Joseph in vision, is a monument of unconquerable zeal. The imposing splendor of the pulpits, the orders of the Melchizedek and the Aaronic priesthoods, and the veils which are let down or drawn by machinery, dividing the place of worship into several apartments, presents before us a strange compound of Jewish antiquity and Roman Catholic mummery. The reproof which the prophet addresses to ancient Israel that they dwelt in sealed houses while the Temple of God was laid waste, can never be applied to these Mormons.—Stimulated by strong faith and zeal, you will see them muster all their forces for miles around to hear the brethren speak in tongues, and proclaim the wonderful works of God. In this view they give to those who call themselves sober Christians a most severe rebuke. If they had half the zeal of these misguided Mormons, the world would tremble, and the millennial day would speedily be ushered in. Yours, in the bonds of the Gospel.

Truman Coe.

William S. West

Source: *A Few Interesting Facts, Respecting the Rise and Progress and Pretensions of the Mormons*, Warren, Ohio: 1837.

"O! TRUTH, thou blessed offspring of the world above, Be thou my bosom friend, the object of my love."

1837

The object of this little work is to call upon the citizens of these United States, to arouse from your slumbers, for the enemy of truth is abroad in the land. Our beloved country is overrun with the propagators of the most mischievous delusion that has been recorded since the creation of man; and the consequence is that thousands are annually embracing it. This is evident, for it is but about seven years since they arose, and they assert that they now number at leas forty thousand. And their, traveling elders are continually sending letters in Kirtland, from various parts of the United States, and the Canada, giving accounts of their extensive travels, the numbers they have baptized, &c. For the truth of this, see Latter Day Saints Messenger and Advocate, (which I shall hereafter notice as the Mormon Advocate.) Therefore, as friends is the present generations, and more especially to those which are to follow, it is our duty to arouse from our careless stupidity, and inform ourselves by ever means in our power: for knowledge is the best counsellor, and in the midst of counsellors there is safety. I am aware that a lengthy catalogue of shameful lies designed to injure this people, have been put in circulation by those from whom we might expect better things. These lies have strengthened the Mormons, because they knew them to be false, and blinded the world by giving erroneous ideas. The author of this work having ascertained that people in general were very ignorant of the movements of the Mormons, determined as publishing to the world some of the most important facts in his possession; but not being contented with his present store of information, he immediately repaired to Kirtland, where he spend a few days in viewing their growing village, and magnificent temple, their Egyptian mummies and records, asking questions, &c.

The lot on which the Temple is situated is in the best part of the village, and is forty rods long, and twelve wide. This lot is the personal property of Joseph Smith, Jr. For the truth of this see revelation given to Enoch, eighth paragraph, to be found in the Mormon Book of Doctrine and Covenants, page 243. And we learn from the sixth paragraph of said revelation, that other public buildings are to be erected on the same lot, all of which must of course be under Smith's control. The fact that the Mormons have been duped to give this valuable lot to their prophet Joseph Smith, and expend more than $30,000 in building a Temple on it is a positive proof that they are dupes indeed. This Temple is built of stone, and the outside is finished with a hard cement, it is 80 feet long, and sixty wide. It is lighted with:

32 Gothic	windows	each	75 panes
3 Venetial	do [ditto]	do	118
10 Dormer	do	do	24
2 Square gable	do	do	20
1 Circular	do	do	36
2 Half circle	over doors	do	7
4 Basement	do	do	18
Total multiplied and added	3156		

In front, at the height of 45 feet from the ground is this inscription, in gilt letters: HOUSE OF THE LORD BUILT BY THE CHURCH OF THE LATTER-DAY SAINTS, A.D. 1834.

I paid twenty-five cents for going through the Temple, and seeing the mummies and records, which excited my curiosity so much that I went the next day and examined them again. Upon entering the first story the keeper took off his hat, I did the same and asked him if that was the rule, he said it was. Indeed, the sublime appearance of that apartment, when the vails are unfurled, seem to enjoin sacred reverence. There is a pulpit in the west end for the Melchizedek priesthood, composed of four seats parallel with each other, those in the rear suitably elevated, and each seat calculated for three officers and accommodated with a suitable desk, which is ornamented with a cushion and fringe, and a curve for each occupant, on the front of which is the initials of his office, in gilt letters. The desk of the front seat consists of the leaves of the communion table, upon which are the initials of its occupants, in letters of stain. There is also a pulpit in the east end for the Aaronic priesthood, which is of the same construction.

The veils by which the house in divided into quarters, are of canvass, painted white, and are rolled up or drawn at pleasure, by means of cords which come down the pillars concealed, and are worked with cranks; also each official seat is completely veiled, both sides and front; these are also worked with cords which come in the seats concealed. The second story is not finished; but is to be of the same pattern, except the official seats which are not so much elevated. I have been particular in describing this apartment, because I have never seen any account of it before the world. For further accounts of the Temple see Mormon Advocate of July, 1835, also of Jun. 1837. The Mormons have four mummies, and a quantity of records, written on papyrus, in Egyptian hieroglyphics, which were brought from the catacombs near Thebes, in Egypt. They say that the mummies were Egyptian, but the records are those of Abraham and Joseph, and contain important information respecting the creation, the fall of man, the deluge, the patriarchs, the book of Mormon, the lost tribe, the gathering, the end of the world, the judgment, &c. &c. This is as near as I can recollect; if there is an error I hope some of the Mormons will point it out, and I will recall it. These records were torn by being taken from the roll of embalming salve which contained them, and some parts entirely lost; but Smith is to translate the whole by divine inspiration, and that which is lost, like Nebuchadnezzar's dream, can be interpreted as well as that which is preserved; and a larger volume than the Bible will be required to contain them. For further account of these mummies and records, see Mormon Advocate, of December, 1835.

It is possible that a record written by Abraham, and another by Joseph, containing the most important revelation that god ever gave to man, should be entirely lost by the tenacious Israelites, and preserved by the unbelieving Egyptians, and by them embalmed and deposited in the catacombs with an Egyptian priest, there to lay in oblivion for may ages, and finally obtained by Antonio Lebolo and brought to Kirtland, Ohio, and bought by the Mormons, that Joseph Smith, the money-digger, might add them to his fictitious bible, and blasphemous revelations!! I venture to say no, it is not possible. It is more likely that the records are those of the Egyptians; and who is so slothful and vile as to sit in submissive silence while these wicked impostors are so active in filling the world with false bibles, false revelations, false pretensions, false doctrine and fanaticism. I answer no one, who is possessed of one grain of common sense, two grains of understanding, and three drops of philanthropic blood. Let it no longer be said, that the Mormons are incapable of doing any harm; let them alone and they will destroy themselves, &c., for a knowledge of their proceeding unfolds many cunning plans to accomplish deep designs. "A stitch in time saves nine." And had they been properly exposed when they commenced operations, they never would have troubled the good people of Ohio: but the Smith family were so worthless, and so full of pretensions which had all come to naught, that they were beneath public notice, and no excitement prevailed: but it was not know that Sidney Rigdon was at the bottom of it, which evidently was the case. See Mormonism Unveiled, [*sic*] page 278, 290, inclusive.

When I was in Kirtland I saw a certain young man of good information, who gave me an explanation of certain fictitious names, which are found in the following pretended revelation, which is but one of ninety-nine that I now have before me: it is to be found in the Mormon Book of Doctrine and Covenants, page 240. [Current LDS Edition, D&C 104.]

Revelation given to Enoch, concerning the order of the church for the benefit of the poor.

1. Verily I say unto you my friends, I give unto you counsel and a commandment, concerning all the properties which belong to the order, which I command to be organized and established, to be an united order, and an everlasting order for the benefit of the church, and for the salvation of men until I come, with promise immutable and unchangeable, that inasmuch as those whom I commanded were faithful, they should be blessed with a multiplicity of blessings; but inasmuch as they were not faithful, they were nigh unto cursing. Therefore inasmuch as some of my servants have not kept the commandment, but have broken the covenant, by covetousness and with feigned words, I have cursed them with a very sore and grievous curse, for I the lord have decreed in my heart, that inasmuch as any man, belonging to the order, shall be found a transgressor; or, in other words, shall break the covenant with which ye are bound,

he shall be cursed in his life, and shall be trodden down by whom I will, for I the Lord am not to be mocked in these things: and all this that the innocent among you, may not be condemned with the unjust; and that the guilty among you may not escape, because I the Lord have promised unto you a crown of glory at my right hand. Therefore inasmuch as you are found transgressors, ye cannot escape my wrath in your lives: inasmuch as ye are cut off by transgression, ye cannot escape the buffetings of satan until the day of redemption:

2. And I now give unto you power from this very hour, that if any man among you, of the order, is found a transgressor, and repenteth not of the evil, that ye shall deliver him over unto the buffetings of satan; and he shall not have power to bring evil upon you. It is wisdom in me: therefore a commandment I give unto you, that ye shall organize yourselves, and appoint every man his stewardship, that every man may give an account unto me of the stewardship which is appointed unto him: for it is expedient that I the Lord should make every man accountable, as stewards over earthly blessings, which I have made and prepared for my creatures. I the Lord stretched out the heavens, and builded the earth as a very handy work; and all things therein are mine; and it is my purpose to provide for my saints, for all things are mine; but it must needs be done in mine own way: and behold this is the way, that I the Lord have decreed to provide for my saints: that the poor shall be exalted, in that the rich are made low; for the earth is full, and there is enough and to spare, yea, I prepared all things, and have given unto the children of men to be agents unto themselves. Therefore if any man shall take of the abundance which I have made, and impart not his portion, according to the law of my gospel, unto the poor, and the needy, he shall, with the wicked, lift up his eyes in hell, being in torment.

3. And now, verily I say unto you, concerning the properties of the order: let my servant Pelagoram have appointed unto him the place where he now resides, and the lot of Tahhanes, for his stewardship, for his support while he is laboring in my vineyard, even as I will when I shall command him; and let all things be done according to counsel of the order, and united consent, or voice of the order which dwell in the land of Shinehah. And this stewardship and blessing, I the Lord confer upon my servant Pelogoram, for a blessing upon him, and his seed after him; and I will multiply blessings upon him, inasmuch as he shall be humble before me.

4. And again, let my servant Mahemson have appointed unto him, for his stewardship, the lot of land which my servant Zombre obtained in exchange for his former inheritance, for him and his seed after him; and inasmuch as he is faithful I will multiply blessings upon him and his seed after him. And let my servant Mahemson devote his moneys for the proclaiming of my words, according as my servant Gazelam shall direct.

5. And again, let my servant Shederlaomach have the place upon which he now dwells. And let my servant Olihah have the lot which is set off joining the house which is to be for the Lene-shine-house, which is lot number one; and also the lot upon which his father resides. And let my servant Shederlaomach and Olihah have the Lane-shine-house and all things that pertain unto it; and this shall be their stewardship which shall be appointed unto them; and inasmuch as they are faithful behold I will bless, and multiply blessings upon them; and this is the beginning of the stewardship which I have appointed them, for them and their seed after them; and inasmuch as they are faithful, I will multiply blessings upon them and their seed after them; even a multiplicity of blessings.

6. And again, let my servant Zombre have the house in which he lives, and the inheritance, all save the ground which has been reserved for the building of my houses, which pertains to that inheritance; and those lots which have been named for my servant Olihah. And inasmuch as he is faithful, I will multiply blessings upon him. And it is my will that he should sell the lots that are laid off for the building up of the city of my saints, inasmuch as it shall be made known to him by the voice of the Spirit, and according to the counsel of the order; and by the voice of the order. And this is the beginning of the stewardship which I have appointed unto him, for a blessing unto him, and his seed after him; and inasmuch as he is faithful, I will multiply a multiplicity of blessings upon him.

7. And again, let my servant Ahashdah have appointed unto him, the houses and lot where he now resides, and the lot and building on which the Ozondah stands, and also the lot which is on the corner south of the Ozondah; and also the lot on which the Shule is situated: And all this I have appointed unto my servant Ahashdah, for his stewardship, for a blessing upon him and his seed after him, for the benefit of the Ozondah of my order, which I have established for my sake in the land of Shinehah; yea, verily this is the stewardship

which I have appointed unto my servant Ahashdah; even this whole Ozondah establishment, him and his agent, and his seed after him, and inasmuch as he is faithful in keeping my commandments, which I have given unto him, I will multiply blessings upon him, and his seed after him, even a multiplicity of blessings.

8. And again, let my servant Gazelam have appointed unto him, the lot which is laid off for the building of my house, which is forty rods long, and twelve wide, and also the inheritance upon which his father now resides; and this is the beginning of the stewardship which I have appointed unto him, for a blessing upon him, and upon his father, for behold, I have reserved an inheritance for his father, and his support: therefore he shall be reckoned in the house of my servant Gazelam, and inasmuch as he is faithful, even a multiplicity of blessings.

9. And now a commandment I give unto you concerning Zion, that you shall no longer be bound as an united order to your brethren of Zion, only on this wise: after you are organized you shall be called the united order of the stake of Zion, the city of Shinehah. And your brethren, after they are organized, shall be called the united order of the city of Zion; and they shall be organized in their own names, and in their own name; and they shall do their business in their own name, and in their own names: and you shall do your business in your own name, and in your own names. And this I have commended to be done for your salvation and also for their salvation in consequence of their being driven out and that which is to come. The covenants being broken through transgression, by covetousness and feigned words: therefore, you are desolved as a united order with your brethren, that you are not bound only up to this hour, unto them, only on this wise, as I said, by loan, as shall be agreed by this order, in council, as your circumstances will admit, and the voice of the council direct.

10. And again, a commandment I give unto you concerning your stewardship which I have appointed unto you: behold all these properties are mine, or else your faith is vain, and ye are found hypocrites, and the covenants which ye have made unto me are broken: and if the properties are mine then ye are stewards, otherwise ye are no stewards. But verily I say unto you, I have appointed unto you to be stewards over mine house, even stewards indeed: and for this purpose I have commanded you to organize yourselves, even to shinelah my words, the fullness of my scriptures, the revelations which I have

given unto you, and which I shall hereafter, from time to time, give unto you, for the purpose of building up my church and kingdom on the earth and to prepare my people for the time when I shall dwell with them, which is nigh at hand.

11. And ye shall prepare for yourselves a place for a treasury, and consecrate it unto my name; and ye shall appoint one among you to keep the treasury, and he shall be ordained unto this blessing: and there shall be a seal upon the treasury, and all the sacred things shall be delivered into the treasury, and no man among you shall call it his own, or any part of it, for it shall belong to you all with one accord: and I give it unto you from this very hour: and now see to it, that ye go to and make use of the stewardship which I have appointed unto you, exclusive of the sacred things, for the purpose of shinelah those sacred things, as I have said: and the avails of the sacred things shall be had in the treasury, and a seal shall be upon it, and it shall not be used or taken out of the treasury by any one, neither shall the seal be loosed which shall be placed upon it, only by the voice of the order; or by commandment. And thus shall ye preserve all the avails of the sacred things in the treasury, for sacred and holy purposes: and this shall be called the sacred treasury of the Lord: and a seal shall be kept upon it that it may be holy and consecrated unto the Lord.

12. And again, there shall be another treasury prepared and a treasurer appointed to keep the treasury, and a seal shall be placed upon it; and all moneys that you receive in your stewardships, by improving upon the properties which I have appointed unto you, in houses or in lands, or in cattle, or in all things save it be the holy and sacred writings, which I have reserved unto myself for holy and sacred purposes, shall be cast into the treasury as fast as you receive moneys by the hundreds or by fifties, or by twenties, or by tens, or by fives, or in other words, if any man among you obtain five talents let him cast them into the treasury; or if he obtain ten, or twenty, or fifty, or an hundred, let him do likewise; and let not any man among you say that it is his own, for it shall not be called his, nor any part of it; and there shall not any part of it be used, or taken out of the treasury, only by the voice and common consent of the order. And this shall be the voice and common consent of the order: that any man among you, say unto the treasurer, I have need of this to help me in my stewardship: if it be five talents, or if it be ten talents, or twenty, or fifty, or an hundred, the treasurer shall give unto him

the sum which he requires, to help him in his stewardship, until he be found a transgressor, and it is manifest before the council of the order plainly, that he is an unfaithful, and an unwise steward; but so long as he is in full fellowship, and is faithful, and wise in his stewardship, this shall be his token unto the treasurer that the treasurer shall not withhold. But in case of transgression the treasurer shall be subject unto the council and voice of the order. And in case the treasurer is found an unfaithful, and an unwise steward, he shall be subject to the counsel and voice of the order, and shall be removed out of his place, and another shall be appointed in his stead.

13. And again, verily I say unto you, concerning your debts; behold it is my will that you should pay all your debts; and it is my will that you should humble yourselves before me, and obtain this blessing by your diligence and humility, and the prayer of faith, and inasmuch as you are diligent and humble, and exercise the prayer of faith behold I will soften the hearts of those to whom you are in debt, until I shall send means unto you for your deliverance. Therefore write speedily unto Cainhannoch, and write according to that which shall be dictated by my spirit, and I will soften the hearts of those to whom you are in debt, that it shall be taken away out of their minds to bring affliction upon you. And inasmuch as ye are humble and faithful and call on my name, behold I will give you the victory: I give unto you a promise, that you shall be delivered this once, out of your bondage: inasmuch as you obtain a chance to loan money by hundreds, or thousands, even until you shall loan enough to deliver yourselves from bondage, it is your privilege, and pledge the properties which I have put into your hands, this once, by giving your names, by common consent, or otherwise, as it shall seem good unto you: I give unto you this privilege this once, and behold, if you proceed to do the things which I have laid before you, according to my commandments, all these things are mine, and ye are my stewards, and the master will not suffer his house to be broken up: even so. Amen.

Names	*Explained*
Pelagoram	Sidney Rigdon
Tahhanes	Tannery
Shinehah	Kirtland

Mahemson	Martin Harris
Zombre	John Johnson
Gazelam	Joseph Smith, Jr.
Shederlaomach	Dr. F. G. Williams
Olihah	Oliver Cowdery
Lane-shine-house	Printing office
Ahashdah	N. K. Whitney
Ozondah	Storehouse
Shule	Ashery
Cainhannoch	Supposed to be New York or Buffalo

While in Kirtland this revelation afforded me much amusement. I frequently asked for an explanation of it, and the meaning of those names. Some said it was a revelation given to Enoch, the third from Adam, concerning the order of the church that was established in his day, and the names were those of persons and places that then existed. This is according to the purport of the revelation; but others told me that they were the Latin names of certain persons that lived in Kirtland, and acknowledged that Pelagoram was Sidney Rigdon. I conversed with two men in particular, who were very free to instruct me in the way of their belief, so I asked them the meaning of these names: one of the began to tell me that they were the names of certain persons who lived in the days of Enoch: I asked him if Pelagoram did not mean Sidney Rigdon, upon which the other advised me to learn things of less importance before I sought into such deep matters, said he was in haste, and they both left me.

Ebenezer Barr, of whom I requested an explanation of this revelation, read it in full, and then handed me the book, saying there it is.

I told him that I wanted to know the meaning of those words.

"O! said he that is another thing."

Can't you tell me what they mean?

"I shall not."

Are they the names of men who live in Kirtland, or did they live in the days of Enoch?

"They are names of certain persons who live in Kirtland."

Who are they?

"I shall not tell you."

Why?

"Because if I should you would sound it to the four winds: it is not to be made known to the world."

This caps the climax. Mormons' God must be an inferior being, to give a revelation to his children veiling them in fictitious names, that they may escape the scrutiny of the world. And shall he be compared with Israel's God? God forbid!1

When I was in Kirtland, I ascertained from a variety of sources, too numerous to mention, that the Mormons had been in serious difficulty, many had been dissatisfied with their leaders, and wanted a new prophet, but the majority adhered to Smith. One day, when I went to the Temple, I saw a number of men about it, busy in conversation, Smith was among them, and the topics of discussion were the bank, money, the steam saw mill, etc.; the prophet was kept very busy, but at last he started toward the bank, when a man said to him, "brother Joseph, I want to speak with you a minute," upon which he exclaimed, "my God, I wish I was translated!" He did not stop to speak with him, but went on grumbling that every one wanted to speak with him a minute, etc. This prophet says that slavery was instituted by God, and is right. See Mormon Advocate of April 1836. The Mormons pretend to have wrought many notable miracles, but I defy the whole fraternity to mention one that has been wrought through their instrumentality, and in case they will give reasonable proof that they have wrought one, I will pledge myself to say nothing more in opposition to their wishes.

They also pretend that the authenticity of their new bible is proven by numerous passages of Scripture, one of which is the 11th verse of the 85th Psalm, where the Psalmist says, "truth shall spring up out of the earth." But the Psalmist could not have had reference to the Book of Mormon, for there is an abundance of proof that the Book of Mormon is false. ÊIn support of this assertion I will state, in the first place, that there is sufficient testimony that the historical part of the Book of Mormon was written at Conneaut, Ashtabula county, Ohio, about the year 1811, by one Solomon Spalding, who called it the Manuscript found, and intended it for a romance; that he went to Pittsburgh for the purpose of getting it printed, left it at the office of Patterson & Lamdin, and soon after died; that Rigdon became an intimate in this office about the year 1825, that the printing copartnership was soon after dissolved, and that Lamdin died: see Mormonism Unveiled, pages 278, and 290 inclusive. Now if this manuscript did not fall into the hands of Sidney Rigdon where is it? Any person who knows where it is, or has ever seen it, or heard of it, is called upon to communicate the information to Wm. S. West, of Braceville, Trumbull county, Ohio. Also any other information respecting this deception, that can come well authenticated, will be thankfully received; for I am confident that a knowledge of the truth respecting Mormonism, will place it on a par with Mahometanism. All business communications must be post paid.

In the second place, I will notice that the three witnesses to the Book of Mormon saw the plates only in their imagination: see Booth's third letter. This proves that they saw no plates at all, and there never were any to be seen. Who will have to answer for the many lies told about those plates under the solemn circumstances of God called to witness? O the height of presumption.

In the third place, we are told by the Book of Mormon that the people of Jared were brought to America by a combination of miracles, at the time of the dispersion from Babel. This was 101 years after the flood, and 2247 years before Christ. This people became very numerous, and flourished until 600 years before Christ, when, by their wars they became extinct, and were succeeded by Nephi and his party, from which the American Indian have descended. This alone is sufficient to justify my assertion for there are found throughout the whole continent murderous traits of many ancient nations, differing materially from the present race of Indians, and also from each other: see American Antiquities. The celebrated traveler Mr. Ash, states that hundreds of mummies, in all probability of Egyptian origin, were found in Kentucky in the year 1775; see American Antiquities, page 110. These mummies must have been embalmed before the Christian era. It is the opinion of many celebrated antiquarians that for many centuries after the flood the Island Atlantis afforded an easy passage from Europe to America: see American Antiquities. "There is a strong resemblance between the northern and independent Tartars and the tribes of North American Indians, but not the South American. Besides this reason, there are others for believing our aborigines of North America, were descended from the ancient Scythians, and came to this country from the eastern part of Asia," Josiah priest: see American Antiquities, third edition revised, page 55. Therefore it is a reasonable conclusion that America was settled soon after the flood, and has ever since been subject to the rise and fall of nations.

Part Eight

Nothing Unusual, but They Knew It Was True

A miraculous event is not required to gain a testimony of the Gospel. Many of the journal accounts in this compilation point to some type of heavenly manifestation that led them to the truthfulness of the Church. However, as great as this is, it is not required for a confirmed testimony.

I remember sitting in gospel doctrine class and the discussion had evolved to the different manifestations experienced by various members that led to their conversion. Earlier in the discussion, it was established that all are considered converts to the Gospel, whether they were born into it or they had to search for the truth and as such, all are entitled to some manifestation that they could point to as the defining moment when they knew the Church was true. Many in the class said that they did not feel that burning that Moroni speaks of in the Book of Mormon at the time of their conversion, but that there were other heavenly manifestations that led them to the truth of the Gospel.

I am a convert, the type that was born into the Church. For many years I leaned on my parent's testimony, though I didn't discover this until I was a month into my mission. As grateful as I was that my parents' testimonies were that strong, I realized that I had to know if the Church was true for myself and stand on my own two feet. I put Moroni's challenge to the test. Kneeling in a humble trailer in my first area of Guilford, Maine, I prayed for a knowledge of the truth and within seconds of beginning the prayer, I felt a burning go through the torso of my body, confirming to me that what I was teaching was indeed the truth and left absolutely no doubt that I was doing the right thing.

The following journal accounts of George Morris, Joseph Hovey, Levi Jackman, and Isaac Leany are indicative of the fact that experiencing a miraculous heavenly manifestation in the form of an angel is not necessary to gain a testimony. I find Joseph Hovey's experience interesting because it is through good member and missionary work that he and his wife join the Church, as our leaders would have us do today.

George Morris (1816–1897)

Source: Autobiography (1816–1849). Typescript, BYU–S.

On the 6th of January, 1840, I married Jane Higginbotham, an orphan girl about 19 years of age; she had a baby on January 23rd, 1841, and died April 17, aged 20 years and 3 months. She was interred by the side of my mother. We had been married in Parrish Church at Ashton, Cheshire, England. The baby was a girl and was named Jane after her mother. She died October 9th, 1841, and was interred with her mother. These bereavements caused me to feel sorrowful, to reflect much about religion, to read the scriptures, and to pray for light that I might understand the principles of salvation. I had always been earnestly engaged seeking after the truth; I had made a practice of attending as many of the meetings of the different sects and parties as I could get to, of identifying myself with several of them, and of enjoying myself pretty well for a short time with each of them but I could not rest satisfied long with any of them. I learned in a very short time about all they professed to know about religion and it came far short of satisfying me. I had visited all the sects and parties around the country within reach and had concluded to stand aloof from them all for I considered that they were all lacking the true principles of religion. After that I would frequently meet some of the ministers of the different sects to which I belonged who would claim me as a member of their church saying that they had converted me, to which I would reply that there was where the trouble was; that if the Lord had converted me I should have stayed converted. They would call me a backslider and labor with me to bring me back into the fold again. I told them that I could not feel as they said they felt. I could not enjoy religion as they said they enjoyed it; I could not jump and clap my hands and shout "Glory, Hallelujah, Amen," as they did; I could not say "He is coming just now," "We have got Him just now." I said that it looked to me more like they were crazy than religious. They would then try to scare me with hell fire, damnation, the bottomless pit and ever-enduring torment and then wind up by praying that the Lord would shake me over the pit of hell and show me my awful condition before it was too late. But I had become such a hardened sinner that all their powerful reasoning had no effect at all upon me for I did not think that I was half as bad as they said I was.

I had never allotted myself to get into the habit of swearing or using bad language, stealing or fighting; I never had anything to do with litigation; I was very conscientious in all my dealings and strict in keeping my promises. I will mention a little incident which will verify this fact.

I was coming from the market one Saturday night, and there was an old man on the side of the road selling some books. There was one that I wanted, but I lacked a halfpenny of having enough to pay for it. "Well you can take it," said the old man. "You are an honest boy; you will pay me sometime." "Well," I said, "if you will allow me to take it, I will pay you the halfpenny next Saturday night." When Saturday night came I walked two miles expressly to take the halfpenny to him, having no other business to call me that way. When I handed it to him he said, "Oh I knew you were an honest boy. I would not be afraid to trust you with a sovereign, and the Lord will bless you all your life."

About six months before I was married, my half-brother James Silverthorn married my wife's older sister. They had two children. The younger was called Martha and the older called Elizabeth. Their mother's name was Mercy, and she was the daughter of Matthew and Nancy Higginbotham. They had two uncles; Matthew and James. About this time my brother Joseph got severely burned in the coal mines by an explosion of fire damp. It was in the year 1840, and he was visionary and flighty in his mind ever after. I had come to the time when I first heard the sound of the everlasting gospel. It was in the month of March, 1841. Some of the Elders had just made their appearance in the small town where I lived and called Dukenfield and Cheshire England. The way it came to me was as follows. I was sitting in my shop making shoes. The door was open, and some little children stopped before the door to play. My attention was arrested by hearing them talking about people they called "dippers." They said that they dipped people over head in water and talked gibberish in their meetings, and the children tried to imitate speaking in tongues. I asked them where they held their meetings, and they said, in an old room up town and pointed it out to me. So I made them visit the next week.

I heard something at the first meeting that suited me better than anything that I had ever heard from any of the sectarians. I was not very hasty in joining the church; I took time to investigate the principles of the Gospel pretty thoroughly, attended all the meetings that I could get to, borrowed a Book of Mormon from one of the Elders, and commenced reading it very earnestly and prayerfully. I had not read far before the spirit of the Lord bore testimony to me that it was the truth of heaven. I continued reading until I had read it through and got testimony after testimony concerning the truth of the work and divine authenticity of the Book of Mormon and concerning a Prophet, Seer and Revelator having been raised up in those last days with all the power, authority and Priesthood necessary to build up the church of Christ upon the earth. I received testimony that the Elders preached the truth from heaven, that the organization of the church was according to the mind and will of heaven, and concerning the gifts of the Spirit and the gathering.

Before I was baptized I walked eight miles to attend a fast meeting held by the Saints in the carpenters hall in Manchester, fasted, and at four o'clock in the afternoon they had what they called a tea party. But there was no tea there; they had hot water with plenty of good cream and sugar and plenty of something good to eat. I partook with them as though I had been one of them, and felt in my heart that it was the richest feast in my life, and the best company that I had ever enjoyed. The gift of tongues, the interpretation of tongues, and the spirit of prophesy was poured out richly upon the Saints and they sang the sweet songs of Zion. Such a heavenly influence rested down upon the assembly that it was in very deed a rich foretaste of heaven.

For about a week before I was baptized I took a way one Sunday afternoon up by a beautiful riverside into a retired place for the purpose of meditation and reflecting undisturbed upon than of salvation which had occupied my mind very forcibly for some time. I prayed to my Heavenly Father in secret and confessed my sins. I had one of the most refreshing seasons that I ever experienced in my life, for my soul was truly humble before the Lord. My sins were made manifest to my mind; my ignorance and my imperfections were shown to me, and I felt my weakness so keenly that I wept again and again over my condition. As I lay prostrate on the ground I poured out my soul in prayer before my Heavenly Father in the name of Jesus Christ confessing my sins and asking forgiveness from the Lord. I covenanted with the Lord that I would forsake all my sins and begin from that very hour to lead a new life and serve him the remainder of my life to the best of my abilities if I could but obtain his Holy Spirit to assist me for I felt that I could not do it in my own strength. He heard my prayers and poured out his Holy Spirit upon me mightily which caused me to weep for joy and rejoice that the Lord had been so merciful and good unto me all through my checkered life. My heart was made as light as a feather that very hour for a change had taken place which caused me to feel like I was in a new world; the rippling in the river was like sweet music in my ear, and the birds sang sweeter than I had ever heard them before. I looked forward with joy to the time when I should be baptized and enter in through the door into the kingdom of God, for I had seen it and had a foretaste of its joys, which to me were sweeter than honey from the honeycomb.

I have now nearly got through with the history of my early life; I will mention one or two more little incidents before I commence with my baptism. There was a firmness and decision of character accompanied me through my youthful days that was really exhibited by the young men of my acquaintance. When I lived at that tavern during my 15th year I never spent as much of my wages as would buy one pint of ale while the other young men spent all their wages in drink. Another circumstance was that when I worked with the boiler makers and coal miners, they had a custom of paying us our wages on a Saturday night at some public house where they had to spend some for the good of the house. I would pay my share of the money but would not drink. Then I would leave saying that I had some important business to attend to [for I could not endure their obscene language and ribald songs, their cursing, tobacco fumes—I could not endure it.] When I could avoid it, of course, they would curse and abuse me and tell me that I thought myself too good for their company; but that did not make me like them any better.

There was one more thing which happened when I was a very small boy which I feel very delicate about mentioning. My father was an inveterate smoker according to his means and circumstances; he was out of tobacco and there was no bread in the house for the children's breakfast nor flour to make any and but one penny to buy anything with. A controversy arose between my mother and him whether the penny should go to buy tobacco or bread; but, of course, father being the strongest party, it had to go for tobacco. It seemed as though my mother's heart would break with grief, and it made such an impression upon my little mind that I vowed that I would never use tobacco while I lived. I have kept my vow inviolate to this day.

Now we got through with my history up to the time of my baptism. At the time I had that joyful season in that retired place on the riverside, I made up my mind to be baptized the following Sabbath morning. The week that intervened seemed like an age almost; I felt so much afraid lest something might intervene to prevent it. But when Sunday morning arrived I arose at a very early hour, it was about four o'clock and called upon the Elder that I had selected to baptize me. We resorted to the place where I had spent the previous Sunday afternoon, and he baptized me. His name was John Albiston, Jr. In my ignorance and simplicity I requested him to baptize me a second time, considering that once was hardly sufficient in my case, but the Elder said that it was all sufficient and to do anything more would be doing beyond the order of heaven and would not be acceptable.

Additional Information: George remained a dedicated Latter-day Saint to his death.

See http://www.allthingsancestor.com/ancestors-of-thomas-watrous/george-morris-1817-1897 (04/11/2014).

Joseph Hovey (1812–1868)

Source: Autobiography (1812–1847). Typescript, BYU Harold B. Lee Library.

In the year 1839, I, Joseph, moved to Pike County, Illinois. I practiced medicine there for two years with good success. June 8 of this year my wife bore me another son. We named him, Joseph Grafton.

At this time the members of the Church of Jesus Christ of Latter-day Saints were exterminated from the state of Missouri by Governor Boggs. Some fifteen or twenty thousand souls, both women and children were forced to leave their homes in Missouri. One George White Pitkin, an elder of said Church, came and took up his residence near my home. This afternoon he came to our house for some medicine. My wife, knowing that he was one of the newcomers, Mormons, from Missouri, questioned him. By and by he gave us a short account of his persecutions and the Church at large. We were entirely ignorant of this and this was the first time we were informed of the Church of Jesus Christ or the Book of Mormon. He instructed us on the subject of the gospel in plain terms. We obtained the Book of Mormon and other books from our friend and these carried conviction to our hearts, especially the Book of Mormon.

I, Joseph, for the first time bowed myself before God in secret and implored his mercy and asked him if what I had read out [of] the Book of Mormon was true and if the man, Joseph Smith, was the one who translated these marvelous records. I, Joseph, asked God for a testimony by the Holy Spirit and truly I got what I asked for and more abundantly. Therefore, my wife, Martha, and I did truly rejoice in the truth we had found in those records. We also searched the Bible daily and found that it did corroborate with the Book of Mormon. We were, therefore, born again and could see the kingdom. Hence, July 4, 1839, we were baptized with water and received the Holy Ghost by the laying on of hands. One brother, Mr. Draper, baptized us.

Additional Information: Joseph Hovey served a full mission to southern Utah, was called to be the first bishop of Millville in Cache

County, and eventually moved back to Salt Lake City, where he spent the remainder of his life laboring to help complete the Salt Lake Temple.

See http://www.findagrave.com/cgi-bin/fg.cgi?page=gr&GRid=65738 (04/11/2014).

Levi Jackman (1797–1876)

Source: Autobiography (1797–1833). *A Short Sketch of the Life of Levi Jackman* by Levi Jackman. Typescript, BYU–S.

In the year 1830, we moved to the Ohio Portage County. The next winter Joseph Smith and others came to that country with the Book of Mormon, and bore testimony to its truth, etc. After a fair investigation I believed it, and embraced it. On the 4th day of May, 1831, my wife and her mother were baptized. On the 7th I was baptized. Harvey Whitlock baptized us and many more in that place.

A few days after this I was ordained an elder by Oliver Cowdrey [Cowdery]. This season Joseph Smith with about twenty elders went to the west part of the state of Missouri to find location for the saints. They returned the next fall after having picked on Jackson County for the place. This season a few families moved to the place. The work spread with much power and signs followed the preaching of the work, and very many received it. In November, at a conference, I was ordained a high priest with many others. It was decided that as many as could (with few exceptions) should move west the next spring.

Wishing to see some of my brothers who lived in Pennsylvania before I went west, I started in March, in company with Peter Whitmer, to see them.

The first evening after we arrived at my brothers in Columbus, we attended a Methodist meeting and were invited to preach. It was new work to us, but we did the best we could. When we were through we were opposed, and abused by their leader. We were invited to preach the next evening in a school house in another part of town.

At the appointed time we went to the place. The house was full. A stand with a lamp and candle burned on it, with two chairs to point the place for us.

If ever I felt small it was at that time. Brother Porter testified to the Book of Mormon, made a few remarks and sat down. I found good liberty in speaking, and the people did honor to the name of gentlemen and ladies, and I hope some good will result from the interview. We soon returned home.

Additional Information: "In 1847 he was selected as a member of the original pioneer company and became one of the first Mormons to see the Salt Lake Valley. In addition to recording the details of the trek, he saw the Mormon experience as a parallel with ancient Israel's entering the promised land: "Like Moses on Pisgah's top, we could see a part of the Salt Lake Valley, our long anticipated home." His diary describes the cutting of a road through the mouth of Emigration Canyon and on entering the Valley it 'seemed like bursting from the confines of prison walls into the beauties of a world of pleasure and freedom.' Jackman lived in the Salt Lake Valley and later settled in Salem, Utah, where he died on 23 July 1876."

See http://net.lib.byu.edu/imaging/into/pco1847/jackman/jackfs.html (04/11/2014).

Isaac Leany (1815–1873)

Source: Autobiography of William Leany. Typescript, BYU Harold B. Lee Library and Struggles of an 1847 Pioneer by Isaac Leany.

Grandfather's [Isaac Leany] first known American ancestor, John Leany, was a native of Ireland. While yet a young man, John married Miss Margaret Means and soon after his marriage came to America, bringing his wife and his father. The family settled in Pennsylvania prior to the French and Indian War.

Like most Irishmen, John seemed always ready to fight for justice, so in 1754 he enlisted as a Pennsylvanian Provincial, and served under Lieutenant General Washington, at what was known as Braddock's Defeat. Then at the outbreak of revolutionary war, John enlisted and served three years under General Washington. After his discharge his father, who was then quite old, was drafted into the service. As the father was too old to stand army life, John took his place, and served another three years. During his service in the army John was with Colonel Dan Morgan at the Battle of Cowpens, with Nathaniel Green at the Battle of Gilford Courthouse, and was under the command of General Washington at the surrender of Lord Cornwallace at Yorktown.

After the war he moved with his family to York District South Carolina(?). Here Culbert Leany, Isaac's father, was reared. Culbert Leany went to Kentucky in 1811 where he helped to survey, build roads and bridges, and lay out and develop Simpson County, Kentucky.

In 1812 he married Miss Margaret Cook, and the following year enlisted under General Jackson for defense of New Orleans against the British. On the day of the battle, June 18, 1813, his oldest son was born, and on December 19, 1815 his wife presented him with twin boys, William and Isaac. They with their brothers and sisters grew up under the disadvantages of frontier life.

Grandfather told of an interesting occurrence while on the old homestead. He said there were spots of soil so rich that the grain would grow tall and rank, falling before it could ripen. Many fragments of human bones were found in these places. One day he picked up a man's thigh bone, so long that when placed under his chin he could hardly reach the end with his fingers. In the Book of Mormon, speaking of those few that were left at the last great battle, it is said they were large and mighty men, as to the strength of men.

Grandfather while a young man was actively interested in religion, and it was at one of the open air meetings near his home in Kentucky that he first heard a Mormon elder explain the gospel of Jesus Christ. Isaac knew at once that he had found what he had been looking for. Desiring to be near the Saints he went to Illinois, and it was while here he met a young lady whom he married. Leaving Illinois, Isaac went to Missouri where he shared with the rest of the Saints the terrible persecutions of the mob. The 29th of October, 1838 found him with a small number of Saints working at a place called Haun's Mill in Missouri. It was on this day that the mob came upon them demanding that they sign a treaty of peace and deliver their weapons of war. They were allowed no word in the matter and had to comply. Grandfather had no faith in the mob's promise of peace.

Part Nine

Ministers and Mormonism

To conclude are the journal accounts of Robert Gardner and Reverend George Moore. Reverend Moore lived in Quincy at the time the Saints first arrived in Illinois. He made a number of trips to Nauvoo to study its people, but more so, its Prophet. I included this as it is most likely a representation of the generic reports issued by the clergy at the time. It also is an indication of the falsehoods provided by the clergy to their parishioners. The people trusted their ministers. They were perceived as men of God and, as such, were incapable of misleading them or bearing false witness. Moore's account is suggestive of why mob violence was unleashed on the Saints, despite being a peaceful people.

Robert Gardner's account gives a hint of the pressure applied by ministers on people that showed a desire to make the switch to Mormonism.

Robert Gardner (1819–1906)

Source: Autobiography (1819–1848). Typescript, BYU Harold B. Lee Library

I think it was in the year 1844 that an elder named John Baraman brought the gospel of Jesus Christ to our neighborhood but I did not oppose but I went to their meetings to hear and judge for myself. The Methodist minister used to hold meeting in his house but where the meeting come at the same time as the Mormon meeting he would go two miles to hear what the Mormon's taught. I would tell them they could go ahead hold their meeting. My wife and father and mother would take care of them. They advised me not to go near them for if I did I would be deceived but I went when I pleased and never went out of my way to shun meeting them.

The Methodists soon drew their meeting from my house but I continued to go hear what the Mormon's taught. He would then compare their doctrine with the doctrine of Christ and his apostles till he was satisfied it was from God. Then he applied for baptism, this the first days of January 1845. He remarked I never will forget the time we went a mile and a half into the woods to find a suitable place. We cut a hole in the ice. It was 18 inches thick. His father William baptized him. He was confirmed on a log near the water edge under the hands of William Gardner and Samuel Bolton the latter being mouth. He often said I cannot describe my feelings that I had at that time but he felt like little child and was very careful what I said or thought lest I might offend my Heavenly Father. My secret prayers and all my leisure time I kept a pocket Testament with him all the time and I found something new on every page and I began to turn down leaves and I found such strong proofs in favor of Mormonism. He said he only got three weeks in school and the rest he picked up in business and from his mother not having education has been a great drawback to him through life. It has made him feel awkward in society and made him prefer a backseat for fear of exposing his ignorance. He said he might have been some use to community if he got an education and it would have been quite a comfort to himself in place of fretting for the want of it.

He often said to his children to educate their children if it was only common book learning that they need to use everyday of their life even if they have to do without some of the things of the fashions that are outside of the Kingdom of God.

I wish them to profit by what I have suffered in not having an education when he was seventeen or eighteen years old, a temperance man come around and I signed the pledge not that I was given to drinking, but they advised him to sign it to encourage others that was give to drink to sign it. And that pledge he kept for eight years although he lived in a neighborhood where whiskey was most as common as water at all public gatherings and I was often urged to drink and often sneered because I would not way back in 1838 he joined the Methodist church and though it was all right but he found they were not sincere and he could not stand a hypocrite.

In the beginning of January 1845 in company with a few Saints we went a mile and half into the woods and cut a hole in the ice about 18 inches thick and was there baptized in the township of Brook in a stream called Brown's Creek. I was there baptized by his brother William who had been ordained elder, and I was confirmed by another elder, named Samuel Bolton. I can't describe my [feelings] but I felt as humble as a little child to think I had lived to have my sins remitted and received the Holy Ghost.

I had no trouble in believing the Book of Mormon for I had a burning testimony in my bosom every time I took the book. It was so plain to me I thought I had nothing to do but run and tell my neighbors and they would believe it all. Mother was a Methodist but never fought against the gospel but believed it right along after awhile she was taken very sick not expected to live. She wished to be baptized. Our neighbors said if you put her in the water we will have you tried for murder for she will surely die. But we put her on a sled and took her two miles through the snow and then cut a hole in the ice and baptized her in the presence of those who came to see her die. One man declared if she did not [die] that night he would be a Mormon next day. The next day he met her going to her daughter's; she was on foot. He gazed at her as if he had seen a ghost. He gave her the road but never spoke nor never joined the church.

Additional Information: Robert served two missions after reaching the Salt Lake Valley. He later settled in southern Utah.

See https://www.lds.org/general-conference/2009/04/get-on-with-our-lives?lang=eng (04/11/2014).

George Moore (1811–1847)

Source: Excerpts from the diary of George Moore in Donald Q. Cannon, "Reverend George Moore Comments on Nauvoo, the Mormons, and Joseph Smith," Western Illinois Regional Studies 5 (Spring 1982):6–16.

[The diaries of George Moore consist of six volumes, covering the period 1828–1845. They are located at Harvard University Archives and the American Antiquarian Society in Worcester, Massachusetts. Parts of the diaries have been published in Kenneth W. Cameron, Transcendental Epilogue (Hartford, Conn.: Transcendental Books, 1965). The only volume used in this study is the one which covers the period from December 27, 1840–May 12, 1845 and is located in the American Antiquarian Society. It is cited in this work as Diary.

Reverend George Moore was born on May 4, 1811 in Sudbury, Massachusetts. Following his graduation from Harvard Divinity School, he became a Unitarian minister. After preaching in various communities in Massachusetts, he served as a Unitarian missionary and pastor in Quincy, Illinois. He was living in Quincy at the time Latter-day Saints were gathering in Nauvoo.]

[During the years 1840–1845, George Moore made several visits to Nauvoo, Illinois, faithfully recording in his diary the things he observed. Following a visit to the city on Friday, June 3, 1842, he wrote:]

Visited the Mormon [Nauvoo] Temple. The situation is beautiful, commanding an extensive view—about a half mile back from the river, on the bluff—overlooking a large band of the river—the city of Nauvoo—and a fine prairie on the other side of the river. Dimensions, about 100 feet by 70. The basement of this temple is laid—and in the basement is the baptismal font, supported by 12 oxen. In this I learned that persons are baptized for the dead, and for restoration to health.

Saw the basement of the "Nauvoo House," on the river bank near Jo [Joseph] Smith's house. Dimensions 120 feet by 100, or thereabouts. This is to be 4 stories high—and of stone. [Diary, 105.]

[He was fascinated by the Mormon people and their customs. Concerning a Mormon meeting and those in attendance he wrote:]

I don't know that I ever before saw such a congregation of stolid faces. [Diary, 8.]

[Moore then went on to say that most of the Mormons were poor and many suffered for lack of the necessities of life. The Minister from Quincy found the Mormon sermons boring, but apparently never tired of writing about them. Concerning the sermons during one meeting he wrote:]

When I entered, one of their number was speaking about the elder and younger son in the parable of the Prodigal Son. He made wretched work as a speaker—he hesitated—and what he said amounted to nothing at all—he did not seem to know himself what he was talking about. But he soon gave way to another—a man of about 50 years of age—who spoke for nearly an hour at the top of his voice. There was but little connection in what he said. He would run from one subject to another—just as an old sailor will tell a long yarn, in which the great essential is to keep talking. [Diary, 8–9]

[George Moore had heard that the Mormons spoke in tongues and he was most anxious to hear them practice this ancient custom. In this desire, however, he was disappointed and had to rely on accounts given by others. If he was disappointed in this interest, however, he compensated for it by observing other gifts of the spirit such as the gift of healing. Discussing the conversion of one of his parishioners, Mr. [Joseph L.] Heywood, Reverend Moore reported on his miraculous healing:]

He then told me he had received that which was satisfactory to himself—that Elder [Orson] Hyde laid hands upon him, and prayed over him, while he was suffering from a severe nervous head-ache, and the head-ache departed—and that he believed this was a miracle wrought upon himself.

[Another Mormon told George Moore how his withered leg was healed, and went on to describe how his wife's crooked arm had been straightened. Clearly, in the mind of Dr. Moore, the Latter-day Saints believed in and practiced faith healing. [Diary, 157–58.]

Concerning the so-called Mormon peep stone, Reverend Moore had this to say:]

At Nauvoo, they have what is called a "peep stone," and two boys, who are believed to have the power of looking into this stone, and seeing what people are doing at a distance, and of such implicit faith in this, that they go to see the peep-stone boys as soon as they lose any thing. But I hear that Joe [Joseph] Smith gives no countenance to this superstition." [Diary, 179.]

[Like other nineteenth-century observers of the Latter-day Saints, Moore saw parallels between Mormonism and Mohammedananism. For example, he wrote that the Mormons believed in the idea of an earthly paradise, which was one of Mohammed's great ideas. Rev. Moore also believed the Mormons sought an outward, tangible evidence of their beliefs, not just an inward spiritual manifestation. This desire for outward show he observed in the Mormon propensity for military parades and maneuvers—that is, the war games and reviews of the Nauvoo Legion.]

As George Moore visited Nauvoo and shared the association of Mormons, he also noted a pragmatic tendency. Because of their financial difficulty they constantly looked for ways to save money. Hence, the "strange" practice of performing marriages on the ice-covered Mississippi. A Mormon elder would accompany the bride and groom to a point more than halfway across the river, and there on the snow-covered ice, unite them in matrimony, thus avoiding payment for a certificate in the Hancock County Court. [Diary, 175.]

While George Moore's comments on Mormon beliefs and customs are of interest, his most meaningful comments concern the conversion of some of his parishioners to the Mormon faith. A careful examination of Moore's observations indicates that he thought highly of the people involved, but could not understand how they could become Mormons. His comments about Mrs. [Hannah L.] Case are a good example of his high regard for her, but also show his disapproval of her decision to unite with the Mormons:]

Tuesday Evening, September 13 (1842)

An event took place this morning, which has occupied my mind through the day. Mrs. [Hannah L.] Case, who is a member of the Episcopal Church, but who has usually attended my church, was this morning baptized into the Mormon faith. When I first heard of it, I was very much surprised. And I determined to go at once and see her. I found her at home—just returned from the river where she had been immersed by a Mormon Elder. I conversed with her about the step which she had taken—told her if she knew anything of the recent disclosures of the corruptions in the Mormon Church. But I found her full in the faith that the Mormon church is the true church. Mrs. [Hannah L.] Case is an excellent woman, with a heart glowing with charity for all—she has read a good deal, and is thoughtful and pious. But withal she has a mind easily biased—much taken with novelties—and in her universal charity is apt to excuse sin, or rather the sinner. She has for some time been reading the Book of Mormon and several of the Mormon publications, and has had a Mormon woman living with her, or visiting her home. But she has not intimated to any of her friends, so far as I can learn, that she was impressed with the truth of the Mormon faith, until last evening, when she sent word to her sister that she intended to be baptized this morning and that if she wished to witness the performance of the rite, she could. Her sister was taken by surprise—was troubled—called to see her—and tried to dissuade her from her purpose for the present. But no—she could not wait. It seems as though she must have some distrust of her own convictions, for she has not consulted with any of her long-tried friends. When I talked with her about this, she returned the reply of fanaticism, "I take no counsel of flesh and blood, but of my Father in heaven." Well, she has taken the step—a very rash one, as I believe—she has the very best intentions in it, I doubt not—and I look upon her as still as good as ever. I cannot but look upon her as very credulous—and as having less judgment, nay less intelligence than I supposed. But yet I would not say, she is wrong. What she regards in the Mormon faith as good and pure I have no doubt is so—and placing her own interpretations upon their views, I suppose she thinks she has received new light. But she is a good and true woman—and I hope will yet be guided into the truth, whether she finds it in the Mormon Church, or any other. [Diary, 132–33.]

[When one of his deacons joined the Church of Jesus Christ of Latter-day Saints, Moore expressed similar concerns. That the course of events troubled him is seen by the fact that his journal entries for three consecutive days concern this matter. The relevant portions of those entries follow:]

Monday Evening, December 19 (1842)

I little thought, when I was recording some causes of discouragement, last evening, that I should be called upon, today, to record the apostasy of one of the deacons of my church. But so it is, as I am told. He returned, today, from Nauvoo, where he was baptized into the Mormon faith. This is a most strange delusion. And this step has been taken by Mr. [Joseph L.] Heywood in a singular manner. He has surprised all his friends by it. He has not intimated to any one that he was going to change his faith. He has not conversed with any, so far as I know, in whom he has been accustomed heretofore to place confidence. But, all at once, by a visit to the Mormon City, has been suddenly converted. I trust that he is sincere in this course, and that his sincerity will erelong, bring him back from his error, his delusion.

Tuesday, December 20 (1842)

Called on Mr. [Joseph L.] Heywood. He told me that he had been baptized into the Mormon faith. In the course of conversation, he professed to believe that Joseph Smith is the best and purest being on earth, a perfect human being, the prophet of the Almighty. I asked him what evidence he had of this. He said he had seen and conversed with Mr. Smith, and had heard the testimony of his friends and family who ought to know him best. I asked for some stronger evidence. He then told me he had received that which was satisfactory to himself—that Elder [Orson] Hyde laid hands upon him, and prayed over him, while he was suffering from a severe nervous headache, and the head-ache departed,—and that he believed this was a miracle wrought upon himself. I asked for stronger evidence still. He then told me a story which Elder Hyde had related to him. Elder Hyde was in England, was called in to lay hands upon, and pray over, a blind boy—he saw no effects from his prayer—immediately left the house—on his arrival in the country, at St. Louis, he met some individuals who told him the child had been healed. Elder Hyde says that letters may be procured from England certifying to this fact. This was the strongest evidence that Mr. Heywood could offer for believing that Joseph Smith is the prophet of God. I told him I regarded him as perfectly deluded, and that I believed he would see cause to regret the step he had taken.

Thursday, December 22 (1842)

Called upon Mrs. Heywood. Found her very unhappy in regard to her husband's course. She said that he never intimated to her that he had any intention of joining the Mormons. She regards him as a complete dupe of Joe [Joseph] Smith. [Diary, 157–58.]

[Reverend Moore's failure or even inability to understand why his members embraced the Mormon Church is shown in his comments about the death of Mrs. Case.]

Sunday, December 17th (1843)

Mrs. Hannah L. Case died today—a most excellent Christian. She formally worshipped with my congregation, but more than a year since united herself with the Mormons, and has remained firm in the faith of Mormonism ever since. But the name by which she was called mattered but little; she was a truly Christian woman, and has done much in this place for the cause of our holy religion. She was eminent for her charity, and her humility, and her deep and fervent piety. She died of a lingering consumption, fully resigned to her Heavenly Father's will. May he who is the father of the orphans guide and bless the three sons who survive.

Tuesday Evening, December 19th (1843)

Was called upon, this afternoon to take part in the services at the funeral of Mrs. Case. I made the prayer, and read a hymn, and Elder Hyde of the Mormon faith made a very long address about the resurrection of the body. This address seemed to me a tissue of errors and absurdities from beginning to end. It was boisterous talk, and had nothing in it that I could perceive calculated to give comfort to those that mourn. The gentle spirit of Mrs. Case must have been grieved if she knew aught that was going on. [Diary, 241–42.]

[While he thought Mrs. [Hannah L.] Case was a good Christian, he clearly believed she had been deluded by the Mormons. George Moore hoped his former member found eternal happiness, but he was certainly very skeptical about her future state.

During his visits to Nauvoo the Unitarian minister had an opportunity to visit with the prophet Joseph Smith. In his diary, he recorded their conversations as well as some character sketches and physical descriptions of the Mormon Prophet. Moore's first meeting with Joseph Smith occurred on Friday, June 3, 1842. He recorded his visit with the prophet in this manner:]

Called on the "Prophet Jo [Joseph] Smith." His carriage was at the door and he was about going away, but he received me very kindly, asked me into his house. I remained about 10 minutes. He was very communicative. We conversed about the golden plates, which he professes to have dug up and translated into the Book of Mormon. "Those plates are not now in this country," he said—"they were exhibited to a few at first for the sake of obtaining their testimony—no others have ever seen them—and they will never again be exhibited."

He showed me some specimens of the hieroglyphics, such as, he says, were on the gold plates. He asked me if I was a Clergyman—and of what denomination—and what were the fundamental doctrines of our faith—on my telling him that we believed in divine Unity—in one God in one person—he said, we don't agree with you there. We believe in three Gods, equal in power and glory. There are three personages in heaven, but those three are not one. I suppose, from what I hear, that Smith makes it a point not to agree with any one in regard to his religious opinions, and adapts himself to the person with whom he talks for the time being. . . . He expressed a desire to have a long conversation with me, but he had an engagement, and I was soon going away, so that we could not have much conversation. Our interview was short, but pleasant. [Diary, 105–106.]

[Besides commenting on the circumstances surrounding this conversation and Mormon doctrine, the Quincy minister penned a physical description of the Mormon Prophet.] This 'prophet' is a man of large frame—tending to corpulency—has blue eyes, light complexion, one or two of his front teeth gone—he has a rather benevolent expression of countenance. [Diary, 106.]

[As he left Joseph Smith's home he noted the following:]

As I came out, I found two large cannon, mounted in his yard. Can this be a prophet of God, thought I, who must have cannon for a guard, and must convert all his followers into soldiers—into a "Nauvoo Legion"—and excite in them a warlike spirit? What a return in this to Judaism, nay to Judaism, but to barbarism? And yet this imposter (for I cannot call him any thing else) has his thousands of followers. Nauvoo contains a population of from 5 to 10,000—being variously estimated—and the converts to this system, if system it may be called, are coming in by hundreds. How happens it that an ordinary man by such ordinary means can exert such an influence and sustain himself? It is strange, it is passing strange—it is wonderful—and yet so it is. It shows this most certainly, that there is a great deal of credulity in man. [Diary, 106.]

[Being personally acquainted with Joseph and living just a few miles down the Mississippi from Nauvoo, the Unitarian minister was both an interested and timely observer of the events leading up to the death of the Prophet. Consequently, he made the following entry in his diary:]

At the present our whole community is excited in regard to the Mormons. They have demolished a printing-press in Nauvoo, in violation of the laws of the states. Joe [Joseph] Smith, the prophet, was arrested for his act on a legal process, and was rescued by a writ of habeas corpus issued by his own municipal court. The whole community became excited, armed themselves to support the civil officer in his duty, sent for the governor; and now seem determined to carry out the law. Meantime, Nauvoo has been declared under martial law. The governor has arrived—ordered out several regiments of militia—sent off for arms—called upon the Mormons to send a committee, unarmed, to Carthage, there to be examined by him—the committee appeared, and the investigation was not satisfactory.

Now, I am told, the governor has sent 12 men to Nauvoo to arrest Joe [Joseph] Smith—and that the Mormons have laid down their arms. Such are some of the rumors afloat here. Nothing is talked of but the Nauvoo news. The military companies, instead of attending church this evening, have had meetings at their armories, and are expecting to be called out in the morning to march to the seat of war. I know not what will be the result of this excitement. May God in his infinite wisdom so rule in the hearts of men as to subdue their evil and revengeful passions, and to prevent any bloodshed! [Diary, 265–66.]

[A few days later he wrote this about the death of Joseph Smith and his brother:]

Quincy, Friday Evening, June 28th

The war alarm has sounded through our city. At day-break, on this morning, the bells were rung and the citizens called out to attend a meeting at the courthouse. The news had come down in the boat that Joe [Joseph] Smith and his brother Hyrum had been killed in the prison at Carthage. Threats had been made by many of the Mormons to destroy the towns of Carthage and Warsaw, and it was supposed that their whole body might be infuriated so as to be ready to do anything. This was stated at the meeting in the courthouse. Also, that the governor went yesterday to Nauvoo with 60 men to see the Mormons and quiet them, and to receive the arms of the state in their possession. Fears were entertained for the safety of the governor and his guard. It was immediately determined that a force should be raised to go to the protection of Warsaw. And at 9 o'clock about 300 troops left on the Boreas for Warsaw. The Quincy Rifle Company—Quincy Guards (German

Company)—Irish Volunteers—and a volunteer company under command of Captain Johnson—all went off amidst much cheering for "the Constitution and the Laws."

I never before witnessed so much excitement. And I have been unable to keep quiet in the midst of it. Every thing in the morning wore a warlike aspect. Even some apprehensions were expressed in regard to the safety of Quincy. But news has come by boat, this evening, that all was quiet at Nauvoo, that they had received the bodies of the Smiths to bury them, that some of their leaders had advised them in public speeches to keep quiet, and to make no attack upon the property or lives of others. They will probably remain at Nauvoo, and act on the defensive, if attacked.

The attack on Smith was first made, according to the report which we have received, by Higbee, a seceding Mormon—the guard of the prison resisted attack, but the mob forced their way into the prison—and there killed Joe [Joseph Smith] and Hyrum [Smith]. The prophet fought to the last with pistols—rushed to a window in order to jump out—and fell head long having received a shot in his head. It seems not to have been a cold-blooded murder on the part of the people of Carthage. I know not what to think of the matter. It was perfectly astounding when I first heard of it. I sincerely trust that peace will now be restored. [Diary, 266–67.]

[Several things are of interest here. Obviously, Moore and other non-Mormons were afraid of an attack by the Mormons. He also called attention to the mobilization of troops to defend the communities and keep the peace. Moore's description of the assault on Carthage Jail is similar to the most common accounts. It is interesting, however, to note that he did not blame the people of Carthage for the murder.

Commenting further on the reasons for the martyrdom, Reverend Moore wrote the following:]

How truly did Jesus say, "They that take the sword shall perish by the sword!" Smith has taken up the sword to defend himself—has ever inculcated the war spirit among his followers—and now behold the result! A dreadful and appalling result, but still the direct consequence of his military system. If they (the Mormons) had been a peaceful sect, and had never used arms as a religious body, they would have received ample protection in their religion. But how could this be expected from an imposter? [Diary, 267–68.]

[Here, Moore blames the death of Joseph Smith on the prophet's military activities. In a sense, the Unitarian minister is suggesting that the existence of the Nauvoo Legion may have caused the murder of the Mormon prophet.

Still interested in the Mormons, Moore continued to observe them and to record his thoughts in his journal. Three months after the prophet's death, he wrote:]

A glorious Autumn day. Would that I could say it has been a glorious day at Church! But, instead of that, the peace of the Sabbath has been broken by martial music. Soldiers paraded our streets at noon. Our two independent companies have again marched to Nauvoo. They were ordered out by the governor, and commanded to report themselves at Nauvoo on Wednesday next. I know not what to make of this new move. It is conjectured by some that it is a political movement on the part of the governor. The pretence for ordering out the troops is that the people of Warsaw have invited the people from the neighboring counties and from Iowa and Missouri to attend a grand wolf hunt there on Friday next, and have also notified the Mormons that they must leave before that time,—and that this wolf hunt is a concealed movement by which they intend to drive the Mormons out of the state. Under this pretence the governor has called out the troops from several counties, and they are now marching towards Nauvoo. What will be the result of this movement, time must determine. I fear that the very attempt to obviate the difficulty, may bring on some collision. [Diary, 294.]

About the Author

Dan was born in northwest Montana and raised in Calgary, Alberta. He served for two years in the Massachusetts Boston Mission and married Kate Nelson in the Cardston Alberta Temple. He has six children and soon-to-be seventeen grandchildren. He is a graduate of both Lethbridge Community College and Utah State University. Dan loves to hike and read. He currently serves as the first assistant in his high priest group.

0 26575 14412 3